A SHORT HISTORY OF ITALY (476-1900)

BY

Henry Dwight Sedgwick

A SHORT HISTORY OF ITALY (476-1900)

Published by Wallachia Publishers

New York City, NY

First published circa 1957

Copyright © Wallachia Publishers, 2015

All rights reserved

ABOUT WALLACHIA PUBLISHERS

<u>**Wallachia Publishers**</u> mission is to publish the world's finest European history texts. More information on our recent publications and catalog can be found on our website.

TO H. D. S., C. D. S., R. M. S., W. E. S., A. C. S., F. M. S., and T. S.

O passi graviora ...
... forsan et hæc olim meminisse juvabit.

PREFACE

This volume is a mere sketch in outline; it makes no pretence to original investigation, or even to an extended examination of the voluminous literature which deals with every part of its subject. It is an attempt to give a correct impression of Italian history as a whole, and employs details only here and there, and then merely for the sake of giving greater clearness to the general outline. So brief a narrative is mainly a work of selection; and perhaps no two persons would agree upon what to put in and what to leave out. I have laid emphasis upon the matters of greatest general interest, the Papacy, the Renaissance, and the Risorgimento; and my special object has been to put in high relief those achievements which make Italy so charming and so interesting to the world, and to give what space was possible to the great men to whom these achievements are due.

H. D. S.

New York, October 1, 1905.

A SHORT HISTORY OF ITALY: A SHORT HISTORY OF ITALY: CHAPTER I: THE FALL OF THE EMPIRE IN THE WEST (476 A. D.)

In the year 476 an unfortunate young man, mocked with the great names of the founders of the City and of the Empire, Romulus Augustus, nicknamed Augustulus, was deposed from the throne of the Cæsars by a Barbarian general in the Imperial service, and the Roman Empire in Italy came to its end. This act was but the outward sign that the power of Italy was utterly gone, and that in the West at least the Barbarians were indisputably conquerors in the long struggle which they had carried on for centuries with the Roman Empire.

That Empire, at the period of its greatness, embraced all the countries around the Mediterranean Sea; it was the political embodiment of the Mediterranean civilization. In Europe, to the northeast, it reached as far as the Rhine and the Danube; it included England. Beyond the Rhine and the Danube dwelt the Barbarians. Europe was thus divided into two parts, the civilized and the Barbarian: one, a great Latin empire which rested upon slavery, and was governed by a highly centralized bureaucracy; the other, a collection of tribes of Teutonic blood, bound together in a very simple form of society, and essentially democratic in character.

The Empire, composed of many races, Etruscan, Ligurian, Iberian, Celtic, Basque, Greek, Egyptian, and divers others, had been created and maintained by the military and administrative genius of Rome. Over all these people Roman law and Roman order prevailed. All enjoyed the Pax Romana. From Cadiz to Milan, from Milan to Byzantium, from Byzantium to Palmyra, stretched the great Roman roads. Coins, weights, and measures were everywhere the same. The inhabitants of Africa, Asia, and Europe, enfranchised by an Imperial edict, were thankful to be Roman citizens. To this day Roman law, the Romance languages, and the Roman Catholic Church testify to the vigour and solidity of Roman dominion. The city of Rome was, and had been for centuries, the head of the world. From east and west, from north and south, booty, spoils, taxes, tribute had flowed into Rome. Even after the seat of government had been removed to Constantinople (A. D. 330), visitors from the new capital were astounded to behold the Roman temples, baths, amphitheatres, forums, circuses, and palaces, all glittering with marble and bronze. But the riches acquired by conquest and tribute had brought seeds of evil with them. Society was divided into the very rich and the very poor; the simple laborious life of the freemen of ancient Rome was gone; the regular occupations of production had been abandoned to serfs and slaves; moderate incomes and plain living had disappeared. The middle class had been thrust down to the level of the plebs. In the country the small proprietors had been reduced to a position little better than that of the serfs, while the great landlords had got vast tracts of land into their hands. Nearly half the population were slaves. Taxes had become heavier and heavier as the exigencies of the Empire grew; great numbers of officials were maintained, and great mercenary armies. The rich controlled the government, and shifted almost the whole burden of taxation from their own shoulders to those of the poor. In the cities, each imitating Rome so far as it could, had grown up a vicious unemployed class, living on the distribution of bread which was paid for out of the public revenues.

On the farther side of the Rhine and the Danube, in marked contrast with this society, the Teutonic Barbarians tilled their lands and herded their flocks. They dwelt in little communities which were banded together into tribes; and these in turn were united in a sort of loose confederation, which assumed the semblance of a nation only when under the necessity of military action, and then the adult male population constituted the army. Their buildings were of the humblest character, their clothes rude, their arts primitive; they could neither read nor write, and their men cared for little besides hunting and fighting. They were, however, a free, self-respecting, self-governing people, electing their king, and meeting in one great assembly to enact their laws. On the Roman borders the Barbarians had become Christians, unfortunately not Trinitarians, but mere Arians, heretics in the eyes of the orthodox Catholics; so their Christianity hardly served to smooth their relations with the Romans.

The differences between these two divisions of Europe were about as great as between ourselves and the Don Cossacks. A Roman gentleman living in Gaul, for example, would have a villa in Auvergne, built high upon the hills in order to get the breezes and the view. Here was a bath-house, a fish-pond, separate apartments for the women, a pillared portico that overlooked a lake, a winter drawing-room, a summer parlour, etc. In this agreeable place, in his times of leisure, the owner would stroll about his grounds, play tennis, cultivate his garden, read Virgil and Claudian, compose epigrams, write letters to his friends in the vein of Horace's Satires, gossip about the doings at the Imperial court or talk philosophy. The pleasant, luxurious life of Roman gentlemen was not very different from luxurious life in America to-day.

The Barbarians in their native forests were hardly aware of Roman civilization; and those on the border made a marked contrast with the Romans. The young kings were superb athletes, sparing at table, and attentive to their kingly duties. The Barbarian elders admired Roman civilization, but were "stiff and lumpish in body and mind." The young men, six feet or more in height, with long, yellow hair, were great eaters of garlic and indelicate viands; they went about bare-legged, booted with rough ox-leather, and wore short-sleeved garments of divers colours, belted tight, with swords dangling at their backs, shields at side, and battle-axes in their hands.

It would be a mistake, however, to draw a very sharp line between these two opposing divisions of Europe. The Teutons were called Barbarians because they were not Romans, but many of them had been trained in the Roman armies and had lived in Constantinople, Trier, or Milan, and were well accustomed to Roman military arts and discipline; in fact, the Roman army was recruited mainly from among the Barbarians. Roman traders dealt with them regularly. In one way and another the Barbarians, especially their leaders, had come under the educating influence of Roman civilization, and they regarded that civilization with an amazement and a respect that at times deepened into awe.

But though a sharp line cannot be drawn, yet at bottom Romans and Barbarians were far apart. It was impossible that two societies of such divergent civilization should exist side by side in peace; one must conquer the other. The struggle between the Empire and its enemies had been almost continuous since the days of Julius Cæsar, and for several centuries the Empire had prevailed; but social disintegration within had proceeded rapidly, and by the beginning of the fifth century the Empire's doom had come. Rome herself, the original home of empire, lay "nerveless, dead, unsceptred," open to any takers; and takers came. The Visigoths, under Alaric, captured the city in 410 and were merciful; the Vandals, under Genseric, captured it in 455 and were cruel.

The fall of Rome, which we now see to have been inevitable, came, however, with a terrible shock to the civilized world. St. Jerome, who had gone to the wilderness near Bethlehem in order to meditate upon the prophets, wrote: "My voice is choked and my sobs interrupt the words which I write; the city is subdued which subdued the world.... Who could believe that Rome, which was built of the spoils of the whole earth, would fall, that the city could, at the same time, be the cradle and grave of her people; that all the coasts of Asia, Egypt, and Africa should be filled with the slaves and maidens of Rome? That holy Bethlehem should daily receive, as beggars, men and women who formerly were conspicuous for their wealth and luxury?"

The city of Rome had been deemed immortal; it had become almost sacred from long veneration; and when Rome fell, the Empire in the West had not a prop to rest upon. Spain was taken by the Suevi and the Visigoths, Gaul by the Franks, Burgundians, and Alemanni, England by Angles and Saxons, Africa by the Vandals; and, with the deposition of Romulus Augustulus, Italy, too, became the prize of a Barbarian general.

The succeeding period of European history, in Gaul, Spain, Africa, and Italy, is the mingling or attempted mingling of the old populations of the Empire with the Barbarian conquerors. The process had, indeed, as I have intimated, begun before the fall of the Empire. For several generations Barbarians had not only been received as colonists and taken as soldiers, but even whole tribes had been admitted within the Roman boundaries. Imperial statesmen had realized that the Empire could only be upheld by an infusion of Barbarian virility, and they had favoured the process. But assimilation had not taken place, and now that the Empire had passed into the hands of the Barbarians there were two social strata,—the rude martial conquerors on top, and the civilized, feeble, subject race, ten times as numerous, underneath. It was obvious to the wiser Barbarian chiefs, trained as they were in Roman ways, that if they were to get stable dominion and civilized government, they must adopt the complicated Imperial machinery. They saw that unless the Barbarians learned Roman civilization, they would need hundreds of years to create any such civilization of their own. This was especially true in Italy. Odoacer, the general who deposed Romulus Augustulus, well knew that a state which had its military service all Barbarian and its civil service all Roman could not stand firm. Barbarian sovereignty needed support, especially legal support, in the eyes of the subject population. Such legitimacy could only come from the Empire. Odoacer and other intelligent Barbarians turned instinctively to Constantinople for recognition. They did not think that they had overturned or suppressed the Empire. Nobody thought that there were two Empires, one Eastern and one Western, one enduring and one destroyed in 476. To the Roman world the Empire had always been single, had always been a unit. The division into eastern and western parts had been made for convenience of administration; the Empire itself had never been divided. Even after the western countries of Europe had been overrun by the Barbarians, the Emperor at Constantinople remained the supreme and sole source of authority and law. The very Barbarians could not free themselves from this theory, however little heed they paid to it in practice. Odoacer acknowledged the sovereignty of the Empire without question. He merely wished to control the civil and military administration in Italy.

Before beginning a sketch of the attempts to found a permanent Barbarian government in Italy and to combine Barbarians and Romans in one people, it is necessary to speak of a rising power which already constituted the most important element in the situation. The Church was not only the one vigorous body in Italy, but it had already begun to foreshadow its future greatness. In the time of Constantine (323-337) and his immediate successors, the bishops of Rome had no primacy over other bishops, but they had claims to precedence, which they soon put to good use. Their city was the cradle and home of Roman dominion. St. Paul had lived and died there. Above all, as was universally acknowledged, the apostle Peter had founded their bishopric. Theirs, in an especial sense, was the Church to which Christ referred when He said to the apostle, "Thou art Peter, and upon this rock I will build my church; and the gates of hell shall not prevail against it." The bishops of Rome also derived immense advantage from the absence of a temporal prince; whereas their chief rivals, the patriarchs of Constantinople, were wholly eclipsed by the presence of the Emperor. The removal of the great offices of government to Constantinople and the absence of any real civil life, had left Rome even then a mere ecclesiastical city, and the head of the Church became the most important personage there. It was so generally acknowledged that Roman bishops were entitled to that precedence in rank over other bishops, which Rome enjoyed over other cities, that in 344 an Ecumenical Council submitted a most important question to the decision of the Roman See. One hundred years later the great pope, Leo I, merely gave utterance to the general opinion when he said: "St. Peter and St. Paul are the Romulus and Remus of the new Rome, as much superior to the old as truth is to error. If ancient Rome was at the head of the pagan world, St. Peter, prince of the Apostles, came to teach in the new Rome, so that from her the light of Christianity should be shed over the world."

The Roman Church gathered to herself whatever remained of the administrative ability of ancient Rome. With acute practical sense she condemned those subtle doctrines that kept springing up in the East, late flashes of Greek metaphysics; and though she may have cut herself off from certain spiritual Neoplatonic thought, and have set her heart too much upon domination, yet by her very adherence to dogma, by her very insistence upon uniform law and obedience, by steadfastly maintaining the purity and the unity of the Faith, she became the great cohesive force in Europe, and by creating Christendom contributed immensely to the cause of European civilization. Partly by good fortune, partly by her success in making her cause prevail, Rome was always orthodox. She remained staunchly Trinitarian. She fought the Arians, who believed that the Son, created by the Father, could not be identical with Him and could not have existed from the beginning. She fought the Nestorians, who alleged that the Virgin was the mother of Christ only in so far as He was man. She fought the Monophysites, who denied that Christ had two distinct natures, human and divine. She fought always gallantly, and always, or almost always, in the end triumphantly. In those days ecclesiastical affairs were inseparable from political affairs;

no man dreamed of severing them either in fact or in theory; the State and the Church were one fabric under a double aspect. The idea of the State apart from the Church, or the Church apart from the State, was no more imagined than the Darwinian theory.

If we now go back to Odoacer, and to his Barbarian successors, we shall find that in their endeavours to establish an Italian kingdom they were confronted by a threefold task,—to blend the Barbarian conquerors and the subject Latins, to establish friendly relations with the Empire, and to win the confidence and support of the Orthodox Church. In all the long period of Barbarian dominion, each Barbarian chief in turn had to face the imminent danger that these three political powers, the subject people, the Church, and the Empire, should make common cause against him. The Barbarians, in fact, were always unsuccessful. They never were able to make Italy into one kingdom. These three enemies were too strong for them. The inherent difficulties of the situation appear at once on the deposition of Romulus Augustulus, and give whatever interest there is to Odoacer's brief career. Over that career, which bridges the years 476 to 489, we need not pause, for Odoacer's attempt to establish a permanent government over all Italy was so ephemeral, and also so similar in all essential features to that of the Ostrogoths, his successors, that an account of their attempt may serve for his as well.

CHAPTER II: THE OSTROGOTHS (489-553)

The Ostrogoths were a fine people; and historians have speculated sadly on the immense advantage, the vast saving of ills, that would have accrued to Italy had they succeeded in their attempt to establish a kingdom. Such a union of strength and vigour with the gifted Italian nature might well have produced a happy result. But my business is merely to indicate why and how the attempt failed.

The Ostrogoths (East Goths), one branch of the great Gothic nation, of which the Visigoths (West Goths) were the other, immediately prior to their invasion of Italy inhabited Pannonia (now Austria) on the south side of the Danube. They were a warlike people, and had given much trouble to the Eastern Emperors, who had been obliged not only to bestow upon them territory, but also to pay tribute. The reigning Emperor eagerly seized the first opportunity to rid himself of them. He suggested to their king, Theodoric,—hunter, soldier, statesman, a big-limbed, heroic man, passionate but just,—that he should lead his people into Italy, conquer Odoacer, and rule as Imperial lieutenant. As Italy was far pleasanter than Pannonia, Theodoric gladly accepted the suggestion.

The Goths, not more than two or three hundred thousand persons all told, effected their tedious emigration in 488-489. It was an easy matter to defeat the unstable Odoacer, and the Latins made no resistance. Theodoric, now master of Italy, both by right of conquest and by Imperial commission, set himself, in his turn, to the task of uniting Barbarians and Romans throughout the peninsula under one stable government. His difficulties were great. In the first place the immigrating people whom he led, though mainly Goths, were a medley of various tribes, and constituted an alien army of occupation in the midst of an unfriendly population, perhaps ten times their number. This Roman population, which had completely given up the use of arms, and never took part in any fight more formidable than a riot, was largely urban and lived in the cities which were scattered over Italy, almost the same that exist to this day. In the north were Turin, Pavia, Ferrara, Milan, Bergamo, Verona, Aquileia; on the east coast, Ravenna, Rimini, Ancona; on the west coast and in the centre, Genoa, Pisa, Lucca, Perugia, Spoleto, Rome, Benevento, Naples, Salerno, Amalfi; and in the south, the old Greek cities. All the ordinary business of life was in Roman hands; lawyers, physicians, weavers, spinners, carpenters, masons, cobblers, were Roman. Many of the workmen on great estates were also Roman. The Goths were primarily men-at-arms, and only exercised such rude crafts as were required in village communities. The leaders became military landowners. Naturally each race looked upon the other with suspicion, dislike, and contempt. It is obvious that there was need of both time and statesmanship before the two races would understand each other, share occupations, inter-marry, and feel themselves countrymen.

Theodoric's policy falls under three heads,—relations with the subject population, with the Emperor, and with the Church. With the Romans Theodoric was just and considerate; he limited the division of lands among his followers, so far as he could, to those lands which Odoacer's followers had had; he left civil administration chiefly in Roman hands; he let Romans live under

Roman law and Goths under Gothic law. He employed as his chief counsellor Cassiodorus, a great Roman noble of wealth and learning; he issued a code compiled from the Imperial codes; he reduced the taxation. Following the custom of the late Western Emperors, he dwelt in Ravenna, where S. Apollinare Nuovo, S. Spirito, a baptistery, and a mausoleum still testify to his presence. When the State had been put in order, Theodoric made a royal progress to Rome (500), where he was welcomed with Imperial honours. He promised to uphold all the institutions established by Roman Emperors, and showed himself as much interested in the city as if he had been a Roman. He provided carefully for the preservation of all the monuments of antiquity, repaired the walls, the aqueducts, the cloacae, and drained the Pontine Marshes. He spoke of Rome as "the city which is indifferent to none, since she is foreign to none; the fruitful mother of eloquence, the spacious temple of every virtue, comprising within herself all the cherished marvels of the universe, so that it may in truth be said, Rome is herself one great marvel." He renewed the distribution of bread, celebrated games in the circus, and treated the Senate with great distinction. In fact, until his breach with the Church, which turned all the orthodox population against him, he walked closely in the Imperial footsteps and was very successful in his relations with the Latin people.

Dealings with the Emperor were more difficult. Immediately after his victory over Odoacer, Theodoric had asked the Emperor for the regalia (the crown jewels and Imperial vestments) of the West, which had been sent to Constantinople upon the deposition of Romulus Augustulus. This embassy had been at first fobbed off, but finally the regalia were sent him in token of full recognition of his authority. In the mean time Theodoric's army without waiting for permission from the Emperor had proclaimed him king; and in practice Theodoric always acted as an independent king. In theory, however, he accepted the inclusion of Italy in the Empire as a fundamental principle, and acknowledged that his position was merely that of ruler of one of the Imperial provinces. The Emperors, compelled by impotence to acquiesce in Theodoric's lieutenancy of Italy, wished him in their hearts all possible bad luck, and bided their time to make trouble for him. But this ill will was concealed beneath the surface, and for about thirty years his relations with the Empire, with some interruptions, were amicable enough.

Before speaking of Theodoric's relations with the Church, which were a matter of politics, and had to be considered by him on general grounds of policy, it is necessary to speak of the relations between the Church and the Emperor, for the latter affected the former. There were always difficulties, active or latent, between the Roman Church and the Empire. There was jealousy between old Rome and new Constantinople. There was misunderstanding between the Latin and Greek mind. There was friction between Papal and Imperial authority. These troubles will appear more clearly as we proceed. At this time it is only necessary to say that during the first thirty years of Theodoric's reign, his period of success and prosperity, there was discord between Pope and Emperor, a kind of schism. The Byzantine Emperors, often men of cultivation, living in the most civilized city of the world, interested themselves in theology, and liked nothing better than to tinker with the Faith. To this, also, they were pushed by political needs. Their subjects were divided into the orthodox and the heterodox; and this diversity of belief was always a menace to political unity. To heal the breach, the reigning Emperor devised a scheme of compromise, a via media, on which he hoped all would unite. The Papacy, incensed by this trifling with orthodoxy, and by the assumption of an Imperial right to interfere in matters of faith, denounced the compromise. A schism was the consequence, which lasted until the reign of the Emperor Justin (518-527), when the crafty statesman who guided Justin's policy, his nephew, the famous Justinian, effected a reconciliation. For Justinian already cherished an ambition to win back Italy for the Empire; and he knew that that could not be done without the support of the Papacy. In 519 a papal embassy bearing the olive branch was warmly welcomed at Constantinople; both Emperor and nephew condemned the compromise and accepted the orthodox Catholic faith. Thus the breach was healed.

During the period of this breach between Empire and Papacy, the Gothic king had managed his relations with the Church very prudently. Although an Arian (like all Barbarians except the Franks), he was exceedingly just to the Catholics. He carefully refrained from taking part in the domestic affairs of the Church, until he was compelled to do so in the interest of order. While in Rome he maintained a most correct attitude. But though he acted with great moderation and only followed Imperial precedents, the Church resented his interference. Do what Theodoric would, the Papacy was his natural enemy. It felt instinctively that a king of Italy must always overshadow the Pope, just as at Constantinople the Emperor eclipsed the Patriarch, and that only upon condition of keeping Italy without a strong government within its borders could the Church attain its full stature. The ecclesiastical power was already inimical to civil authority. The attitude of the Church toward Theodoric presaged the history of the Holy Roman Empire during the Middle Ages, and the kingdom of Italy in our day. Nevertheless, until the reconciliation of Emperor and Pope, Theodoric had no serious trouble.

About the year 524 the crafty Justinian, strong in his complete reconciliation with the Papacy, felt the time ripe to set about the recovery of the lost provinces of the West, and made the first hostile move. Perhaps, however, it is unjust to assign a purely political motive to Justinian's action, for in his active Byzantine brain, policy, theology, law, art, and ambition were curiously blended. An Imperial edict was issued, persecuting Arians in various ways, and in particular commanding that all Arian churches throughout the Empire should be handed over to Catholics. This action of course received the approval of the Pope, and was most effective in alienating the Arian Goths from the Catholic Latins. Theodoric, who had been consistently tolerant to Catholics, was very angry and threatened to retaliate by suppressing the Catholic ritual throughout Italy. This threat threw the Papacy into closer alliance with the Emperor, and aggrieved the Latin people. A new generation had grown up in peace and comparative prosperity under Theodoric's rule, and, forgetful that for these blessings it was indebted to the Goths, began to give free play to its Latin prejudices. Thus the three natural enemies of Gothic rule gradually drew together: the Empire, from desire to recover Italy; the Papacy, to be rid of a ruler; and the Latins, out of national prejudice.

Intrigues were started between Constantinople and some leading men in Rome. How far the conspiracy went nobody knew. The king was in no mood to act judicially. Several senators were arrested on the charge of high treason, tried before partial or irregular tribunals, and put to death. Of these senators the most famous was Boethius, who stands at the end of Roman civilization, as Dante stands at the beginning of modern civilization. The long centuries between the two constitute the Middle Ages. It is interesting to note that Dante in his desolation after the death of Beatrice took to console him the book which Boethius wrote in prison, the "Consolations of Philosophy."

Boethius came of the most distinguished family in Rome. He and both his sons had been consuls. He was a student of Plato, Aristotle, and of the Neoplatonists; he had translated treatises on mathematics from the Greek, and had written on philosophy and theology. He was an encyclopedia of knowledge; when a hydraulic watch was wanted, or an especially magnificent sundial, or a test to detect counterfeit money, or a musician to be sent to a foreign potentate, he was the man to be consulted. His "Consolations of Philosophy," which had immense vogue all through the Middle Ages in every language, furnishes his apology, his case against Theodoric, and gives the Latin view of the Barbarians. He says: "The hatred against me was incurred while I was in office, because I opposed the acts of oppression to which the Romans were subjected. The greed of the Barbarians for the lands of the Romans, always unpunished, grew greater day by day; they sought men's lives in order to get their goods. How often have I protected and defended wretches from the innumerable calumnies of the Barbarians who wished to devour them." To this Roman defence must be opposed the statement of a contemporary historian: "Everything about the Barbarians, even the very smell of them, was hateful to the Romans; nevertheless it often happened that they, especially the poor, preferred the oppression of the Barbarians to that of the Imperial officials. The rich Romans impose taxes but they do not pay them; they make the poor pay them. And when peradventure the taxes are diminished the relief goes not to the poor but to the rich; so that, when it is a matter of paying it concerns the people, and when it comes to the matter of reducing taxes it is as if the rich were the only persons taxed at all. Not Franks, Huns, Vandals, nor Goths behave so shamelessly."

In spite of trials and executions Theodoric's anger and suspicion increased; he compelled the Pope to go to Constantinople to ask that the Arians be treated fairly and the Arian churches restored. The Pope returned having obtained some favours for the Catholics, but nothing for the Arians; whereupon Theodoric threw him into prison, and kept him there till he died (526). He then nominated a successor, who was promptly elected by the frightened Romans. This high-handed action stimulated discontent so much that it seemed as if the time for a Byzantine invasion had come, but Justinian, not having fully spun his web, delayed. Perhaps he feared Theodoric and wished to wait for his death. He did not have to wait long. That summer Theodoric died, and with him Italy's best hopes died too.

With Theodoric's death ended the possibility of a Gothic monarchy. Even in his reign a process of deterioration had set in among the young generation. The decadent civilization of Italy wrought with fatal effect upon the simple Goths; the luxurious ways, the idle habits, even the refinements of the Latins, robbed them of their vigour and independence of character. The conquerors became divided among themselves; some inclined to the old Gothic traditions, some to the Latin ways. The royal house affords a conspicuous instance of this deterioration; the boy king succumbed to debauchery, his mother fell a victim to her Latin sympathies, and his cousin, last of the royal line, a student of literature and philosophy, showed himself perfectly incapable of action and was deposed by his soldiers. Justinian, the spider, had been biding his opportunity; now it had surely come. The Goths were disintegrated; the Papacy and Latin people were with him; and his great general, Belisarius, fresh from the brilliant conquest of the Vandal kingdom in Africa, was ready for the task. In 535 the war for the reconquest of Italy began.

The Goths were confused, divided, and without a leader, whereas Belisarius was a man of military genius, and his army was composed of veterans. The issue could not remain long in doubt. Naples, Rome, and finally Ravenna, fell, and the reconquest would have been complete, but that Justinian, jealous of a too successful general, recalled Belisarius. The Goths improved their respite, and their king, Totila, a very valiant soldier, for a time retrieved their falling fortunes. Justinian, however, who had a remarkable knowledge of men, appointed general-in-chief an extraordinary little old man, Narses, who, devoid of all military experience, had passed his life in the Imperial civil service. Narses handled his men as if he had been born and bred in a camp, and, after a comparatively brief campaign in which Totila was killed, compelled the last remnant of the Gothic army to surrender (553).

Thus ended the first attempt to erect a Barbarian kingdom in Italy. Its failure proved that without the support of the Catholic Church it was impossible to establish a kingdom of Italy, for the Church controlled the Latin people, and though these never fought, they had an hundred ways of helping friends and hindering foes.

CHAPTER III: THE LOMBARD INVASION (568)

The Imperial dominion over all Italy had lasted scarce a dozen years before another Barbarian nation, the Lombards, came and repeated the experiment in which the Goths had failed. The period of Lombard dominion lasted two hundred years (568-774). It is rather an uninteresting time; nevertheless, like most history, it has a dramatic side. It makes a play for four characters. The Lombards occupy the larger part of the stage, but the protagonist is the Papacy. The Empire is the third character. Finally, the Franks come in and dispossess the Lombards. The plot, though it must spread over several chapters, is simple.

The scene of the play was pitiful. For nearly twenty years (535-553) Italy had been one perpetual battlefield; whichever side won, the unfortunate natives had to lodge and feed a foreign army, and endure all the insolence of a brutal soldiery. Plague, pestilence, and famine followed. The ordinary business of life came to a stop. Houses, churches, aqueducts went to ruin; roads were left unmended, rivers undiked. Great tracts of fertile land were abandoned. Cattle roamed without herdsmen, harvests withered up, grapes shrivelled on the vines. From lack of food came the pest. Mothers abandoned sick babies, sons left their fathers' bodies unburied. The inhabitants of the cities fared no better. Rome, for instance, had been captured five times. Before the war her population had been 250,000; at its close not one tenth was left. It is said that in one period every living thing deserted the city, and for forty days the ancient mistress of the world lay like a city of the dead. With peace came some respite; but the frightful squeeze of Byzantine taxation was as bad as Barbarian conquest. Italy sank into ignorance and misery. The Latin inhabitants hardly cared who their masters were. They never had spirit enough to take arms and fight, but meekly bowed their heads. Such was the scene on which these three great actors, the Lombards, the Papacy, and the Empire, played their parts. It is now time to describe the actors. We give precedence to the Empire, as is its due.

This remnant of the Roman Empire, with its capital on the confines of Europe and Asia, was an anomalous thing. It is a wonder that it continued to exist at all. In fact, there is no better evidence of the immense solidity of Roman political organization than the prolonged life of the Eastern Empire. The countries under its sway, Thrace, Illyria, Greece, Asia Minor, Syria, Palestine, Egypt, had no bond to hold them together, except common submission to one central authority. By the end of the sixth century, the Roman Empire was really Greek. The Greek language was spoken almost exclusively in Constantinople, Latin having dropped even from official use. Yet the Empire was still regarded as the Roman Empire, and was looked up to by the young Barbarian kingdoms of Europe with the respect which they deemed due to the Empire of Augustus and Trajan. For instance, a king of the Franks addresses the Emperor thus: "Glorious, pious, perpetual, renowned, triumphant Lord, ever Augustus, my father Maurice, Imperator," and is content to be called in return, "Childipert, glorious man, king of the Franks." Yet it must be remembered that Constantinople at this time was the chief city of Europe. Greek thought and Greek art lingered there. Justinian had just built St. Sophia. In fact, Constantinople continued for centuries to be the most civilized city in the world.

The Imperial government was an autocracy; all the reins, civil, military, ecclesiastical, were gathered into the hands of the Emperor. Its foreign policy was to repel its enemies, Persians to the east, Avars to the north, Arabs to the south; its domestic policy was to hold its provinces together and to extort money. The Emperors, many of whom were able men, usually spent such time as could be spared from questions of national defence and of finance in the study of theology, for at Constantinople the problems of government were in great measure religious. Next to the actual physical needs of life, the main interest of the people was religion. A statesman who sought to preserve the Empire whole, of necessity endeavoured to hold together its incohesive parts by means of religious unity. This political need of religious unity is the explanation, in the main, of the frequent theological edicts and enactments.

The Emperors governed Italy, after the reconquest, by an Imperial lieutenant, the Exarch, who resided at Ravenna, under a system of administration preserved in mutilated form from times prior to the fall of Romulus Augustulus. An attempt was made to keep civil and military affairs separate, but the pressure of constant war threw all the power into military hands. The peninsula, or such part of it as remained Imperial after the Lombard invasion, was divided for administrative and military purposes into dukedoms and counties, which were governed by dukes and generals. The Byzantine officials were usually Greeks, bred in Constantinople and trained in the Imperial system; they regarded themselves as foreigners, and had neither the will nor the skill to be of use to Italy. Their public business was to raise money for the Empire, their private business to raise money for themselves.

In spite of these oppressions the Latin people preferred the Greeks to the Lombards, partly because of their common Greco-Roman civilization, partly because the Empire was still the Roman Empire; and this popular support stood the Empire in good stead in the long war which it waged with the Lombards. The Latin people did not fight, but they gave food and information. The Empire, however, was ill prepared for a contest. The recall of Narses removed from Italy the last bulwark against Barbarian invasion. The Imperial army was weak, cities were poorly garrisoned, fortifications badly constructed; and, but for the control of the sea which enabled the Empire to hold the towns on the sea-coast, the whole of Italy would have fallen, like a ripe apple, into the hands of the invaders. The Empire, in fact, was exhausted by the effort of reconquest and had neither moral nor material strength to spare from its home needs.

The Lombards, if inferior in dignity to the Empire, played a far more active part in this historic drama. They came originally from the mysterious North, and after wandering about eastern Europe had at last settled near the Danube, where part of them were converted to Arian Christianity. Discontented with their habitation, and pressed by wilder Barbarians behind them, they were glad to take advantage of the defenceless condition of Italy. They knew how pleasant a land it was, for many of them had served as mercenaries under Narses. The whole nation, with a motley following from various tribes, amounted to about two or three hundred thousand persons. They crossed the Alps in 568.

There were many points of difference between these invaders and the Goths. The Lombards had had little intercourse with the Empire, and were far less civilized than their predecessors, and far inferior in both military and administrative capacity. Their leader, Alboin, cannot be compared in any respect with Theodoric. Moreover, Theodoric came, nominally at least, as lieutenant of the Emperor, and affected to deem his sovereignty the continuation of Imperial rule; whereas the Lombards regarded only the title of the sword and invariably fought the Empire as an enemy.

The invaders met little active resistance; if they had had control of the sea, they would readily have conquered the whole peninsula. They overran the North and strips of territory down the centre within a few years, and afterwards gradually spread little by little; but they never conquered the South, the duchy of Rome, or the Adriatic coast. For the greater part of the two hundred years during which the Lombard dominion existed, the map of Italy bore the following aspect: the Empire retained the little peninsula of Istria; the long strip of coast from the lowlands of Venetia to Ancona, protected by its maritime cities, Ravenna, Rimini, Pesaro, Sinigaglia; and the duchy of Rome, which spread along the Tyrrhene shore from Civita Vecchia to Gaeta; Naples and Amalfi; the territories of the heel and toe; and also Sicily and Sardinia. The boundaries were never fixed. Of the Lombard kingdom all one need remember is that it was a loose confederation of three dozen duchies; and that of these duchies, Spoleto, a little north of Rome, and Benevento, a little northeast of Naples, were the most important, as well as the most detached from the kingdom. In fact, these two were independent duchies, and rarely if ever took commands from Pavia, the king's capital, except upon compulsion.

At the time of the invasion the Lombards were barbarians; and they did not make rapid progress in civilization. Fond of their native ways, of hunting and brawling, they were loath to adopt the arts of peace, and left most forms of craft and industry to the conquered Latins. Nevertheless, it was impossible to avoid the consequences of daily contact with a far more developed people, and their manners became more civilized with each generation. The royal house affords an indication of the change which was wrought during the two hundred years. Alboin, the original invader (died 573), killed another Barbarian king, married his daughter, and forced her to drink from a cup made of her father's skull. The last Lombard king, Desiderius (died about 780), cultivated the society of scholars, and his daughter learned by heart "the golden maxims of philosophy and the gems of poetry." Each advance of the Lombards in civilization was a gain to the Latins, who, especially in the country where they worked on farms, were little better than serfs. The two races drew together slowly. The conversion of the Lombards from Arian to Catholic Christianity (600-700) diminished the distance between them. Intermarriage must soon have begun; but not until the conquest by the Franks does there seem to have been any real blending of the races.

The most conspicuous trait in the Lombard character was political incompetence. It would have required but a little steadiness of purpose, a little political foresight, a little spurt of energy, to conquer Ravenna, Rome, Naples and the other cities held by the Byzantines, and make Italy into one kingdom. Failure was due to the weakness of the central government, which was unable to weld the petty dukedoms together. This cutting up of Italy into many divisions left deep scars. Each city, with the territory immediately around it, began to regard itself as a separate state, with no sense of duty towards a common country; each cultivated individuality and jealousy of its neighbours, until these qualities, gradually growing during two hundred years, presented insuperable difficulties to the formation of an Italian national kingdom.

In spite of their political incompetence the Lombards left their mark on Italy, especially on Lombardy and the regions occupied by the strong duchies of Spoleto and Benevento. For centuries Lombard blood appears in men of vigorous character; and Lombard names, softened to suit Italian ears, linger on among the nobility. In fact, the aristocracy of Italy from Milan to Naples was mainly Teutonic, and the principal element of the Teutonic strain was Lombard.

CHAPTER IV: THE CHURCH (568-700)

One great political effect of the Lombard conquest was the opportunity which it gave the Papacy, while Lombard and Byzantine were buffeting each other, to grow strong and independent. Had Italy remained a Greek province the Pope would have been a mere provincial bishop, barely taking ceremonial precedence of the metropolitans of Ravenna, Aquileia, and Milan; had Italy become a Lombard kingdom, the Pope would have been a royal appointee; but with the Lombard kings fighting the Byzantine Exarchs, each side needing papal aid and sometimes bidding for it, the Pope was enabled to become master of the city and of the duchy of Rome, and the real head of the Latin people as well as of the Latin clergy. In fact, the growth of the Roman Catholic Church is the most interesting development in this period. The Lombards gave it the opportunity to grow strong and independent, but the power to take advantage of the opportunity came from within. This power was compact of many elements, secular and spiritual. From the ills of the world men betook themselves with southern impulsiveness to things religious; they sought refuge, order, security in the Church. In the greater interests of life among the Latins the rising ecclesiastical fabric had no competitor. Paganism had vanished before Christianity, philosophy before theology. Literature, art, science had perished. Italy had ceased to be a country. The ancient Empire of Rome had faded into a far-away memory. The wreck of the old nobility left the ecclesiastical hierarchy without a rival. In the midst of the general ruin of Roman civilization the Church stood stable, offering peace to the timid, comfort to the afflicted, refinement to the gentle, a home to the homeless, a career to the ambitious, power to the strong. By a hundred strings the Church drew men to her; in a hundred modes she sowed the prolific seeds of ecclesiastical patriotism. She was essentially Roman, and gathered to herself whatever was left of life and vigour in the Roman people. With a structure and organization framed on the Imperial pattern, she slowly assumed in men's minds an Imperial image; and Rome, a provincial town whose civil magistrates busied themselves with sewers and aqueducts, again began to inspire men with a strange confidence in a new Imperial power.

In addition to the strength derived from her immense moral and spiritual services, the Church had the support of two potent forces, ignorance and superstition. The general break-up of the old order had lowered the common level of knowledge. Everybody was ignorant, everybody was superstitious. The laws of nature were wholly unknown. Every ill that happened, whether a man tripped over his threshold, or a thunderbolt hit his roof, was ascribed to diabolic agencies. The old pagan personification of natural forces, without its poetry, was revived. The only help lay in the priest, a kind of magical protector, who with beads, relics, bones, incense, and incantation defended poor humanity from the assaults of devils. Thus, while all civil society suffered from ignorance, while every individual suffered from the awful daily, hourly, presence of fear, the Church profited by both.

Beside these intangible resources, the Church, or to speak more precisely the Papacy, had others of a material kind. For centuries pious men, especially when death drew near, had made great gifts of land to the bishops of Rome, until these bishops had become the greatest landed proprietors in Italy. Most of their estates were in Sicily, but others were scattered all over Italy, and even in Gaul, Illyria, Sardinia, and Corsica. In extent they covered as much as eighteen hundred square miles, and yielded an enormous income. This income enabled the Popes to maintain churches and monasteries, schools and missionaries, to buy off raiding armies of Lombards, and also to equip soldiers of their own. These estates the Church owned as a mere private landlord. During the Gothic dominion and the restoration of Imperial rule, she had no rights of sovereignty. But later on, during the disturbed period of border war between Lombards and Greeks, we find the Popes actually ruling the duchy of Rome.

The corner-stone of the great papal power, however, was laid by the genius of one man, who organized the monastic sentiment of the sixth century and put it to the support of the Papacy. There had been monks in Italy long before St. Benedict (480-544), but as civil society disintegrated, men in ever greater numbers fled from the world, and sought peace in solitude and in monastic communities. St. Benedict perceived that the monastic rules and customs derived from the East were ill suited to the West; so he devised a monastic system, and formulated his celebrated Rule, which became the pattern for all other monastic rules in Europe. He founded a monastery at Subiaco, a little village near Rome, and afterwards the famous abbey on Monte Cassino, a high hill midway between Rome and Naples, which became the mother of all Benedictine monasteries and shone like a light in the Dark Ages. Benedict's ideal was to help men shut themselves off from the temptations of life and realize, as far as they could, the prayer "Thy kingdom come ... on earth as it is in Heaven." He ordained community of property, and required a novitiate. Most strictly he forbade idleness, and with special insistence exhorted his brethren to till the ground with their own hands. Intellectual interests followed; and Benedictine monks became the teachers not only of agriculture, but of handicraft, of art and learning. His Order spread fast over Italy and Gaul, and in time over Spain, England, and Germany. Its communities, like the old castra romana, upheld the authority of Rome and enforced her dominion.

The attractions of the monastic life at Monte Cassino are well set out in a letter written (after St. Benedict's day) to one of the abbots, by a man of the world who had once lived there: "Though great spaces separate me from your company, I am bound to you by a clinging affection that can never be loosed, nor are these short pages enough to tell you of the love that torments me all the time for you, for the superiors and for the brethren. So much so that when I think about those leisure days spent in holy duties, the pleasant rest in my cell, your sweet religious affection, and the blessed company of those soldiers of Christ, bent on holy worship, each brother setting a shining example of a different virtue, and the gracious talks on the perfections of our heavenly home, I am overcome, all my strength goes, and I cannot keep tears from mingling with the sighs that burst from me. Here I go about among Catholics, men devoted to Christian worship; everybody receives me well, everybody is kind to me from love of our father Benedict, and for the sake of your merits; but compared with your monastery the palace is a prison; compared with the quiet there this life is a tempest."

What Benedict did for the monastic orders, another great man, St. Gregory (540-604), did for the Papacy itself. Gregory the Great, the most commanding figure in the history of Europe between Theodoric and Charlemagne, was a Roman, made of the same stuff as Scipio and Cato, and presented the interesting character of a Christian and an antique Roman combined. Born of a noble Roman family, Gregory was educated in Rome, and entered the service of the state, in which he rose to the high office of prefect of the city; but, dissatisfied with civil life, he abandoned it and became a monk. He wanted to give himself up wholly to a monastic life, but deemed it his duty to accept office in the papal service, and filled the distinguished position of papal ambassador (to use a modern term) at the Imperial court at Constantinople. In 590 he was elected Pope, half against his will, for he desired to be either a monk or a missionary; but he felt that the hopes of civilization and the future of religion lay in the Papacy, and he applied himself with energy to his new task. This task was as complex and multifarious as possible. It concerned all Europe, from Sicily to England. Rome itself was in a deplorable condition, left undefended by the Exarch, and threatened by the Lombards of Spoleto, who harried the country to the very gates, murdering some Romans and carrying others off as slaves. Gregory had to take complete control of the city, military and civil. He wrote: "I do not know any more whether I now fill the office of priest or of temporal prince; I must look to our defence and everything else. I am paymaster of the soldiers." He kept up the courage of the Romans, and tried to draw spiritual good out of their plight. It was impossible for a contemporary eye to see that under present wretchedness lay germinating the seeds of empire; yet Gregory acted as if he beheld them. In spite of apprehensions of the end of the world he organized the Church to endure for centuries. Both at home and abroad he displayed a tireless activity.

Among the foreign events of his pontificate are the conversion of England by Augustine (597) and the ministry of St. Columbanus (543-615) among the Franks, Alemanni, and Lombards. It , was Gregory who saw the handsome fairhaired boys from England standing in the market-place and said, "Non Angli sed angeli." He had the true imperial instinct, and always encouraged the clergy in distant parts of Europe to visit Rome and to apply to Rome for counsel and aid. The respect in which he was held may be inferred from the titles given him by Columbanus: "To the holy lord and father in Christ, the most comely ornament of the Roman Church, the most august flower, so to speak, of all this languishing Europe, the illustrious overseer, to him who is skilled to inquire into the theory of the Divine causality, I, a mean dove (Columbanus), send Greeting in Christ." Gregory also maintained close relations with the clergy in Africa, and received homage from the Spanish bishops, for Spain had recently been converted from Arianism to Catholicism. He was by no means content to confine his dealings to the clergy, but was in frequent correspondence with kings and queens of western Europe, as well as with the Emperor and Empress in Constantinople. His immense energy made itself felt everywhere. He made rules for the liturgy; and mass is still celebrated partly according to his directions. He reformed church music and founded schools for the Gregorian chant. He administered the papal revenues, superintending the management of farms, stables, and orchards. He founded monasteries, he supported hospitals and asylums.

Benedict and Gregory are the two great figures of this period, and, though no worthy successor followed for several generations, they did their work so well that the Papacy, like a great growing oak, continued to spread its power conspicuously in the eyes of the world, and also, out of sight, in the hearts and habits of men.

The relations between the Papacy and the Empire were difficult. The Popes were subjects of the Emperor. The whole ecclesiastical organization throughout the Empire was subject to the Imperial will, just as the civil or military service was. The Papacy did not like this position of subordination and resented any interference in papal affairs. Though Odoacer, Theodoric, and Justinian had always asserted their right to exercise a supervision over papal elections, the Popes had never acquiesced willingly, and even in those early days showed a marked disposition to take exclusive control of what they deemed their own affairs. It might be supposed that the Papacy, mindful of the great danger of a Lombard conquest of Rome, would have clung to the Empire; but after the Lombards had become Catholics the gap between the Romans and the Greco-Oriental Empire was nearly as wide as that between them and the Lombards. There was a fundamental difference between the Greek mind, floating over metaphysics and speculative theology, and the Roman mind, bound to political conceptions and practical ends. A theology which would satisfy a congregation in St. Sophia would not suit the worshippers in St. Peter's. The Empire, obliged to adapt theological niceties to political necessities, favoured any creed of compromise, which should promote political concord and unity. Rome, with its despotic, imperial instincts, felt that orthodoxy was its strength, and maintained an inflexible creed. The two were an ill-yoked pair, and quarrels were inevitable.

The relations between the Papacy and the Lombards were more simple. They varied between war, and friendship real or feigned. In the beginning, and even, as we have seen, in Gregory's time, there was war; but then began the conversion of the Lombards to Christianity, and intervals of peace followed, during which the Lombard king saluted the Pope as "Most Holy Father," and the Pope replied "My well-beloved Son."

CHAPTER V: THE COMING OF THE FRANKS (726-768)

We now come to the separation of the Latin world from the Greek world in both political and ecclesiastical affairs, and to the reconstruction of Europe by the alliance of the Franks and the Papacy. The plot continues to be very simple. The Empire, pressed by dangerous enemies, tried once more to gain political strength by ecclesiastical legislation; the effect of this legislation on the Imperial provinces in Italy was to cause rebellion. The Papacy broke the ties that bound it to the Empire; then, finding itself defenceless before the Lombards, made an alliance with the Franks, who invaded Italy and overthrew the Lombards.

In order to elaborate this plot, we must begin with the great Asiatic movement of the seventh century; for this movement acted as a cause of causes to split the Latins from the Greeks, to exalt the Papacy, and to form the Holy Roman Empire. In one of the tribes of Arabia, without heralding, appeared a man, who at the age of forty became a religious prophet, and by the force of genius constructed one of the great religions of the world. Mohammed's religion worked on the ardent Arabian temperament like magic, and engendered a fierce passion for conquest and proselytizing. Tribes cohered, became both a sect and a nation, and swept like wildfire over the west of Asia and the north of Africa. Mohammed died in 632, but his successors, the Caliphs, carried on his work; under the inspiration of the slogan, "Before you is Paradise, behind you the devil and the fire of hell," they advanced from conquest to conquest. Cities and provinces were torn from the Empire. Damascus, Syria, Jerusalem, Mesopotamia, Armenia, Egypt, Rhodes fell in rapid succession; next Africa, bit by bit. Persia was beaten to her knees. Sicily was raided. Twice Constantinople had to fight for life.

Naturally Byzantine statesmen felt that some radical step must be taken, or all the remnants of the Empire would be reduced to slavery. A vigorous Emperor, Leo the Isaurian (717-741), took the radical step. It was necessarily religious, for, in Constantinople, political action always took a religious complexion. Leo issued a decree forbidding the use of images in churches and in Christian worship (726). Those in place he ordered broken. He acted no doubt from high motives, thinking to ennoble religion and to arouse patriotism; but his people disagreed with him. In the East riots and civil war broke out. These were suppressed, but discontent and persistent opposition remained. In Italy also the excitement was intense. The country had already been irritated by severe taxation, and when the decree of iconoclasm was published, the image-loving Italians rose in a body. The Pope, as most hurt in conscience by the decree, and in pocket by the taxation, was the natural head of resistance. The Exarch attempted to arrest him, but both Latins and Lombards rallied to his defence. In some places open revolt broke out, and a plot was started to set up another Emperor in place of the wicked iconoclast who polluted the Imperial throne. But the Pope, Gregory II (715-731), was a prudent man, and was not ready to take a step which would deprive Rome of its single defence from the Lombards. He opposed the rebellious plan, but in the matter of maintaining the images he stood like a rock. His successor, Gregory III (731-741), went farther, and took decisive action. He convoked a synod, which expelled every image-breaker from the Church (731). This was tantamount to a direct excommunication of the

Emperor, and a declaration of papal independence. The Emperor was powerless to compel obedience. Thus began the great split between the Papacy and the Byzantine Empire, between western and eastern Europe, between the Latin Church and the Greek. Some of the western provinces, Calabria, Sicily, and Illyria, which were practically Greek, remained faithful to the Empire and shared its fortunes for several hundred years more. Ecclesiastically they were removed from the jurisdiction of the Popes to that of the Patriarchs of Constantinople.

This breach between the Papacy and the Empire led inevitably to an alliance between the Papacy and the Franks, which is of such great historical consequence that it must be recounted in some detail. While the Empire and the Papacy were quarrelling over ecclesiastical matters, western Europe had been changing. The Frankish kingdom had been established in what is now Belgium, Holland, and large parts of France and Germany, and was the one great Christian power in Europe. Therefore, when the Papacy had cut loose from the Empire and saw itself defenceless against the Lombards, it had no alternative but to seek help from the Franks. There were also two special reasons for friendship between the Franks and the Papacy. First, the Franks, alone of Barbarians, had been converted to Catholic Christianity. Secondly, in their endeavours to enlarge their eastern borders, the Franks had been greatly assisted by the missionaries, who—in the normal course, missionaries, merchants, soldiers—had prepared the way for Frankish conquest, and had strengthened the Frankish power when established. These missionaries were absolutely devoted to the Roman See; they spread papal loyalty wherever they went, and wrought a strong bond of union between the Frankish kingdom and the Papacy. This union of sympathy and interest was an excellent basis for a political union; and the time soon came for such a development.

When the iconoclastic revolts occurred in Italy, and the Popes broke with the Empire, the Lombard kings thought that their opportunity to conquer all Italy had come. But instead of making one bold campaign against Rome and the South, they merely laid hands on a few border cities. The Popes turned with frantic appeals for help to the only power that could help them, the Franks. Every time the Lombard king made a hostile move, the Pope cried aloud for aid. For some time the Franks deemed that the balance of political considerations was against intervention and refused to take part in Italian affairs. Charles Martel, mayor of the palace and ruler of the Franks in all but name, stood firm on the policy of non-interference; but his son and successor, Pippin the Short, took a different view. Pippin judged that the time had come to depose the royal Merovingian family and to exalt his own, the Carlovingian, in its stead. As the Merovingians had reigned for two hundred and fifty years, the step was revolutionary, and Pippin wished to strengthen his position by the support of the Papacy. He sent messengers to the Pope, Zacharias, to ask advice; and the Pope, according to the chronicler, "in the exercise of his apostolical authority replied to their question, that it seemed to him better and more expedient that the man who held power in the kingdom should be called king and be king, rather than he who falsely bore that name. Therefore the Pope commanded the king and the people of the Franks, that Pippin, who was using royal power, should be called king and should be settled on the throne." The last Merovingian, therefore, was tonsured and stowed away in a monastery, and

Pippin became king of the Franks (751). Without accepting the monkish chronicler's statement, that the Pope commanded Pippin to be king, there can be little doubt that the papal sanction was of very real value to Pippin, and that Pippin let it appear that he was acting rather in conformity with the Pope's will than with his own.

Thus the Pope laid Pippin under a great obligation; it now remained for Pippin to discharge that obligation. It was not long before the time came.

The Lombard king felt that his opportunity was slipping by, and acted with some vigour. He captured Ravenna and threatened Rome. The Pope hurried across the Alps. He anointed and crowned Pippin; he likewise anointed and blessed his son Charles (Charlemagne), and forbade the Franks under pain of excommunication ever to choose their king from any other family. These three great favours, the transfer of the royal title, the coronation rite, and the perpetual confirmation of the Carlovingian sovereignty, called for a great return. Pippin promised that the Adriatic provinces, taken by the Lombards from the Byzantines, should be ceded by the Lombards to the Pope. This promise Pippin fulfilled. He crossed the Alps, defeated the Lombard king, and forced him to cede the Exarchate of Ravenna and the five cities below it on the coast, to the Pope, who thereby became an actual sovereign. Thus Pippin discharged his obligation to the Papacy.

This beginning of the Papal monarchy is so important that the theoretic origin may as well be mentioned here. There was a legend, universally believed, that an early Pope, Silvester (314-335) healed the Emperor Constantine of leprosy, and that the Emperor, in gratitude, made a great grant of territory to the Pope. The fact appears to have been that Constantine, although not cured of the leprosy, did give to Silvester the Lateran palace and a plot of ground around it. This little donation grew in legend like a grain of mustard seed, and served the purpose of the Roman clergy. No good Roman would have been content with a title derived from the Lombards or the Franks. In Roman eyes these Barbarians never had any title to Italian territory; they could give none. The only possible source of legal title was the Empire. In the gift by Constantine to Silvester papal adherents had a foundation of fact. That was enough. It is quite unnecessary to imagine false dealing. People in those days believed that what they wished true was true. This legend was accepted and embodied in concrete form in a document known as the Donation of Constantine, which is so important in explaining the attitude of the Papacy throughout the Middle Ages, that it may be quoted:—

"In the name of the holy and undivided Trinity, Father, Son, and Holy Ghost, the Emperor Cæsar Flavius Constantine ... to the most holy and blessed Father of Fathers, Silvester, bishop of Rome and Pope, and to all his successors in the seat of St. Peter to the end of the world...." Here comes, interspersed with snatches of Christian dogma, a rambling narrative of his leprosy, of the advice of his physicians to bathe in a font on the Capitol filled with the warm blood of babies; how he refused, how Peter and Paul appeared in a dream and sent him to Silvester, how he then abjured paganism, accepted the creed, was baptized and healed, and how he then recognized that heathen gods were demons and that Peter and his successors had all power on earth and in heaven. After this long preamble comes the grant:

"We, together with all our Satraps and the whole Senate, Nobles and People ... have thought it desirable that even as St. Peter is on earth the appointed Vicar of God, so also the Pontiffs his viceregents should receive from us and from our Empire, power and principality greater than belongs to us ... and to the extent of our earthly Imperial power we decree that the Sacrosanct Church of Rome shall be honoured and venerated, and that higher than our terrestrial throne shall the most sacred seat of St. Peter be gloriously exalted.

"Let him who for the time shall be pontiff over the holy Church of Rome ... be sovereign of all the priests in the whole world; and by his judgment let all things which pertain to the worship of God or the faith of Christians be regulated.... We hand over and relinquish our palace, the city of Rome, and all the provinces, places, and cities of Italy and the western regions, to the most blessed Pontiff and universal Pope, Silvester; and we ordain by our pragmatic constitution that they shall be governed by him and his successors, and we grant that they shall remain under the authority of the holy Roman Church."

The date of this document and many statements in it are anachronisms and errors. It was composed about the time of Pippin's Donation, probably by somebody connected with the papal chancery, and may be considered to be a pious forgery representing the facts as the writer deemed they were or else should be. It was officially referred to for the first time in 777, but did not receive its full celebrity until the eleventh century, when the relations of the Papacy and the Holy Roman Empire became the centre of European history.

CHAPTER VI: CHARLEMAGNE (768-814)

The papal theory embodied in the Donation of Constantine was obviously crammed with seeds of future strife; for the present, however, the fortunes of the House of Pippin and of the Papacy were bound together in amity. The constant accession of strength to the former and of prestige to the latter made them the central figures of European politics. The new political form to which their union gave birth slowly shaped itself. In Italy the first step was to get rid of the Lombards. On the death of the Lombard King, Aistulf, there were two claimants for the throne. One of the two, Desiderius, secured the Pope's help by the promise of ceding more cities, and became king. The Pope, writing to Pippin, says: "Now that Aistulf, that disciple of the devil, that devourer of Christian blood is dead; and that by your aid and that of the Franks [a complimentary phrase, for Pippin seems to have done nothing] he is succeeded by Desiderius, a most gentle and good man, we pray you to urge him to continue in the right way." But the "most gentle and good" Desiderius strayed from the right way, and did not cede the promised cities. So the Pope besought Pippin to use force; but Pippin thought that he had done enough, and the Pope was obliged to rest content. Pippin died in 768. One can imagine the consternation at Rome on Pippin's death to learn that the dowager queen of the Franks was arranging a marriage between her son Charlemagne and a daughter of Desiderius, and another marriage between her daughter and a son of Desiderius. The Pope wrote in terror that the plan was of the devil, and forbade it under the pains of everlasting damnation; nevertheless, Charlemagne married the daughter of Desiderius (770).

The Pope's anticipations, however, were not justified; the horrible union of the House of Pippin with the "unspeakable" Lombards came to an abrupt end. Charlemagne, probably from personal dislike, put away his wife, and sent her ignominiously back to her father. Desiderius, angry at the insult, rushed upon his fate; he not only intrigued in Frankish affairs against Charlemagne, but he also seized many of the cities given to the Pope by the Donation of Pippin. He invaded the duchy of Rome, and advanced within fifty miles of the city. This time Charlemagne acted in conformity with the papal entreaties. He crossed the Alps, routed the Lombard army, captured Pavia, took Desiderius prisoner and assumed the title of King of the Lombards (773-774). He went on to Rome, and solemnly confirmed the Donation of Pippin, and also made a further Donation. This latter Donation, which led to disputes between the Papacy and Charlemagne's successors, is a matter of great uncertainty. Subsequent papal advocates claimed that it embraced two thirds of Italy. Probably Charlemagne only intended to restore to the Papacy its private property scattered throughout northern and central Italy, which had been seized by the Lombards.

Charlemagne, having disposed of the Lombards, continued his conquests; across the Pyrenees he annexed the Spanish March, in North Germany he subdued the Saxons and pushed his frontier to the Elbe, to the southeast he subjugated the country as far as the upper Danube. His monarchy now included Franks, Celts, Visigoths, Burgundians, Saxons, Lombards, Romans. How were such widespread territories and such diverse peoples to be united in permanent union? The far-seeing Papacy, in answer to this question, propounded the revival of the Roman Empire of the

Cæsars. Reasons were numerous. The Frankish monarchy, with its conquests, in bulk at least was not unworthy to succeed to Imperial Rome. Throughout this wide territory there was a great network of ligaments; from Gascony to Bavaria, from Lombardy to Frisia, divine service was celebrated in the Latin tongue and with the Roman ritual; bishops, priests, monks, and missionaries acknowledged their dependence upon the Pope and looked to Rome, with its holy basilicas and apostolic tradition, as the centre of Christendom. This Christian unity was a constant argument for political unity. A second argument was the still vigorous Roman tradition. The idea of nationality was as yet undeveloped; Europe had known no other political system than common subjection to the Roman Empire, and all notions of civilization were of a civilization on the Roman pattern. When the Roman Empire in the West had decayed, the Church had adopted the Imperial organization and kept remembrance of the old system fresh in men's minds. The old Empire, moreover, had early lost the notion of dependence on the city of Rome, for the seat of government had been set at Constantinople, at Milan, and at Ravenna; and since the days of the early Cæsars, it had not been necessary for an Emperor to be a native Roman. There was no theoretical difficulty to bar a Frank from the Imperial throne or forbid the seat of government to a Frankish city. In fact, nobody could conceive of the Empire as other than Roman, and the Frankish kingdom could only become an empire by becoming the Roman Empire.

The Papacy had special reasons for these views. Under the Empire Christianity had grown up; under the Empire it had obtained power and dominion, and had become the state religion. The Church might quarrel with Emperors, but it regarded the Empire—the source of secular law and order—as its joint tenant in the world. The one represented religious unity, the other represented civil unity. In addition to these large arguments, local reasons affected the Papacy. Shortly before the expulsion of the Lombards from Italy, the lack of a strong government had been wofully felt. One usurper and then another had been put in St. Peter's chair in riot and bloodshed. It had become plain as day that the Papacy of itself, without the support of a potent secular power, was not able to maintain its dignity, nor even to enforce order in the very city of Rome. The Papacy could not endure without the Empire. The very titles which the Frankish kings had gradually received led up to the Imperial title. Gregory II had called Charles Martel "Patrician," a vague title of honour held by the Exarchs; Gregory III had offered to him the titles both of Patrician and of Consul; Stephen II bestowed upon Pippin the title of Patrician of the Romans; Charlemagne's own titles were King of the Franks, King of the Lombards, Patrician of the Romans; and his son had been crowned by the Pope, King of Italy (781). The title next in order was undoubtedly Emperor of the Romans. Charlemagne himself was a man of gigantic stature and great strength, indefatigable in action, and delighting in hunting, swimming, and martial exercise. His mind also was mighty, restlessly pondering questions of state, of church, of war, of social improvement. He was the greatest of Barbarians, cast by Nature in an imperial mould.

On the other hand there was one conspicuous difficulty in the way of reviving the Roman Empire; this difficulty was that the Roman Empire still existed, and that there was a living Emperor, the legitimate successor of Cæsar Augustus. But that Empire was virtually Greek, and the Emperor no more like Cæsar Augustus than like Hercules. The city by the Tiber had as good title to be the Imperial city as her younger rival by the Bosphorus; the Roman Republic (whatever that ill-defined title may mean), represented by the Pope, had as fair a claim to elect the Emperor, as the army and office-holders at Constantinople. In fact, to Papal and Roman eyes, the rights of Rome were much greater than those of Constantinople.

To us, as we look back, nothing seems more natural than that the great Frankish king, after the conquest of Italy, should have brushed aside the theoretical difficulty of an existing Roman Empire and assumed the Imperial title, Emperor of the Romans. History moves more slowly. Charlemagne was a Frank, accustomed to Frankish usages and ideas; he hesitated to adopt formally a wholly different conception of sovereignty and society. His nobles probably agreed with the advice given by Pope Zacharias to Pippin, that the man who held the power should receive the corresponding title, but being Franks they thought the dignity of Frankish king sufficient. So matters stood with nothing between Charlemagne and the Imperial crown but a theoretic difficulty, and a certain reluctance. Unexpectedly and in quick succession, events in Constantinople swept away the theoretic difficulty, and events in Rome gave the Pope sufficient energy to overcome the reluctance.

At Constantinople, the dowager Empress blinded and deposed her son the Emperor (797), and assumed to rule as sole Augusta. This wickedness, and the ancient doctrine that, though a woman might lawfully share the Imperial throne, she might not reign alone, combined to render plausible a theory readily adopted in the West, that the Imperial throne had become vacant. The event in Rome was this. A savage gang of nobles and ecclesiasts attacked Pope Leo III in the street, beat him, half-blinded him, cut his tongue, and imprisoned him in a monastery (799). He escaped and fled to Charlemagne in Germany. His enemies followed and charged him with various crimes. Charlemagne sent him back to Rome in the company of some great nobles, who were commissioned to investigate the charges, and went himself also. There, in St. Peter's basilica, in the presence of Frankish nobles and Roman ecclesiasts, with Charlemagne presiding, the Pope took a solemn oath of innocence (December 4, 800). Such an oath according to the jurisprudence of the time was necessarily followed by acquittal; and the Pope's innocence necessarily proved the guilt of his accusers, who were punished.

Such crimes, east and west, were insufferable. Something had to be done. Everybody looked to Charlemagne. His position as head of Christendom was acknowledged even beyond the bounds of western Europe. The Patriarch of Jerusalem, a subject of the Caliph Haroun al Raschid, sent to Charlemagne the keys of Calvary and of the Holy Sepulchre and the banner of the Holy City. Obviously it was time for the Imperial dignity to be added to Imperial power.

On Christmas day in the year 800, Charlemagne and a great procession of Frankish nobles and Roman citizens made their way through the streets of Rome towards the basilica of St. Peter's, whose gilt bronze roof, taken from a pagan temple, shone conspicuous on the Vatican hill. They walked through the Aurelian gate and across the bridge over the Tiber, then turning to the left, followed the colonnade which extended all the way from Hadrian's Mausoleum to the atrium of the basilica. There they mounted the broad flight of marble steps, at the top of which the Pope and his court awaited the king. Then Pope and king, followed by the procession, crossed the great atrium paved with white marble, past the fir-cone fountain and papal tombs, to the central door of the basilica, which swung its thousand-weight of silver open wide; then, up the long nave, screened by rows of antique columns from double aisles on either side, all rich with tapestries of purple and gold, they proceeded with slow and solemn steps to the tomb of the apostle. Thirteen hundred and seventy candles in the great candelabrum glowed on the silver floor of the shrine, and glittered on the gold and silver statues around it. In the great apse behind the high altar sat the clergy, row upon row, beneath the Pontiff's throne; above, the Byzantine mosaics looked down in sad severity. Here Charlemagne knelt at the tomb, and prayed. As he rose from his knees, the Pope lifted an Imperial crown of gold and placed it on his head, while all the congregation shouted, "Life and Victory to Charles, Augustus, crowned by God, the great and peaceful Emperor!"

Thus was accomplished that restoration of the Roman Empire, which by its attempt to combine Teuton and Roman in political union so powerfully affected the history of mediæval Europe. Charlemagne is reported to have said that the Imperial coronation took him by surprise. However that may be, this great enterprise of a Christian Empire must be regarded, in its final completion, as the joint work of Frankish king and Roman Pope.

CHAPTER VII: FROM CHARLEMAGNE TO NICHOLAS I (814-867)

The period from the death of Charlemagne (814) to the coronation of Otto the Great (962) is a long dismal stretch, tenanted by discord and ignorance. At the beginning stands the commanding figure of Charlemagne,

With Atlantean shoulders, fit to bear

The weight of mightiest monarchies.

But his descendants were unequal to their inheritance, and under them his Empire crumbled away and resolved itself into incipient nations. That Empire, in theory the restored Roman Empire, was in fact strictly Teutonic, though buttressed by the Roman Church. Charlemagne deemed himself head of both Empire and Church. In his eyes the Pope was his subject, and he legislated, as a matter of course, upon ecclesiastical affairs. In secular matters he endeavoured to maintain local administration without detriment to a strong central government. For this purpose he divided the Empire into three divisions, of which he made his three sons nominally kings, really his lieutenants. Under these sons he appointed counts and bishops, as local governors. He maintained his central authority by means of deputies (missi dominici), who traversed the whole Empire, two by two, a bishop and a count together. The maintenance of such a political unity, however, required either the organic strength and momentum of the old Roman Empire, or a breed of Charlemagnes. On the great Emperor's death the forces of disruption made themselves felt at once. His son, Louis the Pious, indeed succeeded to the whole sovereignty of the Empire; but Louis's sons demanded division. They rebelled; and civil war lasted most of Louis's life. After his death the sons fought one another, and finally agreed on a division of the territory, though the Imperial title was kept. One brother took the territory to the east, destined to become Germany; another, that to the west, destined to become France; and Lothair, the eldest, who also received the Imperial title, took Italy and a long, heterogeneous strip between the territories of his brothers. This division was fatal to the Empire. On Lothair's death the Imperial crown descended to his son Louis II (855-875), and afterwards to two other degenerate members of a degenerate family. The last made himself unendurable and was deposed (887). With him ended Charlemagne's legitimate male line, and also the first revival of the Roman Empire.

This Empire had been a civilizing power. It had supported the Papacy, as an oak supports the creeper that clings to it; and in its decline and fall it pulled the Papacy down with it. Without such support the Papacy could maintain neither dignity abroad nor order at home. This lesson the Church learned once through the outrages inflicted upon Pope Leo, but forgot it; and required the experience of a hundred and fifty years to learn it a second time. In theory Papacy and Empire were co-equal powers, religious and secular, together carrying on the noble task of God's government on earth. In practice, as their respective rights and powers had not been definitely set off, they could not agree; each wished to be master. The relations between the two constitute the great axis on which mediæval politics revolve, and for a long time must serve as the main motive of our story. The contest between them for mastery resembles a fencing match, in which the Pope thrusts at the Emperor's crown, the Emperor parries, and lunges back at the papal tiara. For convenience we divide the match into two bouts, and first take the Pope's attack.

At the famous coronation on Christmas day, 800, Charlemagne and Leo stood side by side, co-labourers in the great task of reconstructing Europe. But once the coronation over, the two undefined authorities jostled each other. Charlemagne, to whom government was as much a religious as a secular matter, though he had accepted his Imperial crown at the hands of the Pope, did not regard papal participation necessary for the continuance of the Imperial dignity. At Aachen, 813, he crowned his son Louis the Pious co-Emperor, without the help of Pope or priest. This thrust must have carried discomfiture to the banks of the Tiber. But with Charlemagne's weak successors the astute Papacy scored hit after hit. Louis the Pious submitted to be recrowned by the Pope, so did his son, Lothair, and his grandson Louis II; and their two successors were also crowned by the Pope. This sequence of palpable hits won this bout and secured for the Papacy beyond dispute the prerogative of crowning the Emperors.

If we now turn to that part of the game where Emperor lunged and Pope parried, we find a more complicated situation. A third player takes a hand, to the confusion of the game and to the great detriment of the papal defence. This third player is the Roman people, who believed that the Senatus Populusque Romanus still possessed their ancient prerogatives, and had the right to appoint both Emperor and Pope. Their claim to elect the Emperor was flimsy enough, being merely the memory of an empty form, and is not of enough consequence to stop for; but their claim to interfere in the papal election was of the highest importance. It arose from the anomalous nature of the Papacy. The Pope was bishop of Rome, and as such his election lay in the hands of the clergy and people of Rome; he was also the ruler of central Italy, and as such the barons there were interested in his election; and, in addition, he was head of all the Christian Churches in the West, and so all western Christendom, and the Emperor as its temporal lord, was likewise concerned. The fact was that no definite method of papal election and confirmation had been settled upon during these disturbed centuries. The original practice had been for the Roman churches, priests, and laymen together assembled, to make the election; subsequently the senate, or the army, or the nobles, had represented the lay body of electors; but whoever represented the laymen, they and the clergy made the election; which was then submitted to the Emperor, or his representative, for scrutiny and confirmation. The submission of the Roman election to the examination of a Byzantine Emperor had never been acceptable in Rome, and after the breach over iconoclasm, the practice ceased. Naturally, on the revival of the Roman Empire in the West, the new Emperors claimed the old Imperial right of supervision; naturally, also, the papal party resisted the fresh exercise of the old prerogative. Here was a situation for a scrimmage, but any clear account of the papal elections in Rome, supposing such were possible, would be too minute; this narrative must confine itself to the main passes between the papal party and the Emperors.

After the death of Charlemagne (no papal election occurred during his lifetime) several Popes were elected and consecrated without previously consulting the Emperor. On the other hand, in the next reign the Imperial deputy made the Romans take oath that no Pope should be consecrated without the approval of the Emperor. What was done at the following election is not known, but at the second the Pope was not consecrated until the Emperor had ratified the proceedings. Thereafter the Imperial right was acknowledged in theory, though in practice the elected Pontiffs did not always wait for Imperial confirmation.

With the fall of the Carlovingian Empire the fencing match ceased for lack of an Imperial contestant. The score stood thus: each had succeeded in the attack, the Papacy had won its right to bestow the Imperial crown, and the Empire had won, though not so definitely, its right to supervise the election of a Pope. We must now pass to this Imperial interregnum knowing that when the Empire shall be revived, the match will begin anew and the combatants, with foils unbated and envenomed, will fight to a finish.

The Imperial interregnum, nominally interrupted by one German and several Italian make-believe Emperors, lasted for three generations; no Imperial power was exercised from 875 to 962. It is a murky period in which shadows wander about; but before taking our candle and descending into the gloom, we will turn to the one bright spot, the career of a great Pope, Nicholas I (858-867).

This Pope, in spite of the decadence of the Papacy, won immense prestige for it by two successful assertions of cosmopolitan authority. The King of Lorraine, brother to Louis II, the Emperor, wished to put away his wife and marry another woman. The innocent queen, with the sanction of the clergy of the kingdom, was divorced and forced to enter a convent; and, with the consent of his clergy, the king married the other woman. The wronged queen appealed to the Pope, who sent his legates to investigate the affair; but the king bribed the legates and succeeded in getting a decision from the local synod in his favour, although, in fact, the whole matter had been a shocking scandal. Thereupon the king sent the archbishops of Cologne and of Trier, the two great ecclesiastical dignitaries of the kingdom, to announce this verdict of acquittal. The Pope, "professing," as his enemies said, "to be imperator of the whole world," seized his opportunity; he espoused the cause of the innocent queen, annulled the fraudulent proceedings, and excommunicated and deposed the two archbishops. The king applied to the Emperor for help, and the Emperor went to Rome, but could obtain no concession. The Pope stood like a rock. He allied himself with France and Germany, and threatened to excommunicate the sinning husband and all his bishops. The king was obliged to submit. The usurping wife was excommunicated and banished, and the papal legate conducted the divorced queen back to the royal palace. Thus the Papacy not only established a great precedent for the supremacy of the spiritual over the temporal power, but also stood conspicuous before the world as the champion of the weak and oppressed and the defender of morality and justice.

It would be difficult to overrate the effect of this papal achievement. It may be that the Papacy stood forth as champion of innocence when policy coincided with righteousness; but it was the righteousness and not the policy which gave the Papacy strength. One can imagine, in days when brutal barons, scattered in strongholds all over the country, were the normal forms of power and authority, what effect such news had upon the people. A pilgrim from across the Alps, a peddler, or some poor vagrant, enters a village huddled at the foot of a hill, on which stands a great castle where a drunken lord revels with his mistresses, and recounts to the assembled peasants, serfs, and slaves, how the Holy Father, in the name of God, had commanded a greater lord, in a greater castle, to put away his mistress and bring back his wife, and how that lord had got down on his knees and had done the Holy Father's bidding.

The second case was the victory of papal authority over the spirit of nationality in the Church. When the incipient nations of France and Germany, having separated from the Empire, had begun to be self-conscious, the spirit of nationality naturally showed itself in ecclesiastical matters as well as in political matters. There was obvious likelihood that the nations would govern themselves ecclesiastically as well as politically. Should they do so, the papal supremacy would fall just as the Imperial supremacy had fallen, and the unity of the Church would be shattered just as the Empire had been. Here was certainly a great danger to the Papacy, and probably a great danger to Christianity and civilization; at least so Nicholas thought. He resolved to meet it boldly. His opportunity came when a French (West Frankish) bishop appealed to Rome against the action of his metropolitan. The metropolitan objected that there was no precedent for papal action in such a case; he did not deny that the Pope had certain appellate functions, but said that if the Pope interfered directly in the discipline of bishops, the power of the metropolitan would be impaired. It is needless to say that this argument did not produce the result that the metropolitan desired. There was nothing the Papacy wanted more than that its central government should act directly everywhere, and that all bishops should be dependent upon Rome; that was the very principle of papal supremacy. The issue would determine whether the Papacy was to be an autocratic power, or a limited court of appeal. Nicholas was able to take advantage of the troubled political situation to enforce direct papal authority, and so added an immense prerogative to the papal power.

Apart from this imperial ecclesiastical principle the latter episode is especially interesting on account of the character of the evidence produced by the Pope to maintain his position. This evidence consisted of a new compilation of Church law which appeared somewhat mysteriously about this time. Theretofore Church law had consisted of a collection of precepts taken from the Bible, from the early Fathers, from decrees of Councils, and also of letters, called decretals, written by the bishops of Rome, but none of these decretals was earlier than the time of Constantine. The fact, that there were no papal decretals prior to Constantine, seemed to imply, at least to the sceptically minded, that papal authority had really begun at the time of Constantine and not at the time of St. Peter. To the ardent papist such an idea was incredible. Nicholas now produced a new batch of documents. Among these was the Donation of Constantine, of which I have spoken. Others were papal decretals, which purported to come from Popes of the third and second centuries, and to prove that papal jurisdiction over other bishoprics had been exercised almost as far back as the time of St. Peter. These new appearing documents placed the Pope not only above kings, but above metropolitans and provincial synods, and justified Nicholas in acting directly in the case of the West Frankish bishop, in the King of Lorraine's matrimonial affairs, and also in assuming to act as "imperator of the whole world." These documents, known as the Isidorian Decretals, were probably composed by some priest in France, not long before their use by Nicholas. For six hundred years they were believed to be genuine, and during that time rendered the Papacy great service by ranging the sentiment of law throughout Europe (at least until the revival of Roman law) on the side of the Papacy in its struggle with the Empire.

CHAPTER VIII: THE DEGRADATION OF ITALY (867-962)

These triumphs were due to the brilliant vigour of Pope Nicholas; but that triumphant position could not last, it was fictitious. The Papacy needed the support of a strong secular power, and when the Carlovingian Empire dissolved, it had nothing to rest on, neither genius nor military force, and fell into deep degradation.

To illustrate that degradation one episode will suffice; but there must first be a word of prologue. The Papacy, as has been said, occupied an anomalous position. From this sprang many troubles. As soon as the pressure of Imperial authority was removed, the Papacy tended to become the prize of municipal politics, and different parties in Rome (if the turbulent mobs may be called so) struggled to get possession of it. One party, with interests centred on local matters, indifferent to the greatness of the Papacy and its European character, and willing to have the Pope a mere local ruler, directed its efforts to getting rid of all Imperial and foreign control. The opposite party, with conflicting interests, wished for Imperial control, and constituted a kind of Imperial party, less from any large views, than in the hope of deriving advantages from Imperial support. Strife between the two parties was the normal condition, and often ended in riot and civil war. In this state of affairs, a certain Pope Formosus (891-896), who belonged to the Imperial faction, went so far as to invite the German king to come down to Rome and be crowned Emperor. The king actually came and was crowned, but accomplished little or nothing, except to arouse bitter hostility in his enemies. When Formosus died, his successor was elected from the opposite faction. The new Pope held a synod of cardinals and bishops, and before them, the highest Christian tribunal in the world, he summoned, upon the charge of violating the canons of the Church, the dead Formosus, whose body had lain in its grave, for months. The body was dug up, dressed in pontifical robes, and propped upon a throne. Counsel was assigned to it. The accusation was formally read, and the Pope himself cross-questioned the accused, who was convicted and deposed. His pontifical acts were pronounced invalid. His robes were torn from him, the three fingers of the right hand, which in life had bestowed the episcopal blessing, were hacked off, and the body was dragged through the streets and flung into the Tiber.

This incident sheds light on mediæval Rome, and on the character of the people with whom the Popes had to live. All the Popes, good, bad, and indifferent, whether they were struggling with the Empire on great cosmopolitan questions, or were trying to unite Christendom against Islam, always had to keep watch on the brutal, ignorant, bloody Roman people, who took no interest in great questions, and were always ready to rob, burn, and murder with or without a pretext.

Now that we have brought the Frankish Empire to its dissolution, and the Papacy to its degradation, we must leave the two wrecks for the moment, and stop in these dark years at the end of the ninth century to see how Italy herself has fared. The Italian world was out of joint, intellectually, morally, politically. There can hardly be said to have been a government. For a generation the poor, shrunken Empire had been but a shadow, and when the last Carlovingian died, its parts tumbled asunder. Local barons ruled everywhere. The Imperial title, which represented nothing, and conveyed no power, seemed, however, to have some vital principle of its own, some ghostly virtue; at least sundry kings and dukes thought so and fought for it; but until the coming of Otto the Great it remained a shadow. North of the Alps duchies and provinces united into kingdoms; but the peninsula remained split up into discordant parts. The valley of the Po was divided into various duchies, peopled by a mixed race of Latins and Lombards, whom the pressure of the conquering Franks had welded together. South of the Po lay the Imperial marquisate of Tuscany. Across the middle of the peninsula stretched the awkward strip of domain from Ravenna to Rome, inhabited by a race of comparatively pure Latin blood. This domain, included in the Donations of Pippin and of Charlemagne, nominally subject to the Papacy under the suzerainty of the Empire, was really in the possession of petty nobles, who knew no law except force and craft. South of this so-called papal domain lay the duchy of Spoleto and the Lombard duchy of Benevento, and farther south a few principalities, such as Naples, Amalfi, and Salerno, and finally in the heel and toe of Italy were the last remains of the Greek Empire. To the northeast, on its islands, lay the little fishing and trading city, Venice.

The Italians, as we had better call them now that Barbarian and Latin blood has well commingled, were in a most unenviable condition. Most of those who tilled the soil were serfs, and went with the land when it was sold; some were scarce better than slaves, others were only bound to render service of certain kinds or on certain days, either with their own hands or with beasts. Their lot depended on the humours of the overseers of great estates. Slaves were worse off because they had no personal rights, but they were always decreasing in number despite a slave trade, for there was a strong religious sentiment against slavery, and it was common for dying men to liberate their slaves. In the cities people were better off, for the artisans were free men, and by banding together in guilds (which had existed ever since the old Roman days) secured for themselves a more prosperous condition. But the only thriving places were the cities of the coast, Venice, Genoa, Pisa, Amalfi, where trade was already beginning to lay the foundations of future greatness.

These glimmerings of commerce were the only lights along the whole horizon. Everything else seemed to share the blight that had fallen on the Empire and the Papacy. The clergy, whose duty it was to maintain learning, failed utterly. Even in the happiest days of the Carlovingian Empire, Charlemagne had found it necessary to enact blunt rules for their guidance. "Let the priests, according to the Apostles' advice, withdraw themselves from revellings and drunkenness; for some of them are wont to sit up till midnight or later, boozing with their neighbours; and then these men, who ought to be of a religious and holy deportment, return to their churches drunken and gorged with food, and unable to perform the daily and nightly office of praise to God, while others sink down in a drunken sleep in the place of their revels.... Let no priest presume to store provisions or hay in the church." Learning, supposed to be committed to their charge, went out like a spent candle. Books were almost forgotten, except perhaps here and there, in Pavia or Verona, where a grammarian still invoked Virgil to prosper his muse; or where in an episcopal city, like Ravenna, some chronicler wrote a history of the bishopric. The theory of historic truth on which these chroniclers acted gives an inkling of the mediæval attitude towards facts. Father Agnello, a priest of Ravenna, one of these chroniclers, says himself: "If you, who read this

History of our Bishopric, shall come to a passage and say, 'Why didn't he narrate the facts about this bishop as he did about his predecessors,' listen to the reason. I, Andrea Agnello, a humble priest of this holy church of Ravenna, have written the history of this Bishopric from the time of St. Apollinaris for eight hundred years and more, because my brethren here have begged me and compelled me. I have put down whatever I found the Bishops had undoubtedly done, and whatever I heard from the oldest men living, but where I could not find any historical account, nor anything about their lives in any way, then, in order to leave no blanks in the holy succession of bishops, I have made up the missing lives by the help of God, through your prayers, and I believe I have said nothing untrue, because those bishops were pious and pure and charitable and winners of souls for God."

The monks were no better than the secular clergy. The monasteries had grown large, for many men had joined in order to escape military service, or to obtain personal security, or an easier life, or greater social consideration; they had also grown rich, for many sinners on their deathbeds had given large sums, in hope to compound for their sins. Naturally monastic vows were often broken. Moreover, the little good that monks and priests did they undid by their encouragement of superstition. They first frightened the poor peasants out of their wits by portraying the horrors of hell, and then preached the magical properties of the sacraments and of saints' bones, until the ordinary man, feeling himself the sport of superhuman agencies, abandoned all self-confidence and surrendered himself to priestly control as his sole hope of safety in this world or the next.

Oppressed by anarchy, by division, by a degenerate church, by a gross clergy, and by waxing ignorance, Italy might seem to have had its cup of evil full. There was but one further ill that could be added, a new Barbarian invasion. It came. The triumphant Saracens, having overrun Spain and raided France in the west, having cooped up the Byzantine Empire in the east, now threatened to plant their victorious banners in the very heart of Christendom. As early as Charlemagne's last years they sacked a coast town scarce forty miles from Rome. In 827 they invaded Sicily, invited by a partisan traitor. Within ten years they had made themselves masters of almost all the island, except a few strongholds which managed to hold out for half a century. The beaten Byzantines retired to the mainland; but they did not get beyond the reach of the victorious Saracens, who raided all the Italian coast as far as the Tiber. Troops of marauders hovered round Rome and harried the country-side, robbing and pillaging at will. One band advanced to the very gates of the city, and sacked St. Peter's and St. Paul's, both outside the walls and undefended (846). All the southern provinces were overrun, half of their towns became Saracen fortresses. It seemed as if Italy were to undergo the fate of Spain and become a Mohammedan Emirate.

The danger to Rome roused the country. A Christian league was effected between the Imperial forces in Italy, the Pope, and the coast cities of the south,—Naples, Gaeta, and Amalfi. Pope Leo himself blessed the fleet, and the Christians beat the infidels in a great sea-fight not far from the Tiber's mouth (849). Some of the prisoners were brought to Rome and set to work on the walls which Pope Leo was building round the Vatican hill to protect St. Peter's; and Rome, imitating the days of Scipio Africanus, celebrated another triumph over Africa. The fighting was kept up all over the south. The Greek Emperor made common cause with his fellow Christians, and the immediate danger of conquest was arrested; but throughout this dismal ninth century, and all the tenth, southern Italy continued to suffer from Saracen marauders. The tales told of their cruelty are fearful, and match our tales of Indian raids in the old French-English war. Separate villages and lonely monasteries suffered most. Some good came out of the evil, however, for the chroniclers relate how the abbots and their terrified brethren spent days and nights fasting and in prayer.

Such was the condition of Italy when the Imperial Carlovingian line came to an end. The omnipresence of anarchy was a permanent argument for the need of an Imperial restoration. But the country did not know how to go to work to restore the Empire. At first various claimants asserted various titles, and Italian dukes and neighbouring kings fought one another like bulls, but none were able to establish any stable power. In the midst of these ineffectual struggles one real effort was made. Arnulf, king of the Germans, who regarded himself as the true successor of the great Frankish house and of right Imperial heir, marched down into Italy at the invitation of Pope Formosus, as we have seen, and assumed the Imperial crown (896). The expedition was barren of consequences, but it gives us another glimpse of the anomalous nature of the Papacy, and the different views entertained of it on the two sides of the Alps. The German king wished to be Emperor, and felt that an Imperial coronation at Rome by the Pope was essential. To him and to his German subjects the papal invitation was of high authority. When he reached Rome, however, the seat of the Papacy, he found the gates barred and the walls manned by rebellious citizens, who had locked the Pope in the Castle of Sant' Angelo, and had seized the government of the city. Arnulf easily carried the defences by storm and liberated the Pope. The incident illustrates the contrast between Teutonic respect and Roman disobedience, and describes the papal situation as it was half the time throughout the Middle Ages. Honoured and reverenced by the pious ultramontanes, the Popes were insulted, robbed, imprisoned, and deposed by their immediate subjects. This local disobedience, or, as it should be called, Roman republicanism, was often the insignificant cause of papal actions of far-reaching effect. The Popes were never strong enough of themselves to suppress these republican sentiments and ambitions; they needed support from some power, Italian or foreign. As they would not endure the idea of an Italian kingdom, they adopted the alternative of calling in a foreign power. This was the constant papal policy.

Another instance of Roman republicanism, or disobedience (as one chooses), throws further light on the nature of this thorn in the papal side. Not long after Arnulf's expedition, two women, Theodora and Marozia, mother and daughter, played a great part not only in Roman but also in Italian politics. These two women ruled the city and appointed the Popes. They were bold, comely, much-marrying women, choosing eligible husbands almost by force; both were wholly Roman in the fierceness, vigour, and sensuality of their characters. They were very capable, and, in part directly, in part through their husbands and others, exercised control for some thirty years; and when the daughter disappeared from history, her son, Alberic, took the title, Prince and

Senator of all the Romans, and ruled in her stead.

Thus the last hope of Italians helping themselves perished; for if the Papacy was powerless, there was no help elsewhere in Italy. The usurpation of these viragoes and of Alberic differs in details from the usurpation of the later republicans, and of the Colonna, Orsini, and other barons, who shall appear hereafter in papal history, but for general effect on papal affairs and through them on European affairs, all these usurpations were very similar. The usurpers, in diverse characters, represent that third player in the fencing match, who, though by no means an ally of the Empire, frequently rushed in and struck up the Pope's guard, and continued to interfere for hundreds of years, until the Popes of the Renaissance finally established their temporal power in the city of Rome.

By the middle of the tenth century the disintegration of Italy had become so bad that it caused its own cure. It was obvious that something must be done. The Saracens, strongly established in Sicily, were a standing menace towards the south. From the north wild bands of Hungarians burst across the Alps and harried the land in barbaric raids as far as Rome. Feudal anarchy prevailed everywhere. Monks and clergy were, to say the least, no help. Even the Papacy, the only stable power, had become the appanage of a Roman family. There was but one way out of this chaos. The Roman Empire must be restored. The Latin people never believed that it was extinct but merely lying latent, requiring some happy application of might and right to set it going again on its majestic course. Charlemagne, in his day, had supplied the might. That might had faded away. Where was its substitute to be found? Pope Formosus and King Arnulf had already suggested the only possible answer,—in the eastern portion of the Frankish Empire, the kingdom of Germany. That kingdom, composed of the great duchies of Bavaria, Swabia, Franconia, Saxony, and Lorraine, had become tolerably compact; it was strong at home, and was eager for glory and power abroad. Its ambitious king, Otto, of the Saxon line, was the man to undertake to follow Charlemagne's example. It was too late to hope to restore the Carlovingian Empire in its former boundaries, but with Germany to give strength and Rome to contribute title, there would be the two necessary elements for a renewal of the Roman Empire.

The immediate pretext of Otto's coming down into Italy was highly romantic. A lovely lady, the widow of one Italian pretender to the throne of Italy, was pestered with offers of marriage from another pretender. She refused, and was locked up in a tower by the Lake of Garda, where memories of Catullus and Lesbia still faintly lingered. She contrived to escape, and sent piteous messages for help to the great Otto, then a widower. Discontented factions in the north, and others suffering from oppression, including the Pope who had been rudely roused to the need of Imperial support, also sent messengers asking him to come. Otto came, took Pavia, and acted as King of Italy. He married the lovely widow, and wished to go to Rome to receive the Imperial crown; but Alberic, lord of Rome, would not give permission. Otto went back to Germany and bided his time. In ten years Alberic died leaving a young son, who, although only seventeen years old, inherited enough of his father's power to get himself elected Pope, John XII. Pope John, however, found himself encompassed by powerful enemies both in Rome and out. He too was obliged to recognize the absolute necessity of Imperial restoration, and called upon Otto for aid. The German king came, and was crowned by the Pope, Emperor of the Romans, in St. Peter's basilica, on the second day of February, 962. This coronation was the beginning of a new phase in the Roman Empire. In this phase that Empire is known as the Holy Roman Empire, although it was merely a union of Germany, Italy, and Burgundy.

CHAPTER IX: THE REVIVAL OF THE PAPACY (962-1056)

This Roman Empire (it did not receive its full title of Holy Roman Empire until later) deserved the name Roman because it rested on the Roman tradition of the political unity of the civilized world. This tradition, by means of the ecclesiastical unity of Europe, had survived the Barbarian invasions, had gained strength through Charlemagne's Empire, and now joined together two nations so fundamentally different as Germany and Italy. The Germans were big blond men, beer-drinkers, huge eaters, rough, ill-mannered, arrogant, phlegmatic and brave; the Italians were little, dark-skinned men, wine-drinkers, lettuce-eaters, with pleasant manners, gesticulating, excitable, and unwarlike. Their union affords the strongest testimony to the strength of the Roman tradition. This ill-assorted pair, married in obedience to the will of dead generations, could not live together in peace. The theory of a world conjointly ruled by a supreme secular sovereign and a supreme ecclesiastical sovereign could not be put into successful practice. The Empire was German, the Papacy Italian, and by their very natures they were antagonistic.

Otto's empire was by no means universal, but its suzerainty was acknowledged by Bohemia, Moravia, Poland, Denmark, perhaps by Hungary, and sometimes by France; and therefore, as eastern Europe was either Greek or barbarian, Britain an island, and Spain practically Mohammedan, it sustained fairly well the idea of a universal (i. e., European) empire. The essential parts were Germany to give strength, and Italy to give title and tradition. In theory the process of royal and Imperial election and coronation was as follows. The German electors (the greater nobles), whose number was not limited to seven for two centuries and more, elected a king, who was crowned with a silver crown at Aachen, and, by virtue of his coronation, received the title, King of the Romans. This king then took the iron crown of Lombardy at Pavia, and became King of Italy; and, when he received the gold Imperial crown from the Pope at Rome, became Emperor. The election of the son of the late Emperor to succeed was the custom, but was not obligatory. Germany was not a strongly centralized state, but was composed of several dukedoms, which often fell out among themselves. Italy was still less a political unit. It had no marks of nationality, except its geographical position, its ancient tradition, and a tardily forming language; but even this lingua volgare, which in Otto's time began to have an Italian sound, and to touch the degenerate written Latin with an Italian look, did not prevail throughout the peninsula. In the south Greek was still spoken, and the Holy Roman Empire never had more than the shadow of a title south of Benevento till after Barbarossa's time. The Emperor's authority rested at bottom on the German military power; and as this depended on the obedience of wayward and jealous dukedoms, it was uncertain and intermittent.

The Papacy was far more stable, for fundamentally it was a moral power, and got its energy from men's consciences. It was far better organized than the Empire. The ecclesiastical system spread all over Europe, into every city, village, hamlet, and monastery; countries which reluctantly acknowledged the suzerainty of the Empire, bowed unquestioningly to papal rule. Moreover, the power of the Papacy did not merely consist in spiritual weapons, terrible as the ban of excommunication was in those days, but also in its ability to raise up enemies against its enemy, and to put the cloak of piety over war and rebellion.

The ironical element in the situation was that the Empire itself lifted the Papacy to the position in which it was able to turn and defy the Empire, fight it, and finally destroy it. The Emperors, who entertained no doubts that the Papacy was subject to them, that they were responsible for its conduct and must secure the election of worthy Popes, took the Papacy out of the hands of the Roman faction, purified it, and appointed honest, capable, upright Popes.

A contemporary account of Otto's dealings with that young scamp, Pope John XII, who in morals resembled his grandmother, Marozia, gives a good picture of the nature of the benefits which the Empire conferred on the Papacy: "While these things were taking place, the constellation of Cancer, hot from the enkindling rays of Ph[oe]bus, kept the Emperor away from the hills around Rome, but when the constellation of Virgo returning brought back the pleasant season he went to Rome upon a secret invitation from the Romans. But why should I say secret when the greater part of the nobility burst into the Castle of St. Paul and invited the holy Emperor, and even gave hostages? The citizens received the holy Emperor and all his men within the city, promised allegiance, and took an oath that they would never elect a Pope, nor consecrate him, without the consent and the sanction of the Lord Emperor Otto, Cæsar, Augustus, and of his son, King Otto.

"Three days later, at the request of the Roman bishops and people, there was a great meeting in St. Peter's Church, and with the Emperor sat the archbishops of Aquileia, Milan, and Ravenna, the archbishop of Saxony [and many other Italian and German prelates]. When they were seated, and silence made, the holy Emperor got up and said: 'How fit it would be that in this distinguished and holy council our lord Pope John should be present! But since he has refused to be of your company, we ask your counsel, holy fathers, for you have the same interest as he.' Then the Roman prelates, cardinals, priests, and deacons, and all the people cried out: 'We are surprised that your reverend prudence should wish to make us investigate that which is not hidden from the Iberians, the Babylonians, nor the Indians. He [the Pope] is no longer one of that kind, which come in sheep's clothing but inwardly are ravening wolves; he rages so openly, does his diabolical misdeeds so manifestly, that we need not beat about the bush.' The Emperor answered: 'We deem it just that the accusations should be stated one by one, and after that we will take counsel together of what we ought to do.'

"Then Cardinal-priest Peter got up, and testified that he had seen the Pope celebrate mass without communion. John, bishop of Narni, and John, cardinal-deacon, declared that they had seen him ordain a deacon in a stable, and not at the proper hour. Cardinal-deacon Benedict, with other priests and deacons, said that they knew that he ordained bishops for money, and that in the city of Todi he had ordained as bishop a boy ten years old. They said it was not necessary to go into his sacrileges because they had seen more such than could be reckoned. They said in regard to his adulteries.... They said that he had publicly gone a-hunting; that he had put out the eyes of his spiritual father, Benedict, who died soon after in consequence; that he had mutilated and killed John, cardinal-subdeacon; and they testified that he had set buildings on fire, armed with helmet and breastplate, and girt with a sword. All, priests and laymen, cried out that he had drunk a toast to the devil. They said that while playing dice he had invoked the aid of Jupiter, Venus, and other demons. They declared that he had not celebrated matins, nor observed the canonical hours, and that he did not cross himself.

"When the Emperor had heard all this, he bade me, Liutprand, bishop of Cremona, interpret to the Romans, because they could not understand his Saxon. Then he got up and said: 'It often happens, and we believe it from our experience, that men in great place are slandered by the envious, for a good man is disliked by bad men just as a bad man is disliked by good men. And for this reason we entertain some doubts concerning this accusation against the Pope, which Cardinal-deacon Benedict has just read and made before you, uncertain whether it springs from zeal for justice or from envy and impiety. Therefore with the authority of the dignity granted to me, though unworthy, I beseech you by that God, whom no man can deceive howsoever he may wish, and by His holy mother, the Virgin Mary, and by the most precious body of the prince of the Apostles, in whose Church we now are, that no accusation be cast at our lord the Pope of faults which he has not committed and which have not been seen by the most trustworthy men.'" The accusers affirmed their charges on oath. Then the holy Synod said: "If it please the holy Emperor let letters be sent to our lord the Pope, bidding him come and clear himself of these charges." The wary John did not come, but wrote: "I, Bishop John, servant of the servants of God, to all the bishops. We have heard that you propose to elect another Pope. If you do that, I excommunicate you in the name of Almighty God so that you shall not have the right to ordain anybody, nor to celebrate mass." Nevertheless, John was deposed and a good Pope put in his stead.

Otto's successors, one after the other, followed his example, and treated the Papacy as if it had been a German bishopric. The Emperors, however, had work to do north of the Alps, and did not spend much time in Rome, except Otto III, a romantic dreamer, who wished to live there; and during their absence the turbulent Roman anti-imperial faction used to seize the Papacy, just as Alberic had done, and put up worthless Popes. In spite of them the Emperors' Popes raised the Papacy so high that, as a matter of course, it became the head of the great ecclesiastical reform movement which swept over Europe in the eleventh century, and from that movement drew in so much force and energy that it became the greatest power in Europe, and was enabled finally to overthrow the Empire.

This tide of reform arose at Cluny, a little place in Burgundy, and began as a monastic reform. All over Christendom monasteries had grown rich and prosperous; many monks had forsaken Benedict's rule, had broken their vows and lived with wives and children upon revenues intended for other purposes. Other monks hated this evil conduct, and burning with a passionate desire to stop it, started a great movement of monastic reform. The reform was ascetic in character, as a moral emotion in those days was bound to be. The first reformers gathered at Cluny, about the beginning of the tenth century. From there disciples went far and wide, purging old monasteries and founding new. After a time the reformers passed beyond the early stage of mere moral revolt against godless living, formed a party, and put forward a creed. The party represented antagonism to the world, pitted saints against sinners, the Church against the State. The creed had three tenets. No ecclesiasts should marry, and married men upon ordination should live apart from their wives. No bribery, no corrupt bargain, should taint the appointment and installation of clergy, high or low. No layman should meddle with the entry of bishops upon their episcopal office. These three tenets roused bitter opposition. Celibacy of the clergy had been a rule of Church discipline since early days, and from time to time efforts had been made to enforce the practice, but it had fallen into general disregard. A celibate clergy, with no affections or interests nearer or dearer than the Church, would be a tremendous ecclesiastical force, and far-sighted Popes always sought to enforce the rule. Necessarily the married clergy and many clerical bachelors were violent in opposition. The article against simony nobody openly gainsaid; but many bishops and abbots had obtained their offices by corrupt practices, and many nobles looked forward to rich livings and high ecclesiastical places; both classes opposed a change. The third article, against lay investiture of bishops, which was to be the cause of deadly war between Empire and Papacy, was a logical conclusion from the article against simony; for it was hard to suppose that in the appointment of bishops, kings and princes would disregard all worldly motives and appoint men solely for the good of souls. On the other hand, the great bishoprics and abbeys were among the most important fiefs in a king's gift, and carried with them feudal privileges of sovereignty, such as rights of coinage, toll, holding courts, etc.; in short, they were mere secular fiefs with ecclesiastical prerogatives added. It was natural that the German Emperors should claim the right to appoint and invest these spiritual barons, and insist that their episcopal territories should be subject to the same feudal obligations and the same civic duties as the territories granted to lay barons. This third article was a direct attack on the civil power. If all Imperial participation were to be stricken out, and bishops put into possession of their fiefs solely by the Pope, then vast territories, estimated to be nearly half the Empire, would be withdrawn from civic obligations, even from military service, and the Pope, ousting the Emperor, would become monarch of half the Imperial domains. According to the canons of the Church, the clergy and the people of the diocese elected the bishop, and the Church bestowed on him ring and staff, the signs of episcopal office. The trouble arose over the fief. In feudal times the kings had enfeoffed bishops with great fiefs in order to counterbalance the insubordinate secular lords, and because, in episcopal hands, these fiefs did not become hereditary. When the reformers took the matter up, they found that in practice the kings did not wait for a canonical election of episcopal candidates, but invested their henchmen in return for money or some service which had no savour of sanctity. The episcopal office, as St. Peter Damian complained, was got "by flattering the king, studying his inclination, obeying his beck, applauding every word that fell from his mouth, by acting the parasite and playing the buffoon." The real difficulty lay in the double nature of the episcopal office, half ecclesiastical and half feudal; and, like other great political difficulties, would not yield to a peaceful solution, until there had been a trial of strength between the discordant interests.

The first consequence, however, of the reforming spirit was to ennoble the whole Church, to purify her members, and animate them with a common zeal, and to uplift her head, the Papacy. It carried on, in a larger way and with a greater sweep, the work of ecclesiastical reformation begun by the intervention of the Emperors in the election of Popes, and gave a loftier tone to European politics.

CHAPTER X: THE STRUGGLE OVER INVESTITURES (1059-1123)

The struggle over the lay investiture of bishops did not arise at first. The Papacy was still a dependent bishopric in the gift of the Emperors, who continued to depose bad Roman Popes and appoint upright Germans. Popes and Emperors worked together to enforce celibacy among the clergy and to put down simony. The Emperors could not see, what is evident in retrospect, that when the spirit of reform should have taken full possession of the Papacy, then the Papacy would not rest content to be a German bishopric, but, in obedience to the law which links political ambition to political vigour, would even aim so high as to try to reduce the Empire itself to the condition of a papal fief. The spirit of reform, embodied in a man of genius, did take possession of the Papacy and the great struggle began.

Among the crowd that thronged to Cluny eager for a higher life, was a young Tuscan from Orvieto, Hildebrand by name, of plebeian birth. Small of stature, vehement in spirit, passionate in feeling and action, he was confident in himself and yet sensitive to sympathy. This lad became an eager scholar, but in spite of erudition and fondness for study, he was essentially a man of action, a born leader of men. "What he taught by word he proved by example." He believed absolutely in the tenets of the reformers. He believed with his whole being that the Church was a divine institution to save men's souls, and he could not endure the idea of secular powers and worldly influences intermeddling with God's fabric. His career exhibits the power of a man of genius, who devotes his whole life to what for him is the highest end, and is able to use human enthusiasm for good as his implement.

Hildebrand has been called the Julius Cæsar of the Papacy. He went to Rome about 1048. From that time papal policy became definite, vigorous, stamped with an antique Roman stamp; and open conflict with the Empire was the inevitable result. Hildebrand's first care was to protect the Papacy from the petty-minded Roman faction; he supported papal candidates of high character and even secured the appointment of a German, sagaciously foreseeing that ecclesiastical patriotism would be stronger than national patriotism. These Popes put Hildebrand's views into execution.

Now that the Papacy had been rescued from the Roman faction, the next step was to free it from the Egyptian bondage of subjection to the Empire. Hildebrand was ready to strike whenever a fair opportunity should come. It soon came. The Emperor died, leaving his son Henry IV, a little boy, his successor on the German throne and heir to the Empire. A long minority seemed to reveal the hand of Providence. Hildebrand acted. It had long been obvious that one cause of papal subjection to Roman faction and Imperial tyrant had been the uncertainty of the electoral body. Emperors, Roman nobles, and Roman rabble, all had certain historic electoral rights. Hildebrand resolved to dispossess them all. A synod was held, which declared that the election of the Pope lay in the hands of the cardinals (1059). Some right of approval was left to the Roman people, some right of sanction to the Emperor, but the right of original election was vested in the cardinals, and this gradually developed into an absolute and exclusive right of election. This act was an act of rebellion towards the Empire, a declaration of independence.

Hildebrand said that he strove to make the Church "free, pure, and catholic." This action made it free.

It was not to be expected that the Empire would acquiesce tamely in this rebellion. Imperialists and Romans made common cause against the clerical rebels. But the height of the conflict was not reached till Hildebrand himself was elevated to the Papacy (1073), becoming Gregory VII. He immediately took the offensive. Burning with conviction himself, he appealed to the general enthusiasm both in the Church and throughout the Empire for the cause of God; he ruthlessly denounced simony and proclaimed principles of papal sovereignty absolute and universal. "The Roman Church was founded by God alone; she never has erred and never will err, and no man is a Catholic who is not at peace with her. The Roman bishop alone is universal. He may depose bishops and reinstate them, he may transfer them from one see to another, he may depose emperors, and may absolve the subjects of the unjust from their allegiance. No synod without his consent is general; no episcopal chapter, no book, canonical without his authority. No man may sit in judgment on his decrees, but he may judge the decrees of all." Here certainly was a second Julius Cæsar in ambition. Gregory claimed feudal supremacy over Bohemia, Russia, Hungary, Spain, Corsica, Sardinia, Dalmatia, Croatia, Poland, Scandinavia, and England. Such claims were vague and shadowy; but the claims to interfere between the German king and the German episcopate and clergy were definite and direct. The Papacy declared its own supremacy, and the Imperial duty of obedience.

Gregory had immense moral support at his back, yet moral support would not have sufficed to protect him from the king's anger. Nor would Gregory have ventured on so haughty a course, had he not had allies of another character. These allies were four in number, and require some description. First in importance come the Normans. For years bands of Norman warriors, pious folk, had passed through Southern Italy on their way to the Holy Land. Once a handful had helped a prince of Salerno to repel a Saracen attack. The prince, so the story goes, delighted with their valour, begged them to invite their compatriots to come. The invitation was readily accepted. Bands of gentlemen adventurers came, fought against Saracens, or Greeks, or the independent dukes and princes of Southern Italy, first as mercenaries in anybody's pay, and afterwards on their own account. They soon conquered a domain, and reached out in all directions. Some drove out the last Byzantines and acquired Southern Italy; some crossed to Sicily, performed prodigies of valour against the Saracens, and finally conquered the whole island (1060-90). In their raids northward they trespassed upon papal territory and came into collision with the Church. St. Peter's sword was drawn and brandished, but ineffectually. The Popes then concluded that martial deeds did not become them; and the Normans, on their part, were pious folk; so together they formed a happy solution. The Normans had possession of Southern Italy and Sicily, but merely by right of conquest; they were in the midst of an alien and far more numerous subject people, and wished for a legal title. The Popes, unable to acquire actual possession, did have, thanks to the Donation of Constantine, a legal title, derived, so they claimed, from the original source of legal titles, the Roman Empire. The mode of agreement was obvious; the Popes conferred Southern Italy and Sicily as feuds upon their liegemen the Norman chiefs, and they in return acknowledged the Popes as their lords suzerain. In this manner, "by the grace of God and St. Peter," the Normans founded the kingdom of the Two Sicilies, which for centuries after the Norman line died out continued to acknowledge the overlordship of the Papacy. The Normans were often disobedient vassals, but they knew that the Empire regarded them as robbers, and in the wars between Empire and Papacy remained loyal to their lords the Popes.

The second papal ally was Countess Matilda (1046-1115), mistress of the Marquisate of Tuscany and other domains, which stretched from the papal boundaries up across the Po to Lombardy, and like her mother, her predecessor in title, a brave, capable, devout woman. As the Normans were a defence to the Papacy on the south, so these ladies constituted a bulwark on the north, and often rendered incalculable service to the Popes of this period. Matilda's devotion to Gregory was boundless. "Like a second Martha, she ministered unto him, and as Mary hearkened unto Christ, so did she, attentive and assiduous, hearken to all the words of the Holy Father." She and her mother make clear one source of papal strength. They show us the attitude of the women, who, from sentiments of morality, piety, and superstition, took the religious side of the quarrel, and did not rest till fathers, brothers, husbands, and lovers had also espoused it. One act of feminine devotion fixes Matilda in the memory. Her domains consisted of marquisates, counties, baronies, and various feudal estates, held as feuds of the Empire, over which on her death she had no power of disposition, and also of large private estates, which she was free to give or devise. All these, Imperial feuds and private estates, she gave or rather attempted to give to the Church. This Donation, the most important since that of Charlemagne, gave fresh causes of quarrel between Papacy and Empire. The Papacy attempted to make good its claim to the Imperial feuds; and the Empire, finding it impossible to discover the boundaries between the two species of territories, also claimed the whole.

The third papal ally is to be found in the cities of Lombardy, which had now become rich and important. In these cities, especially in Milan, which was easily first commercially and politically, trade had created a burgher class which already gave evidence of a desire for political power. In Milan itself there was extreme political instability; archbishop, nobles, gentry, artisans, and populace were all ready for a general scrimmage on the slightest provocation. The clergy were numerous and very rich; sons of noblemen held the fat benefices, and almost all led irreligious lives and held celibacy in the meanest esteem. Simony was the rule. In Hildebrand's time the passion for religious reform swept over the lower classes of the city. A new sect arose, the Patarini (ragamuffins), a species of Puritans, who took up the cry against clerical laxity and immorality, and denounced married priests. Religious excitement set fire to social and economic discontent; populace and nobles flew to arms; there were riots and civil war. Several eminent men, close friends of Hildebrand, became popular leaders; and the contest of people and Patarini against nobles and married clergy became an episode in the general strife between Papal and Imperial parties. Similar tumults, caused half by class enmity, half by the passion for religious reform, took place in other northern cities, Cremona, Piacenza, Pavia, Padua; on one side was the party of aristocratic privilege, looking to the Emperor for support; on the other, the party of the people, looking to the Pope.

Gregory's fourth ally was the rebellious nobility of Germany. Had Germany been united and loyal, the German king would easily have been able to assert his power in Italy; but Germany was disloyal and divided. Archbishops of the great archbishoprics, dukes of the great duchies, bishops, counts, and lords, in fact, all the component parts of the feudal structure of Germany, were jealous of one another; each grudged the other his possessions, and were in accord only in jealousy of the royal power. There were always some barons or bishops thankful to have the Pope's name and the Pope's aid in a rebellious design. These animosities the Papacy through its thousand hands diligently fomented.

Ranged against Gregory and his allies were the loyal parts of Germany, the Imperial adherents in Italy, the married clergy everywhere, and all whom Gregory's reforms had angered and estranged. At their head was a dissipated young king, of high spirit, headstrong, ignorant, and superstitious, who entertained lofty notions of his royal and Imperial prerogatives. The characters of these two men would have brought them into collision, even if the irreconcilable natures of Empire and Papacy had not rendered a clash inevitable.

Gregory, almost immediately after his elevation to the pontificate, held a council and denounced simony, marriage of the clergy, and lay investiture. The king, who believed in the existing system, continued to exercise what he deemed his royal rights with a view to improving his political position. Gregory held a second council and utterly forbade lay investiture. Henry continued to disobey. Then Gregory wrote to him that he must renounce the claim of investiture, and humbly present himself in person before the papal presence and beg absolution for his sins; or, if he should fail to obey, Gregory would excommunicate him. Henry and his party, now very angry, retorted by holding a German synod, which charged Gregory with all sorts of offences, moral, ecclesiastical, and political, absolved both king and bishops from their papal allegiance, and, finally, deposed the Pope. Henry himself wrote Gregory this letter:—

"Henry, not by usurpation, but by God's holy will. King, to Hildebrand, no longer Pope, but false monk:—

"This greeting you have deserved from the confusion you have caused, for in every rank of the Church you have brought confusion instead of honour, a curse instead of a blessing. Out of much I shall say but a little; you have not only not feared to touch the rulers of the Holy Church, archbishops, bishops, priests, God's anointed, but as if they were slaves, you have trampled them down under your feet. By trampling them down you have got favour from the vulgar mouth. You have decided that they know nothing, and that you alone know everything, and you have studied to use your knowledge not to build up but to destroy.... We have borne all this and have striven to maintain the honour of the Apostolic See. But you have construed our humility as fear, and for that reason you have not feared to rise up against our royal power, and have even dared to threaten that you would take it from us; as if we had received our kingdom from you, as if kingdom and empire were in your hands and not in God's. Our Lord Jesus Christ has called us to the kingdom, but not you to the priesthood. You have mounted by these steps; by craft—abominable in a monk—you have come into money, by money to favour, by favour to the sword, by the sword to the seat of peace; and from the seat of peace you have confounded peace. You have armed subjects against those over them; you, the unelect, have held our bishops, elect of God, up to contempt.... Me, even, who though unworthy am the anointed king, you have touched, and although the holy fathers have taught that a king may be judged by God only, and for no offence except deviation from the faith—which God forbid—you have asserted that I should be deposed; when even Julian the Apostate was left by the wisdom of the holy fathers to be judged and deposed by God only. That true Pope, blessed Peter, says: 'Fear God, honour the king.' But you do not fear God and you dishonour me appointed by Him. And blessed Paul, who did not spare an angel from heaven who should preach other doctrine, did not except you, here on earth, who now teach other doctrine. For he says, 'But though we, or an angel from heaven, preach any other gospel unto you than that which we have preached unto you, let him be accursed.' You therefore by Paul anathematized, by the judgment of all our bishops and by mine condemned, come down, leave the apostolic seat which you have usurped; let another mount the throne of blessed Peter, who shall not cloak violence with religion, but shall teach the sound doctrine of blessed Peter. I, Henry, King by God's grace, and all our bishops, say to you, Down, down, you damned forever."

To the action of the German synod and to this letter there could be but one answer. Gregory held a synod, excommunicated the king, and released his subjects from their allegiance. The Germans rose in rebellion, taking the excommunication as a ground or perhaps as a pretext; they held a great council in presence of a papal legate, and decided that they would renounce their allegiance unless the king obtained absolution. The king, too weak to cope with the rebels, submitted. He crossed the Alps with his wife and one or two servants, in midwinter, and came to the fortress of Canossa, near Parma, a stronghold belonging to the Countess Matilda, whither Gregory had gone. For three days the king stood outside the gates, dressed as a penitent, and begged for leave to present himself before the Pope. At last, owing to the entreaties of Matilda, the king was admitted. He cast himself upon the ground before Gregory, who lifted him up and bade him submit to the ordeal of the eucharist. Gregory took the consecrated wafer and said, "If I am guilty of the crimes charged against me, may God strike me." He broke and ate; then turning to Henry, said, "Do thou, my son, as I have done." The king did not dare to invoke the judgment of God; he humbled himself, resigned his crown into Gregory's hands, and swore to remain a private person until he should be judged by a council. He was then absolved (1077).

Various events followed this terrible humiliation. The German rebels set up an anti-king, and the king's men set up an anti-pope, and there was war and hatred everywhere. The king's energy triumphed for a time; he even captured Rome, and had it not been for a Norman army, which came to the Pope's rescue, he would have captured Gregory, too. But, despite royal triumphs the scene at Canossa had struck the majesty of the Empire an irretrievable blow; the king of the Germans, Emperor except for a coronation, had admitted in a most dramatic way, before all Europe, the inferiority of the temporal to the spiritual power.

Gregory died in exile at Salerno, Henry died deposed by his rebellious son; and the question of lay investiture still remained unsettled. More deeds of violence were done, more oaths broken, more lives taken; at last an agreement was reached and the long contest closed. Papacy and Empire made a treaty of peace, known as the Concordat of Worms (1122). The Emperor renounced all claim to invest bishops with ring and staff, and recognized the freedom of election and of ordination of the clergy, thus giving up all claim to appoint bishops and other ecclesiastical dignitaries. The Pope agreed that the election of bishops should take place in presence of the Emperor or his representative, and that bishops should receive their fiefs in a separate ceremony, by touch of the royal sceptre, in token of holding them from the Empire. This compromise, which seems absurdly simple, as settled questions often do, was a final adjustment of the immediate quarrel between Empire and Papacy, but left the larger matter of mastery still to be fought out.

CHAPTER XI: TRADE AGAINST FEUDALISM (1152-1190)

The last chapter dealt with the struggle between the two great mediæval institutions, the Empire and the Papacy. This deals with the contest between the Empire, representing the feudal system, and a new social force, the spirit of trade, represented by the Lombard cities. Naturally the Papacy joined in the fray and sided with the Lombard cities; and, before the end, all Italy was divided into two great parties designated by terms derived from Germany: Guelfs, which indicated those opposed to the Empire, and Ghibellines, which indicated friends to the Empire. But the particular issue here fought out was that between feudalism and trade, and the triumph of trade indicates the close of the Middle Ages.

The Emperor Frederick I (1152-90) of the great house of Hohenstaufen is the hero of this period. He was a noble specimen of the knight of the Middle Ages, such as Sir Walter Scott conceived a knight to be. He had a bright, open countenance, fair hair, that curled a little on his forehead, and a red beard (Barbarossa) which impressed the Italian imagination. Valiant, resolute, energetic, bountiful in almsgiving, attentive to religious duties, he was a kind friend and a stern enemy. To his misfortune he was born too late; he belonged to a chivalric generation out of place in a world which had begun to deem buying and selling matters of greater consequence than chivalry and crusades. He thought himself entitled to all the Imperial rights that had been exercised by the Ottos; and, measuring his own prerogatives by their standard, resolved to make good the deficiencies of his immediate predecessors, who for one reason or another had neglected to assert those prerogatives in their plenitude. Barbarossa's situation may be compared to that of Charles I of England, who believed himself lawful heir to all the prerogatives of the Tudors.

Opposed to these old-fashioned views was the hard-headed spirit of commercial Italy. Barbarossa's particular enemies were the Lombard cities, but that was because they were nearest to him. The same mercantile spirit animated all the cities of the peninsula; in fact, it pervaded the maritime cities before it pervaded the Lombard cities, and can best be described by means of a description of them.

The southern cities bloomed earlier than their northern sisters. Amalfi, now a little fishing village which clings to the steep slopes of the Gulf of Salerno, in the eleventh century was an independent republic of 50,000 inhabitants. She traded with Sicily, Egypt, Syria, and Arabia; she decked her women with the ornaments of the East; she built monasteries at Jerusalem, also a hospital from which the Knights Hospitallers of St. John took their name; she gave a maritime code to the Mediterranean and Ionian seas, and circulated coin of her own minting throughout the Levant. Salerno, her near neighbour, had already become famous for her knowledge of medicine, acquired from the Arabs. The speculations of her physicians upon the medicinal properties of herbs went all over Europe. She abounded in attractions. Vineyards, apple orchards, nut trees, flourished round about the city; within there were handsome palaces; "the women did not lack beauty, nor the men honesty." The Normans must have found themselves very comfortable. Naples, Gaeta, and the Greek cities of the heel and toe were also important and prosperous. But these southern cities were soon outdone by their sturdier northern rivals, Pisa, Genoa, Venice.

Pisa, which now lies at the mouth of the Arno like a forsaken mermaid on the shore, is said to have been a free commune before the year 900. She traded east and west; she waged wars with the Saracens, drove them from Sardinia, captured the Balearic Islands (1114), and carried the war into Africa. Rich with booty and commercial gains, she erected (according to a traveller's estimate) ten thousand towers within the city walls, completed her dome-crowned, many-columned, queenly cathedral, and built the attendant baptistery, within whose marble walls musical notes rise and fall, circle and swell, as if angels were singing in mid-air. She received many privileges from the Emperors; her maritime usages were to be respected; she was to enact her own laws, and to judge her citizens. No Imperial Marquess was to enter Tuscany until he had received approval from twelve men of Pisa, to be elected at a public meeting, called together by the city's bells (1085). She spread her power in the Levant. Jaffa, Acre, Tripoli, Antioch were in great part under her dominion, and her factories were scattered along the coasts of Syria and Asia Minor.

Further to the north, mounting hillward from her curving bay, lay Genoa the Proud, who for a time was Pisa's ally against the Saracens, and then became her rival and enemy. Genoa, too, was devoted to commerce and established settlements in Constantinople, in the Crimea, in Cyprus and Syria, in Majorca and Tunis. She, too, had obtained from the Empire a charter of municipal privileges and was a republic, free in all but name.

Venice, their greater sister, first rivalled and then surpassed both Pisa and Genoa. She traces her origin to the men who fled from the mainland in fear of Attila and sought refuge on the marshy islands of the coast (452). In later days others fled before the Lombards, and joined the descendants of the earlier refugees. Here, under the nominal government of the Eastern Empire, the Venetians gradually developed strength and independence, and took into their own hands the election of their Doge (697). The city of the Rivo Alto, the Venice of to-day, was begun about 800. Thirty years later the body of St. Mark the Evangelist was brought from Alexandria, and the foundations of St. Mark's basilica were laid over his bones. Politically Venice maintained her allegiance, shifting and time-serving though it was, true to Constantinople, not from sentiment, but because Constantinople was the first city in the world, the centre of art, of luxury, of commerce. Indeed, Venice was like a daughter or younger sister to Constantinople; all her old monuments, her mosaics, her sculpture, her marble columns, show her Byzantine inclinations. She took an active part in the Crusades, furnished transports and supplies, and mixed religion, war, and commerce in one profitable whole.

These maritime cities constantly fought one another; Pisa destroyed Amalfi, Genoa ruined Pisa, and Venice finally crippled Genoa. The glory they won was by individual effort; whereas the glory of the Lombard cities is that they effected a union, tardy indeed and imperfect, but successful at last in its purpose of enforcing their liberties against the Imperial claims. These Lombard cities included in their respective dominions the country round about, and were, in fact, except for a negligent Imperial control, little independent republics. It has been a matter of long dispute whether these communes were survivals from old Roman times, or sprung from the love of independence brought in by the Teutonic invaders; whatever their origin they virtually began with trade, rested upon trade, and flourished with trade. This trade, which, beginning between neighbouring cities, extended northward over the Alps, was greatly aided by the maritime cities. Ships called for cargoes. The stimulus imparted by the energy of Venetian, Genoese, and Pisan seamen to manufactures and transalpine trade was felt in every Lombard city. For instance, the Venetians, eager to carry a wider range of merchandise over sea to Alexandria or Jaffa, held fairs in the inland cities, exposed the wares they had fetched home, and stirred mercantile industry. A burgher class of traders and artisans grew up. Men met in the market-place, talked business, considered ways and means, discussed the conditions of production and exchange, and became a shrewd, capable class. The moment business expanded beyond the city walls, it bumped into feudal rights at every corner; at every crossroad it found itself enmeshed in feudal prerogatives and privileges. Trade could not endure a system fitted only for a farming community. Trade took men into politics; and in those days politics meant war. The citizens of Milan, Pavia, and neighbouring cities were not wholly unused to civic rights, for they had long had a voice in the election of bishops, and they had their trade guilds. These rights they enlarged whenever they got a chance; and chances came frequently in the quarrels between Emperor and archbishop, or between the greater and lesser nobility. Both sides wanted their support; and they sold it in exchange for privileges, here a little, there a little, and obtained many concessions. Finally, after the burghers had advanced in wealth and social consideration, the petty nobles made common cause with them; and the two combined succeeded in forcing the great lords to join also, and make one general civic union. These great lords, who had been little tyrants in the country roundabout, were compelled to live within the city walls for part of the year and be hostages for their own good behaviour, and were thus converted from enemies into leading citizens. The consequence of these changes was that the former government by a bishop, which in course of time had supplanted the old Carlovingian system of government by a count, was superseded in its turn by a much more popular form of government. The bishop's authority was narrowly limited, the executive power was lodged in consuls, two or more, who were elected annually, and the legislative power was placed in a general council of the burghers (in Milan not more than fifteen hundred men), and in a small inner council, which represented the aristocratic element. By Barbarossa's time the government of the cities had ceased to be feudal, and had become communal. There was inevitable antagonism between Lombardy and the Holy Roman Empire. The league of Lombard cities embodied the revolt of trade against the feudal system, of merchants against uncertain and excessive taxes, of burghers against foreign princes, in short, general discontent with an outgrown political system.

Barbarossa's war with the Lombard cities lasted for twenty-five years, and for convenience may be divided into two periods,—the period before the cities had learnt the lesson of union and the period after. So long as they were divided by mutual distrust and jealousy, Barbarossa was victorious; when they were united they conquered him.

Barbarossa made his first expedition across the Alps in answer to appeals that had been made to him from various parts of Italy. Como and Lodi complained of Milan; the Popes complained of the insubordinate Romans, who had set up a republic and were going crazy over an heretical republican priest, one Arnold of Brescia; the lord of the little city of Capua complained of the Norman king. Barbarossa, with his lofty notions of Imperial authority and Imperial duty, gathered together an army and descended into Italy to settle all troubles. He began by issuing orders to Milan with regard to her conduct towards Como and Lodi. Milan shut her gates. The proud city and the proud Emperor were at swords' points in a moment. A letter from Barbarossa from his camp near Milan, written to his uncle, Otto of Freysing, briefly narrates the circumstances: "The Milanese, tricky and proud, came to meet us with a thousand disloyal excuses and reasons, and offered us great sums of money if we would grant them sovereignty over Como and Lodi; and because, without letting ourselves be swayed one jot by their prayers or by their offers, we marched into their territory, they kept us away from their rich lands and made us pass three whole days in the midst of a desert; until at last, against their wish, we pitched our camp one mile from Milan. Here, after they had refused provisions for which we had offered to pay, we took possession of one of their finest castles, defended by five hundred horsemen, and reduced it to ashes; and our cavalry advanced to the gates of Milan and killed many Milanese and took many prisoners. Then open war broke out between us. When we crossed the river Ticino in order to go to Novara, we captured two bridges which they had fortified with castles, and after the army had crossed, destroyed them. Then we dismantled three of their fortresses ... and after we had celebrated Christmas with great merriment, we marched by way of Vercelli and Turin to the Po; we crossed the river and destroyed the strong city of Chieri, and burned Asti. This done, we laid siege to Tortona, most strongly fortified both by art and nature; and on the third day, having captured the suburbs, we should easily have carried the citadel, if night and stormy weather had not prevented us. At last, after many assaults, many killed, and a piteous slaughter of citizens, we forced the citadel to surrender, not without losing a number of our men."

Such vigour as this reduced Milan and her sister cities to obedience. But Frederick was not content with raids into Italy and spasmodic punishment administered to this rebellious city or to that; he wished to have the Imperial rights and authority definitely settled on a permanent basis; so he convoked a diet on the plain of Roncaglia, not far from Piacenza, to which he summoned bishops, dukes, marquesses, counts, and other nobles of the realm, four famous jurists from Bologna, and two representatives from each of fourteen Lombard cities. Frederick was a just man; he merely wished his legal rights, and proposed to ascertain what those rights were. The determination was left to the lawyers.

By this time lawyers had already begun to play a part in public affairs. Roman law had never been lost. For centuries it had remained side by side with the customs of the conquering Barbarians, less as a code of laws than as the tradition of the subject Latin people; and, when the needs of quickening civilization required a more elaborate system of law than custom could supply, there was the Roman law ready for use. It suddenly leaped into general interest, and rivalled the Church as a career for young men. St. Bernard complained that the law of Justinian was ousting the law of God. In 1088 the great law school of Bologna had been founded. Thither students crowded by thousands; and the opinions of its jurists were received with the deepest respect.

At Roncaglia the body of lawyers appointed to determine Imperial rights, decided, doubtless in accordance with Barbarossa's expectation, in favour of the Imperial side. The feudal nobles were delighted. The archbishop of Milan, the recognized head of the Lombard nobility, said to the Emperor: "Know that every right in the people to make laws has been granted to you; your will is law, as it is said, Quod Principi placuit legis habet vigorem [The Emperor's will has the force of law], since the people have granted to you all authority and sovereignty." In accordance with the spirit of this principle, the regalia, tolls, taxes, forfeits, and exactions of various kinds, were defined, and the right to appoint the executive magistrates in the communes adjudged to the Emperor. In substance the decision of the jurists was the restoration of the Imperial rights as they had been under the Ottos, when the communes were in their infancy.

Frederick's legal triumph was complete, but such a decision could only be sustained by force. The cities would not accept it; they preferred war. In the course of one campaign Milan was razed to the ground (1162), so literally, that Frederick dated his letters post destructionem Mediolani, "after the destruction of Milan." But the cities at last learned the necessity of union and stood shoulder to shoulder. The Papacy, too, which had been friendly to the Emperor during the insurrections in Rome, turned round and joined the cities against him, and Frederick, in retaliation, set up an anti-pope. Nevertheless, the glory of defeating the Emperor belongs to the cities, and not to the Papacy. The decisive battle was fought near Milan on the field of Legnano (1176).

The arbitrament of the sword reversed the decision of the lawyers at Roncaglia. Frederick frankly accepted defeat. A ceremonious conference was held at Venice. At the portal of St. Mark's, Pope Alexander III, no unworthy successor to Hildebrand, raised up the kneeling Emperor and gave him the kiss of peace. Temporary terms were agreed on, and a few years later the Peace of Constance (1183) definitely closed the war. The Emperor relinquished all but nominal rights of sovereignty over the confederate cities. They were to elect their municipal officers, and, with comparatively unimportant exceptions, to administer justice and manage their own affairs. Trade had conquered feudalism. The Middle Ages were near their setting.

No more of Barbarossa's doings need here be chronicled, except what he deemed a brilliant stroke of diplomacy, by which he hoped to unite the crown of the Two Sicilies with the Imperial crown on the head of his son, Henry, and through him on the heads of a long line of Hohenstaufens. The Empire had always asserted a claim to Southern Italy, but its claim had never been made good except during the temporary occupation of an Imperial army; and since the Normans had established their kingdom, Southern Italy had not only been lost to the Empire, but had become the chief prop of the Empire's enemy, the Papacy. If the Empire could acquire Southern Italy, it would hem in the Papacy both south and north, and crush it to obedience. Frederick's son Henry was married to the heiress of the Norman kingdom (1186); and the good Emperor, happy in the prospect before his Imperial line, but happier in that he could not foresee truly, took the cross and led his army towards the Holy Land. He died on the way (1190), leaving behind him a reputation for honour and chivalry, inferior to none left by the German Emperors.

CHAPTER XII: TRIUMPH OF THE PAPACY (1198-1216)

Gregory VII was well named the Julius Cæsar of the Papacy. His great conception of a sovereign ecclesiastical power, supreme over Europe, was destined to be realized. For in the fulness of time came Innocent III, the Augustus Cæsar of the Papacy, who ruled the civilized world of Europe more after the fashion of the old Roman Emperors than any one, except Charlemagne, had done. But in the interval between these two famous Popes, there was a period of reaction in which it looked for a time as if the Empire would plant the Ghibelline flag on the papal citadel. The Popes of this period were men of no marked ability, whereas the young king, Henry VI, had inherited the forceful temper of Barbarossa as well as his theories of Imperial rights, and displayed great vigour, energy, and resolution. Despite the opposition of the Popes, who as feudal suzerains of Sicily were most averse to the alliance, he had married the heiress of the Norman line, and despite the fierce opposition of the Sicilians,—part Arabs, part Greeks, with Italians and Normans mingling in,—he established his authority in the island. Henry was horribly cruel, but he was efficient. He was King of Germany, King of Italy, and King of the Two Sicilies, and had compelled a reluctant Pope to crown him Emperor. He determined to be Emperor in Italy in fact, and to accomplish what his father had failed to do. He undertook to check and suppress the communes by reviving the old feudal system. He reinstated old duchies and counties, and enfeoffed his loyal Germans. Matters looked black for the Guelfs, when, to their great good luck, the fiery young Emperor died, leaving an incompetent widow and a helpless baby (1197). By one of those occurrences, in which Catholics see more than the hand of chance, in the very year after the Emperor's death, a man of political talents of the highest order was elected to the pontifical chair.

In the days of Pope Alexander III, the great antagonist of Frederick Barbarossa, a young nobleman, who took holy orders almost in boyhood, had given early promise of an extraordinary career. This handsome, eloquent, imperious boy, named Lothair, inherited through his father, Thrasmund of the Counts of Segni in Latium, the fierce impetuosity of the Lombards, and through his mother, a Roman lady of high birth (from whom he took his master traits), the tenacity, the adroitness, the political genius of the Romans. He was educated at the universities of Bologna and Paris, where he studied law, theology, and scholastic philosophy. The stormy period of the struggle between Alexander and Barbarossa brought character and talents quickly to the front. Before he was twenty he had distinguished himself, before he was thirty he had been made a cardinal, and at thirty-seven he was elected Pope. According to the practice instituted by the deposed scamp, John XII, of taking a new name, Lothair assumed the title of Innocent III.

Under the guidance of Innocent III (1198-1216), the Papacy attained the full meridian of its glory. When this great Pope, lawyer, theologian, statesman, came to the throne, it was demoralized and weak; before he died, it had set its yoke on the neck of Europe. For the second time in history, orders were issued from Rome to the whole civilized world. A review of his pontificate brings up a panorama of Europe. His task began in Rome. This little city of churches, monasteries, towers, and ruins, which took no pride in great papal affairs, had plunged into one of its fits of republican independence, and, supported by the Emperor, had ousted the Popes from all control. In the course of a few years, by intrigue, tact, and civil war, Innocent got into his own hands the appointment of the senate and of the city governor, and thereby control of the city. He next turned his attention to the Patrimony of St. Peter, that central strip from Rome to Ravenna, given or supposed to have been given by Pippin and Charlemagne to the successors of St. Peter. Here the impetuous Emperor, Henry VI, had seated his German barons, setting up fiefs for them, and reëstablishing the feudal system under the Imperial suzerainty. These German barons were hated by the people. Innocent put himself at the head of the popular discontent, organized a Guelf, almost a national, party, and either drove the Germans out, or forced them to swear allegiance to the Holy See.

In Tuscany also the Guelfs were successful in breaking up the feudal restoration. In fact, since the days of Countess Matilda feudalism had been doomed. The cities had taken advantage of the wars between Papacy and Empire to secure virtual independence; and on Henry's death, with the exception of Ghibelline Pisa, they banded together and agreed never to admit an Imperial governor within their territories. Innocent tried to bring these cities under papal dominion, but they were too independent, and he was obliged to rest content with snapping up scattered portions of Matilda's domains.

Meantime in the kingdom of the Two Sicilies the Emperor's widow had died, and left to Innocent's guardianship her little son, Frederick. Innocent, guardian and suzerain lord, immediately began a struggle with the feudal nobility, just as in Italy, and, after a long and difficult contest, asserted the authority of his royal ward. On the termination of the minority, he handed over the kingdom to Frederick, who, on his part as King of the Two Sicilies, swore fealty to the Pope. Had it not been for his honourable and powerful guardian, Frederick probably would have had no kingdom, and in his oath of fealty he acknowledged his indebtedness: "Among all the wishes which we carry in the front rank of our desires, this is the chief, to discharge a grateful obedience, to show an honourable devotion, and never to be found ungrateful for your benefits—God forbid—since, next to Divine Grace, to your protection we are indebted not only for land but also for life."

In this way Innocent established the Papacy in Italy; sovereign, suzerain, protector or ally, he was the head of the Italian Guelfs and practically of Italy. Let us now look abroad. In Constantinople, the capital of the Greek Empire, Innocent's legate bestowed the Imperial purple upon an Emperor. An odd whirl of Fortune's wheel brought this to pass. Innocent had preached a crusade in the hope of recovering the Holy Land from the infidels, who had succeeded in expelling the Christians. An army of Frenchmen and Flemings answered his summons. They determined to avoid the deadly route overland and go by sea, and applied to Venice for transportation. When they came to pay the bill they did not have the money, and the Venetians insisted that they should help them recapture the city of Zara, on the Dalmatian coast, which had once belonged to Venice but had been lost again. Zara was attacked and taken (1202). One deflection from the straight path of duty led to another. To Zara came the son of the Greek Emperor to say that his father had been deposed, and to beg for help. The Venetians, wishing to wound two commercial rivals at once, Constantinople and Pisa (for the usurping Emperor favoured Pisa), used the suppliant as a stalking-horse, and persuaded the Crusaders once again to divert their immediate purpose and to restore the deposed Emperor to his throne. Again the Crusaders listened to temptation, for the Venetians baited their hook with golden promises; they sailed to Constantinople and restored the wronged Emperor. Matters did not go smoothly, however. Misunderstanding with the Greeks led to disagreements, disagreements to quarrels, and quarrels to war. The Latin Crusaders assaulted Constantinople, carried it by storm, and plundered houses, palaces, churches, shrines, everything; then, with appetites whetted by petty spoils, seized the frail Empire itself (1204). They divided Thrace, Macedonia, Greece, the islands of the Ægean Sea, and all the remnants of the Roman Empire of the East that they could lay hands on. Pious Venice came out best; she took coast and island, town and country, all along from recaptured Zara round by the shores of Dalmatia, Albania, Peloponnesus, and Thessaly, ending with half of Constantinople itself. The Marquess of Monferrat became King of Thessalonica, and his vassal, a Burgundian count, was invested with the lordship of Athens and Thebes. The Count of Flanders was elected Emperor of a Latin Empire. Innocent had been very angry with the deflections to Zara and Constantinople, and had thundered against the polite but inflexible Venetians. When the evil had been done, however, he made the best of it, and behaved with dignity and astuteness. He rebuked the Crusaders for having preferred the things of earth to those of Heaven, and bade them ask God's pardon for the profanation of holy places; but he admitted the advantage that would arise from reconciling the Greeks, schismatics since the days of Leo the Iconoclast, with the Roman See. So his legate bestowed the purple on a suppliant Emperor in the city of Constantinople.

In Germany Innocent also appears as the giver and withholder of crowns. On the death of Henry VI there was a disputed election. The Hohenstaufen party, dreading a long minority, passed over the baby Frederick, and nominated Philip, Henry's brother; the rival party, the German Guelfs, nominated Otto of Brunswick, a nephew of Richard C[oe]ur-de-lion. Civil war followed, and both parties appealed to Innocent who, after deliberation, supported Otto, but exacted a high price. Otto was obliged to guarantee to the Pope the strip of territory from Rome to Ravenna, and those portions of Matilda's domains which were not fiefs of the Empire, also to acknowledge papal suzerainty over the Two Sicilies, and to promise to conform to the papal will with regard to the leagues of the Lombard and Tuscan cities. This guarantee of Otto laid the first real foundation of the Papal States. Hitherto, vague Donations had given pretexts for claims; but Otto's deed was a definite Imperial grant, and conveyed an unquestionable title. In spite of Innocent's support matters went ill for Otto in Germany. Philip's star rose, and Innocent, to whom the cause of the Papacy was the cause of God and justified diplomatic conduct, was on the point of shifting to Philip's side, when in the nick of time Philip was murdered (1208). Otto's claim was now undisputed. No sooner, however, did he feel the crown secure on his head than he shifted his ground. Guelf by birth though he was, he found that he could not be both obedient to the Pope and loyal to his Imperial duties. He turned into a complete Ghibelline, broke his grant to the Pope, attempted to restore the feudal system in the papal territories, and assumed to treat the Two Sicilies as a fief of the Empire. Innocent, outraged and indignant at this breach of faith, excommunicated him (1210). Thereupon, as at the time when Gregory VII excommunicated Henry IV, the German barons rose, deposed Otto, and summoned young Frederick from Sicily to take the German crown. Innocent supported Frederick's cause, but exacted the price which he had formerly exacted from the perjured Otto. Frederick, pressed by present need, and forgetful of Otto's evil precedent, pledged himself as follows: "We, Frederick the Second, by Divine favour and mercy, King of the Romans, ever Augustus, and King of Sicily ... recognizing the grace given to us by God, we have also before our eyes the immense and innumerable benefits rendered by you, most dear lord and reverend father, our protector and benefactor, lord Innocent, by God's grace most venerable Pontiff; through your benefaction, labour, and guardianship, we have been brought up, cherished, and advanced, ever since our mother, the Empress Constance of happy memory, threw us upon your care, almost from birth. To you, most blessed father, and to all your Catholic successors, and to the Holy Roman Church, our special mother, we shall discharge all obedience, honour, and reverence, always with an humble heart and a devout spirit, as our Catholic predecessors, kings and Emperors, are known to have done to your predecessors; not a whit from these shall we take away, rather add, that our devotion may shine the more." Frederick promised that he would not interfere in the election of bishops, and that the candidate canonically elected should be installed. He confirmed the papal title to the Papal States. "I vow, promise, swear, and take my oath to protect and preserve all the possessions, honours, and rights of the Roman Church, in good faith, to the best of my power" (1213).

From this time forward Frederick advanced from success to success. Otto was driven into private life, and the Pope's legate put the German crown on Frederick's head at Aachen (1215). Where Innocent blessed, success and prosperity followed; where he cursed, death and destruction came.

Elsewhere the Pope was equally triumphant. All Europe bent under his imperial decrees. The kings of Portugal, Leon, Castile, and Navarre were scolded or punished. The King of Aragon went to Rome and swore allegiance. The Duke of Bohemia was rebuked, the King of Denmark comforted, the nobles of Iceland warned, the King of Hungary admonished. Servia, Bulgaria, even remote Armenia, received papal supervision and paternal care. Philip Augustus of France, at Innocent's command, took back the wife whom he had repudiated. John of England grovelled on the ground before him, and yielded up "to our lord the Pope Innocent and his successors, all our kingdom of England and all our kingdom of Ireland to be held as a fief of the Holy See"(1213).

Another triumph of darker hue added to the brilliance of Innocent's career. In the south of France, in the pleasant places of Provence and Languedoc, where troubadours praised love and war, and lords and ladies wandered down primrose paths, the humbler folk got hold of certain dangerous ideas. They believed that there was a power of evil as well as a power of good, that Christ was but an emanation from God, that the God of the Jews was not the real God of Goodness, and, worse than all, that the Roman Church, with its sacerdotalism, forms, sacraments, and ritual, was, to say the least, not what it should be. Innocent entertained no doubts that the Roman Church had been founded by God to maintain His truth on earth; as a statesman he regarded heresy as we regard treason and anarchy; as a priest he deemed it sin. He called Simon of Montfort and other dogs of war from the north and urged them at the quarry. The heresy was put down in blood. Here appears the black figure of St. Dominic, encouraging the faithful, rallying the hesitant, and by the fervour of his belief, by his devotion, by his genius for organization, more destructive to heresy than the sword of Montfort.

Thus Innocent sat supreme. He had created a papal kingdom where his predecessors had asserted impotent claims; he had confirmed the Two Sicilies in their dependency upon the Holy See; he had put the Papacy at the head of the Guelf party in Italy, and had made that party almost national; he had enforced the power of the Church throughout Europe, had given crowns to the Kings of Aragon and of England, to the Emperors of Germany and of Constantinople. No such spectacle had been seen since the reign of Charlemagne; none such was to be seen again till the coming of Napoleon. The conception of Europe as an ecclesiastical organization had reached its fullest expression.

CHAPTER XIII: ST. FRANCIS (1182-1226)

In spite of the dazzling success achieved by Innocent, matters were not well with the Church in Italy. Corruption threatened it from within, heresy from without. Simony was rampant; livings were almost put up at auction. Innocent asserted that there was no cure but fire and steel. The prelates of the Roman Curia were "tricky as foxes, proud as bulls, greedy and insatiable as the Minotaur." The priests were often shameless; some became usurers to get money for their bastards, others kept taverns and sold wine. Worship had become a vain repetition of formulas. The monks were superstitious, many of them disreputable. The inevitable consequence of this decay in the Church was heresy. Italy was nearly, if not quite, as badly honeycombed with heretics as Languedoc had been. The Patarini, whom we remember in Hildebrand's time, now become a species of heretics, abounded in Milan; other sects sprang up in towns near by. In Ferrara, Verona, Rimini, Faenza, Treviso, Florence, Prato, anti-sacerdotal sentiment was very strong. In Viterbo the heretics were numerous enough to elect their consul. At Piacenza priests had been driven out, and the city left unshepherded for three years. In Orvieto there had been grave disorders. In Assisi a heretic had been elected podestà (governor).

The great Innocent knitted his brows; he knew well that his noisy triumphs, which echoed over the Tagus, the Thames, the Rhine, and the Golden Horn, were of no avail, if heretics sapped and mined the Church within. It seemed as if the great ecclesiastical fabric, to which he had given the devotion of a life, was tottering from corner-stone to apex; when, one day, a cardinal came to him and said, "I have found a most perfect man, who wishes to live according to the Holy Gospel, and to observe evangelical perfection in all things. I believe that through him the Lord intends to reform His Holy Church in all the world." Innocent was interested, and bade the man be brought before him. This man was Francis Bernadone, known to us as St. Francis, the leader of a small band of Umbrian pilgrims from Assisi, who asked permission to follow literally the example of Jesus Christ. The Pope hesitated. To the cardinals, men of the world, this young man and his pilgrims were fools and their faith nonsense. "But," argued a believer, "if you assert that it is novel, irrational, impossible to observe the perfection of the Gospel, and to take a vow to do so, are you not guilty of blasphemy against Christ, the author of the Gospel?" Thinking the matter over, the Pope dreamed a dream. He beheld the Church of St. John Lateran, the episcopal church of the bishops of Rome, leaning in ruin and about to fall, when a monk, poor and mean in appearance, bent under it and propped it with his back. Innocent awoke and said to himself, "This Francis is the holy monk by whose help the Church of God shall be lifted up and stand again." So he said to Francis and his followers, "Go brethren, God be with you. Preach repentance to all as He shall give you inspiration. And when Almighty God shall have made you multiply in numbers and in grace, come back to us, and we will entrust you with greater things."

So St. Francis, "true servant of God and faithful follower of Jesus Christ," went about his ministry with the blessing of the Church. To the people of Assisi, of Umbria, and afterwards of all Central Italy, his life was a revelation of Christianity. He imparted the gospel anew, as fresh as when it had first been given under the Syrian stars. He embodied peace, gentleness, courtesy, and self-sacrifice. It is not too much to say that he saved the Catholic Church, and put off the Protestant Reformation for three hundred years. His example and influence raised the standard of conduct within the Church; and his love, his devotion, his insistence on the essential parts of Christ's teaching, and his dislike of worldly pomps, deprived heresy of all its weapons. He satisfied the widespread religious hunger better than heresy did. He was so characteristically Italian, and his ministry throws so much light on the state of Italy at the opening of the thirteenth century, that it is worth while to dwell for a few pages on his doings.

Assisi, built for safety on a hill and protected by great walls and gates, was a good example of a little mediæval town. In the centre was the piazza, on which fronted a Roman temple to Minerva, haughtily scornful of its mediæval surroundings. Hard by was the cathedral, where every baby was taken for baptism. On the tiptop of the hill stood a huge castle, where the feudal baron dwelt with his ruffianly soldiers and received his feudal lord, the Emperor, when he stopped at Assisi on his way to Rome. In Francis's boyhood, the people, aided by Pope Innocent, had driven out the German count, and had formed themselves into a free commune, save for their allegiance to the Holy See; but the change was not all gain. The town was divided into discordant classes; the nobility, maintained in idleness by the produce of their estates, the bourgeoisie, engaged in trade (Francis's father was a merchant), the artisans grouped in guilds, and the serfs, who tilled the fields and tended the vineyards and olive orchards. Once rid of the German count, the bourgeoisie endeavoured to rid themselves of the arrogant and idle nobility. Street war broke out. The nobles fled to Perugia, another little town perched on a hill some dozen miles across the plain, and asked for help. Perugia rejoiced in the opportunity. The miseries of a petty war between two little neighbours need no description. Fields and vineyards were devastated, olive orchards destroyed, farm-houses burned. Even in peace the peasants around Assisi lived in constant disquiet, ready to fling down their mattocks and flee to the protection of the city walls.

Within the city the streets were narrow, the houses small. Dirt abounded. War brought poverty, dirt brought the pest, Crusaders brought leprosy. At the gates of the town stood lazar-houses, and in remote spots lepers in the earlier stages of disease gathered together. Yet, despite war, pest, and leprosy, life in Umbria could never have been wholly sad. Certainly the sons of the well-to-do enjoyed themselves and whiled away the time carelessly. Sometimes a great personage stopped on his Romeward way; sometimes strolling players exhibited their shows on the piazza before the Temple of Minerva; sometimes a troubadour, escaped from the persecution in Provence, passed by on his way to Sicily, and sang his songs to repay hospitality. Many an afternoon and night the clubs of young gentlemen gave fêtes champêtres and dances. Francis, as a boy, was gayest of the gay, dancing and piping in the market-place, fighting in the front rank against the nobles of Perugia, but when he grew to manhood he could not bear the contrast between mirth and misery. He sought for some universal joy and found it in the love of Christ. He gathered about him a scanty band of holy and humble men of heart, who took the vow of poverty, and devoted themselves to praising God, comforting the wretched, and tending lepers. The abbot of the neighbouring Benedictine monastery gave them a little chapel, where St. Benedict himself had once said mass, which lay in the plain a mile below the town. This little chapel, named the Portiuncula (the little portion), which is now covered by the great church of Santa Maria degli Angeli (St. Mary of the Angels), so called because the songs of angels were heard there, was the cradle of the Franciscan Order. It was a tiny building, twenty feet wide and thirty long, with a steep pitched roof, plain walls, and big, round-arched door, and was sadly dilapidated. St. Francis and his friends built it up, and it became their church. Round it they built their huts, and encompassed all with a hedge. Here it was that St. Clare, the daughter of a nobleman of Assisi, donned the nun's dress. Here Francis passed the happy years of his life, while as yet his disciples were few and all were animated by his passionate longing for self-abnegation. He followed the New Testament literally, superstitiously one would say were it not that this literal obedience was accompanied by ineffable peace of heart and joy. He specially enjoined poverty. A smock, a cord, and sandals were enough for a true brother. Once a novice begged for permission to own a psalter, and teased him, but Francis answered: "After you have the psalter you will covet and long for a breviary; and when you possess a breviary you will sit on a chair like a great prelate, and say to thy brother, fetch me my breviary." Nor would he suffer the brethren to take heed for the morrow. They were only allowed to ask for provisions sufficient for the day. For he, in the rapture of his love, found infinite pleasure in the literal fulfillment of every word that had fallen from Christ's lips. Francis was an orator; he possessed passion, the great source of eloquence, and stirred prelates and Crusaders as well as peasants and lepers. The world wished for sympathy and he gave it. He seemed to be sick with the sick, afflicted with those in affliction, holy with the good; and even sinners felt him one of themselves. To his disciples he was Jesus come again. Joy and happiness radiated from him. All the world felt the charm and beauty of his love of God, and poetry followed him as wild violets attend the spring.

Thus Francis, by rubbing off the incrustations of twelve hundred unchristian years, revealed the poetry of the gospel to an eager world. One charming trait of his character was his love of animals, especially of birds. He wished the ox and the ass, companions of the manger, to share in the Christmas good cheer; and hoped that the Emperor would make a law that nobody should kill larks or do them any hurt. He was always very fond of larks and said that their plumage was like a religious dress. "Wherefore,—according to his disciple, Brother Leo,—it pleased God that these lowly little birds should give a sign of affection for him at the hour of his death. On the eve of the Sabbath day after vespers, just before the night in which he went up to God, a great multitude of larks flew down over the roof of the house where he lay, and all flying together wheeled in circles round the roof and singing sweetly seemed to be praising God."

His disciples went forth from their headquarters, the Portiuncula, like the Apostles, to preach the gospel, first to the people of Umbria and Tuscany, then on to Bologna and Verona, and soon over the Alps and across the seas. The Order had three branches: the begging friars themselves, tonsured and clad in undyed cloth, with cords about their waists and sandals on their feet; the sister Clares, shut up in nunneries, and dressed most simply; and the third order, people who continued to live in the world, but wished to follow the example of Christ and his blessed imitator and servant, Francis. The first rule of the begging friars had been very strict. For Francis the strait gate that led to eternal life was poverty. Even in his lifetime after his Order had become popular, there was grumbling and opposition; and after his death, the literal observance of his wishes was promptly given up. He would never allow his brethren to own a house or have a church; and yet within two years after his death the great basilica in Assisi was begun, dedicated to him, and hurried to magnificent completion. The Church, which held the doctrine of evangelical poverty fit only for mad men of genius, laid her heavy hand on the Order, and guided and governed it as best suited her purposes. But it would be grossly unfair to the Church to blame her for violating Francis's chief dogma. The total rejection of property, the total disregard of the morrow, seemed to her, as they seem to us to-day, doctrines wholly inapplicable to this world in which we find ourselves.

CHAPTER XIV: THE FALL OF THE EMPIRE (1216-1250)

The Church seized the Franciscan Order as a man in danger grasps at a means of safety, and shaped it to her needs; for, in spite of her brilliant triumphs under Innocent, her needs were great. The Papacy and the Empire approached their final struggle; both felt instinctively that the issue must be decisive. Their fundamental incompatibility had been aggravated by the union of the crowns of Sicily and Germany. Innocent had been pushed by circumstances into supporting Frederick's claim to Germany, and though he had striven to prevent the natural consequences by extorting oaths from Frederick, yet as time went on the danger became clearer. Under Innocent's successor, Pope Honorius, the Papacy lay like a cherry between an upper and lower jaw, which watered to close and crunch it; and this extreme peril is the excuse for the bitterness of the Popes in the contest which followed. The Papacy fought for its life.

The contest affected all Italy. Milan and many cities of the valley of the Po were Guelf; but Pavia and some others were Ghibelline, not that they loved the Emperor, but hated Milan; Florence and the other Tuscan cities, except Ghibelline Pisa and Siena, which hated Florence, were Guelf; Rome was split in two; the Colonna, the Frangipani, and other great families were generally Ghibelline, though permanent allegiance was unfashionable, while the Orsini and others were Guelf. The Gray Friars, who swarmed from the Alps to the Strait of Messina, were steadfast Guelfs, and even carried their loyalty so far, their enemies said, as to subordinate religion to political ends. On the other hand, the aristocracy, which was chiefly of Teutonic descent, held for the Empire.

Frederick himself is the central figure of the period. In his lifetime he excited love and hate to extravagance, and he still excites the enthusiasm of scholars. His is the most interesting Italian personality between St. Francis and Dante. I say Italian, for though Frederick inherited the Hohenstaufen vigour and energy, he got his chief traits from his Sicilian mother. Poet, lawgiver, soldier, statesman, he was the wonder of the world, stupor mundi, as an English chronicler called him. Impetuous, terrible, voluptuous, refined, he was a kind of Cæsarian Byron. In most ways he outstripped contemporary thought; in many ways he outstripped contemporary sympathy. He was sceptical of the Athanasian Creed, of communal freedom, and of other things which his Italian countrymen believed devoutly; while they were sceptical of the divine right of the Empire, of the blessing of a strong central government, and of other matters which he believed devoutly.

Between a stubborn Emperor, a stiff-necked Papacy, and obstinate communes, relations strained taut. The first break occurred between Emperor and Papacy. The Popes honestly desired to reconquer Jerusalem, which had fallen back into infidel hands, and incessantly urged a crusade; but perhaps at this juncture their zeal was heightened by a notion that the most effective defensive measure against the Emperor would be to keep him busy in Palestine. Frederick had solemnly promised to go. He had also solemnly promised to keep the crowns of Germany and of the Two Sicilies separate, by putting the latter on his son's head; but instead of this separation he kept both crowns on his own head, and secured both for his son as his successor. In spite of this violated promise, Pope Honorius, a gentle soul, devoutly eager for the crusade, crowned Frederick Emperor (1220), upon Frederick's renewed promise that he would start on the crusade within a year. The year passed, then another and another, and Frederick, with his crowns safe on his head, did not move a foot towards Jerusalem. The gentle Honorius remonstrated; Frederick made vows, excuses, protestations, but did not go. Finally the mild Pope died, and was succeeded by the venerable Cardinal Ugolino, Gregory IX, (1227-1241). Ugolino was a member of the Conti family of Latium (so preëminently counts that they took their name from their title), and a near relation to Innocent III. His indomitable character proved his kinship. Blameless in private life, a warm friend to St. Francis, deeply versed in ecclesiastical affairs, he had a benign face and noble presence; in fact, to quote the gentle Pope Honorius, he was "a Cedar of Lebanon in the Park of the Church." But, in spite of his virtue, his training, and his fourscore years, he was a very Hotspur, fiery, impatient, and headstrong. It was he who had put the crusader's cross into Frederick's hands and had received his crusader's vow; and now, having bottled up his wrath during the pontificate of Honorius, he could brook no further delay. Frederick made ready to go. Ships and men were gathered at Brindisi, and, in spite of a pestilence which killed many soldiers, the fleet set sail. A few days later word was brought that Frederick had put about and disembarked in Italy.

Gregory was furiously angry, and despatched an encyclical letter to certain bishops in Frederick's kingdom, which sets forth the papal side of the matter: "Out in the spacious amplitude of the sea, the little bark of Peter, placed or rather displaced by whirlwinds and tempests, is so continuously tossed about by storms and waves, that its pilot and rowers under the stress of inundating rains can hardly breathe. Four special tempests shake our ship: the perfidy of infidels, the madness of tyrants, the insanity of heretics, the perverse fraud of false sons. There are wars without and fears within, and it frequently happens that the distressed Church of Christ, while she thinks she cherishes children, nourishes at her breast fires, serpents, and vipers, who by poisonous breath, by bite and conflagration, strive to ruin all. Now, in this time when there is need to destroy monsters of this sort, to rout hostile armies, to still disturbing tempests, the Apostolic See with great diligence has cherished a certain child, to wit, the Emperor Frederick, whom from his mother's womb she received upon her knees, nursed him at her breasts, carried him on her back, rescued him often from the hands of them that sought his life, with great pains and cost studied to educate him until she had brought him to manhood, and led him to a kingly crown and even to the height of the Imperial dignity, believing that he would be a rod of defence, and a staff for her old age."

The encyclical then proceeds to recount Frederick's promises, his delays, evasions, excuses, and the false start from Brindisi, and adds, "Hearken and see if there be any sorrow like the sorrow of your mother the Apostolic See, so cruelly, so totally deceived by a son whom she had nursed, in whom she had placed the trust of her hope in this matter. But we put our hope in the compassion of God that He will show to us a way by which we shall advance prosperously in this affair, and that He will point out men, who in purity of heart and with cleanness of hand shall lead the Christian army. Yet lest, like dumb dogs who cannot bark, we should seem to defer to man against God, and take no vengeance upon him, the Emperor Frederick, who has wrought such ruin on God's people. We, though unwilling, do publicly pronounce him excommunicated, and command that he be by all completely shunned, and that you and other prelates who shall hear of this, publicly publish his excommunication. And, if his contumacy shall demand, more grave proceeding shall be taken."

This ban of excommunication was published over the world; bishops gave it out in their dioceses, priests in their parishes; Gray Friars told of it from Sicily to Scotland. Frederick in answer wrote letters to the kings of Europe, saying that the Roman Church was so consumed with avarice and greed, that, not satisfied with her own Church property, she was not ashamed to disinherit emperors, kings, and princes, and make them tributary. To the King of England he wrote:—

"Of these premises the King of England has an example, for the Church excommunicated his father, King John, and kept him excommunicated till he and his kingdom became tributary to her. Likewise all have the example of many other princes, whose lands and persons she squeezed under an interdict till she had reduced them to similar servitude. We pass over her simony, her unheard-of exactions, her open usury, and her new-fangled tricks, which infect the whole world. We pass over her speeches, sweeter than honey, smoother than oil,—insatiable bloodsuckers! They say that the Roman Curia is the Church, our mother and nurse, when that Curia is the root and origin of all evils. She does not act like a mother, but like a stepmother. By her fruits which we know she gives sure proof.

"Let the famous barons of England think of this. Pope Innocent instigated them to rise in revolt against King John as a stubborn enemy of the Church, but after that abnormally celebrated King made obeisance and, like a woman, delivered up himself and his kingdom to the Roman Church, that Pope, putting behind him his respect for man and fear of God, trampled down the nobles, whom he had first supported and pricked on, and left them exposed to death and disinheritance, so that he, after the Roman fashion, should gulp down his impudent throat the fatter morsels. In this way, under the incitement of Roman avarice, England, fairest of countries, was made a tributary. Behold the ways of the Romans; behold how they seek to snare all and each, how they get money by fraud, how they subjugate the free and disturb the peaceable, clad in sheep's clothing but inwardly ravening wolves. They send legates hither and thither, to excommunicate, to reprimand, to punish,—not to save the fruitful seed of God's word, but to extort money, to bind and reap where they have never sown.

"Against us also, as He who sees all things knows, they have raged like bacchantes, wrongfully, saying that we would not cross the sea according to terms fixed, when much unavoidable and arduous business about the going, and about the Church and about the Empire, detained us, not counting sickness. First there were the insolent Sicilian rebels: and it did not seem to us a good plan nor expedient for Christianity to go to the Holy Land," etc. And he ended, so the chronicler says, with an exhortation to all the princes of the world to beware against such avarice and wickedness, because "you are concerned when your neighbour's house is on fire."

These letters show the temper on both sides. Outwardly, however, peace was observed, and

Frederick really went on the promised crusade; and, though in Syria he found Patriarch, Templars, Hospitallers, and Franciscans all turned against him, he succeeded in making a treaty by which Jerusalem, Nazareth, and Bethlehem were ceded to him, and he crowned himself king in Jerusalem. In the mean time hostilities had broken out in Italy. Frederick incited the Roman barons to drive the Pope from Rome, and the Pope preached a crusade against Frederick. But both sides, having many cares within their respective jurisdictions, at length made peace, and Frederick was enabled to go back to his consuetas delicias, his wonted delights.

This phrase, which was used by the Pope, probably contained an innuendo, for gossip busied itself with Frederick's christianity and morals. He tolerated Saracens in his kingdom, lived on friendly terms with them, and preferred them in his army, for they were indifferent to excommunication; and gossip added that he liked Saracen ladies, hinted at a harem, and alleged that in Syria he had accepted the present of a troop of Moslem dancers. Gossip, spread by the glib tongues of mendicant friars, charged him with saying, "If God had seen my beautiful Sicily, he would not have chosen that beggarly Palestine for His Kingdom," "There have been three great impostors who invented religions, and one of them was crucified." Frederick's real offence in ecclesiastical eyes was that he wished to subordinate the spiritual to the secular power. It was natural, however, that pious folk should look askance at a prince who, while Christendom was fighting Islam, hobnobbed with Mohammedans and seemed to find them more sympathetic than Christians.

Frederick's real consuetæ deliciæ were of another kind. In his Sicilian court we catch the first streaks of the dawn that was destined to brighten into the day of the Renaissance. He himself was a highly accomplished man, spoke Italian, German, Arabic, and Greek, and took an interest in mathematics, philosophy, and in general learning. But poetry was his favourite pleasure. The Italian language, recently emerged from dog Latin, had just begun to serve literary uses, and Frederick's court had the honour of producing the first school of Italian poetry. He, his sons Manfred and Enzio, his chief counsellor Pier della Vigna, and many poets and troubadours drawn thither by his fame, so far outstripped the rest of Italy that all Italian poetry, wherever written, was called Sicilian.

Sicily was the most civilized place in Europe, now that Southern France had been crushed by the Albigensian persecution. The old Greek stock kept some trace of their inheritance; the Arabs had brought their culture; the Normans had added chivalric ideas; the Crusades and commerce had enlarged the intellectual boundaries; and Frederick himself had extraordinary versatility. Mathematicians from Granada, philosophers from Alexandria, were as welcome as the troubadours from Provence. Frederick looked after his own royal estates, managed his stud farm in Apulia, decided when brood mares should be fed on barley and when kept to grass. He was a great sportsman, too, and wrote a book on falconry. He enacted a famous code of laws, far superior in many respects to existing legislation, which was conceived with the definite plan of exalting royal authority over feudal prerogatives and communal customs. He deprived the barons of criminal jurisdiction; forbade private war, carrying weapons, etc; he limited trial by ordeal so far as he could, calling it "a species of divination;" he made minute regulations in matters of business and behaviour, and maintained a paternal authority.

In fact, Sicily, with its culture, poetry, Moslems, and its unorthodox king, succeeded to the heretical position of Southern France. The Papacy felt instinctively that a civilization so happy in the good things of this world, so lax on many points of morality, so careless of the Roman ecclesiastical system, was a perpetual menace to it. In the nature of things, the peace that had been made with Frederick could not last long.

The breach happened in the North. The Lombard cities revolted. Frederick marched against them and won a victory (1237). Then was the zenith of his power; his very triumph was the cause of his undoing. All the Guelfs of Italy roused themselves for the struggle. The Pope took part, and a second time excommunicated Frederick, enumerating a score of sins. A later Pope held a council at Lyons (a place of safety), excommunicated Frederick again, and deposed him from his Imperial throne (1245). Then an anti-emperor was set up. Blow on blow fell upon Frederick. He was terribly routed at Parma, through carelessness. His gallant son Enzio, the poet, was captured by the Bolognese, who would not release him, though Frederick offered to put a rim of gold round the walls of their city. Enzio spent twenty-three years in prison and there died. Pier della Vigna, who "kept both the keys of Frederick's heart," was suspected of high treason and condemned to death. Frederick himself died in 1250, and the Pope shouted for joy at the news, "Be glad ye Heavens, and let the Earth rejoice!" He had good reason, for the Church had lost its most dangerous enemy.

With the death of Frederick the Empire came to its end. The name of Holy Roman Empire continued till 1806, and from time to time for several hundred years German kings came down across the Alps to receive the Imperial crown, but on Frederick's death the old mediæval Empire practically ceased; and Italy, instead of being an Imperial province, became a series of independent states.

The end of the Hohenstaufens themselves reads like the last act of a bloody Elizabethan tragedy. Within a few years the only survivors among Frederick's descendants were his lawful heir, a baby, Conradin, and an illegitimate son, Manfred. Manfred, who had inherited the charm, the address, the energy and brilliance of his father, succeeded in establishing himself in the Two Sicilies, at first as regent for his nephew, and afterwards, for in those troubled times a regency was precarious, as king in his own right. But the Popes were resolved not to undergo a repetition of the danger they had experienced from Frederick, and laid their plans to destroy the last of the "viper's brood," as they called Frederick's family. They followed the old precedent, set in the days when the Papacy had been in danger from the Lombards, and invited a French prince, Charles of Anjou, brother to St. Louis, to come and depose Manfred, and offered him the crown of the Two Sicilies. The crafty, capable, deep-scheming Charles accepted, and came amid great rejoicing among the Guelfs. Rome made him Senator. Florence made him podestà; in fact, all Guelf Italy was at his feet. The Pope proclaimed a crusade against Manfred, collected tithes and taxes for the holy purpose, and provided Charles with an army. Manfred was defeated and killed (1266), and two years later, the valiant Conradin, a lad of sixteen, who came down in the mad hope of regaining his kingdom, was also defeated, taken prisoner, and, after a mock trial for treason, put to death. Thus the Papacy prevented the union of the Two Sicilies with the Empire, and thus the House of Anjou supplanted the last of the Hohenstaufens at Palermo and Naples.

CHAPTER XV: THE FALL OF THE MEDIÆVAL PAPACY (1303)

We are now coming out of the Middle Ages, and the dawn of a new era grows more and more apparent. The Empire, embodiment of an old outworn theory, has already fallen, and its victorious rival, the Papacy, in so far as it embodies the mediæval idea of a theocratic supremacy, is tottering, and it, too, will soon fall before the unsympathetic forces of a new age. So long as the Papacy stood untouched, it looked as potent and sovereign, and spoke with as lofty a tone, as in the days of Innocent; but a hundred years had wrought great changes, and at a push it tumbled and fell.

Hints had already been dropped that the dread thunderbolt, the curse of Rome, which had helped win the proud position of lordship over Europe, had become mere brutum fulmen. Excommunication had been so prodigally used for political purposes that educated men no longer believed that it was really the curse of heaven. Moreover, Europe had not been standing still. The vigorous, compact kingdom of France had come into being, and flushed with a sense of power and importance, determined to take that part in European politics which it regarded as its due. In angry self-confidence the young kingdom confronted the overweening Papacy, savagely tore off its giant's robe, and laid bare its real weakness.

Boniface VIII (1294-1303) was the pontiff under whom the papal empire came to its end. He was a vigorous, energetic, arrogant, eloquent, handsome man, with a wide knowledge of law, diplomacy, and politics. In the cathedral at Florence there is a large statue of him, calm and dignified, almost heroic. He sits with his rochet and tiara on, his right hand raised with two fingers extended as if blessing,—an unusual occupation,—and looks far more of this world than of the other. His contemporary, the Florentine historian, Villani, a Guelf, says: "He was great-minded and lordly, and coveted much honour, ... and was much respected and feared for his learning and power. He was very grasping for money in order to aggrandize the Church and his own relations, making no shame of gain, for he said that he might do anything with what belonged to the Church.... He was very learned in books, very wary and capable, and had great common sense; he had wide knowledge and a good memory, but was extremely cruel and haughty with his enemies and adversaries, ... more worldly than befitted his exalted station, and he did many things displeasing to God." Dante, passionately Ghibelline, calls Boniface "prince of the new Pharisees" and sends him to hell.

Boniface's chief enemies, as was usual in the case of a Pope who had enemies, were Romans. If the Papacy had been able to reduce Rome to real obedience, its history would have been different. The rebellious commune and the rebellious barons were constantly on the watch for favourable opportunities to revolt, or, as they regarded it, to assert their rights and liberties, and Boniface's first struggle came with the great House of Colonna. The Colonnas were haughty; he was imperious. They hinted that he was not legally Pope; he excommunicated them, proclaimed a crusade, captured and destroyed their fortresses in the Campagna, and made them deadly enemies. This victory was achieved at a price thereafter to be paid in full. But for the time Boniface was triumphant, and seemed, to himself at least, to sit as high as the great Innocent a hundred years before.

In the year 1300 he originated the custom, ever since observed, of a papal jubilee to celebrate the centennial year. For centuries Palestine had been the destination of pilgrims, and the holy character of Rome had been passed by, but, now that Palestine was completely lost, Rome reasserted herself as the pilgrims' city, and crowds again visited the Roman basilicas. Eager to encourage a practice which he saw would increase the prestige and the income of the Holy See, Boniface issued his Bull of Jubilee which promised remission of sins to all pilgrims who should visit the basilicas of St. Peter and St. Paul during the year.

Pious folk came from everywhere; on an average there were two hundred thousand at a time. They gave their offerings so generously that, as an eyewitness says, "Day and night two priests stood beside the altar in St. Paul's, holding rakes in their hands, raking in the money." It was noticed, however, that there were no kings or princes in the throng. That year was the summit of Boniface's prosperity.

In the mean time the quarrel with France had already begun. The French king, Philip the Fair, who was the personification of the new lay spirit, enacted a series of laws against the clergy, and, going counter to the accepted doctrine of clerical immunity from secular taxation, levied taxes upon them. This step was portentous. Boniface answered by absolutely forbidding both taxation and payment of taxes. The King of France not only persisted in taxation, but also forbade the exportation of any money from his kingdom, and so deprived the Pope of all his French revenues. Other angry words and acts followed, and a papal bull was publicly burnt in Paris.

Boniface, who had a marked predilection for vehement language, issued a bull, which deserves to be quoted as it sums up the extreme papal doctrine and also incidentally reveals how completely he misunderstood the drift of public opinion. "We are compelled, our faith urging us, to believe and hold—we do firmly believe and simply confess—that there is one holy and Apostolic Church, outside of which there is neither salvation nor remission of sins.... In this Church there is one Lord, one faith, one baptism.... Of this one and only Church there is one body and one head,—not two heads as if it were a monster,—Christ, namely, and the Vicar of Christ, St. Peter, and the successor of St. Peter.... We are told by the word of the gospel that in this His fold there are two swords,—namely, a spiritual and a temporal.... Both swords ... are in the power of the Church; the one, indeed, to be wielded for the Church, the other by the Church; the one by the hand of the priest, the other by the hand of kings and knights, but at the will and sufferance of the priest. One sword, moreover, ought to be under the other, and the temporal authority to be subjected to the spiritual.... That the spiritual exceeds any earthly power in dignity and nobility we ought the more plainly to confess the more spiritual things excel temporal ones.... A spiritual man judges all things, but he himself is judged by no one. This authority, moreover, even though it is given to man, and exercised through man, is not human but rather divine, being given by divine lips to Peter and founded on a rock for him and his successors through Christ Himself; the Lord Himself saying to Peter: 'Whatsoever thou shalt bind,' etc. Whoever, therefore, resists this power thus ordained by God, resists the ordination of God. Indeed, we declare, announce, and define, that it is altogether necessary to salvation for every human creature to be subject to the Roman Pontiff."

In retort the king, knowing that the country was behind him, convoked the States-General of the kingdom; which upheld him, charged Boniface with all sorts of misbehaviour, and called for a general council of the Church to judge the matters in dispute.

The crafty king, however, had determined on other means of revenge than decrees, accusations, and burning bulls; he devised a plot to kidnap Boniface and fetch him prisoner to France. One William Nogaret, once a professor of law in a French university, now deep in the king's counsels, went to Italy, met a vindictive member of the Colonna family, Sciarra Colonna, and the two arranged the details of the plot. There were many conspirators, for not only the Colonnas were eager to revenge themselves, but numerous nobles, dispossessed to make room for the Pope's relations, were ready to lend a hand. The unsuspecting Boniface, now an old man of eighty-six years, was at Anagni (a little fortified town not far from Rome), his native place, but nevertheless honeycombed with treason; here, from the pulpit of the cathedral where Emperors had been excommunicated, he proposed to excommunicate the King of France. Two days before the day set for the excommunication, Nogaret and Sciarra Colonna, with a troop of soldiers, entered the city which had been opened by traitors; many of the townsmen ranged themselves under the French banner. The conspirators broke into the episcopal palace, where they found the valiant old man seated on a throne, in his pontifical garments, with the tiara on his head, and a cross in his hand. Sciarra Colonna dragged him down and would have stabbed him with his dagger but that Nogaret withheld him by main force. The Pope was made prisoner and the palace sacked; but in a few days sympathy turned, papal partisans stormed the palace, rescued Boniface, and carried him to Rome. Here the Orsini, pretending to befriend him, kept him shut up in the Vatican, half crazed by fright and fury, till death happily released him (October 11, 1303). Then men remembered an old prophecy uttered concerning him: "He shall enter like a fox, reign like a lion, and die like a dog." Thus dramatically the hollowness of papal power was revealed.

France did not rest content with this insolent act. A year or two later, a Frenchman of Gascony, the archbishop of Bordeaux, was made Pope by the French king's influence. This Pope, Clement V (1305-14), never went to Rome, but took up his abode at Avignon, a little city on the Rhone, not very far from its mouth. The place was under the overlordship of the Angevin kings of Naples, but really under the influence of the kings of France. Here the Papacy stayed for nearly seventy years, practically a dependency of France. A series of French Popes succeeded one another. They built on the bank of the Rhone a gigantic fortress, regarded Rome, the source of their greatness, as a dismal and dangerous out-of-the-way place, and believed that they had transferred the seat of the Papacy permanently. This period of exile was regarded by the Italians as a Babylonish captivity.

Political degradation was not all. The Roman Curia became a collection of men of pleasure. The ambitious Popes, even Boniface, had had a touch of the heroic in them, and erred through pride, arrogance, and hate; but these Avignonese Popes, though some of them were good men, suffered the papal court to become a place of amusement, banqueting, and dissipation.

CHAPTER XVI: LAST FLICKER OF THE EMPIRE (1309-1313)

After the Papacy had been dragged in servitude to France, the Empire, like a dying soldier who gets on his feet to shout one shout of triumph over his enemy's fall, made a last gallant effort to recover life and strength. The effort was very gallant but very ineffectual, and owes its chief celebrity to its connection with the great man, who summed up and reiterated the Imperial creed, somewhat in the same way that Pope Boniface had summed up and reiterated the papal creed. Both creeds were dead, but each man believed his fervently, and as Boniface's bulls set forth the doctrines of Hildebrand and Innocent III, so Dante's treatises and letters set forth the beliefs of Barbarossa and Frederick II.

The year of Boniface's jubilee is the year to which Dante assigns his journey to the abodes of departed spirits, and as the jubilee marked the close of the mediæval Papacy, so the "Divine Comedy" marks the close of mediæval theology, and Dante himself stands as the greatest mark at the boundary between the old world passing away and the modern world coming in. Giovanni Villani, who was about fifteen years younger, described him in this way: "He was deeply versed in almost all learning, although he was a layman; he was a very great poet, a philosopher, and a complete master of rhetoric in prose and verse as well as in public speech; a most noble writer, very great in rhyme, with the most beautiful style that ever was in our language up to his time and since. In his youth he wrote the book on 'The New Life of Love,' and then when he was in exile he composed twenty ethical poems and many admirable poems on love; and he wrote among others three noble epistles; one he sent to the government of Florence, complaining of his banishment from no fault of his; another he sent to the Emperor Henry, when he was at the siege of Brescia, blaming him for his delay, in the tone of a prophet; the third to the Italian cardinals, during the vacancy after the death of Pope Clement (V), that they should come to an accord and elect an Italian Pope; all in Latin, in lofty style, with excellent reasonings and appeals to authority, which were much praised by men of judgment. This Dante by reason of his knowledge was somewhat arrogant, haughty, and disdainful, and, like an ungracious philosopher, he could not talk easily with unlearned men; but because of his other merits, the learning and the worth of this great citizen, it seems fitting to give him perpetual remembrance in this chronicle of mine, notwithstanding that his noble works left to us in writing bear true testimony to what he was and confer honourable fame upon our city."

Dante, by passages in his "Divine Comedy," but more particularly by his treatise "De Monarchia" (On Universal Empire), enables us to understand how the Empire could raise its head in Italy sixty years after Frederick II had died. In Germany after an interregnum, the House of Hapsburg had mounted the throne, but no one had ventured to cross the Alps for the Imperial crown. Nevertheless, Dante and the Ghibellines could not bring themselves to believe that the old familiar institution had fulfilled its function and was to be cast aside. The conception of Europe as a group of equal nations had not yet arisen, and Ghibellines still believed that a Roman Emperor could put down confusion, anarchy, political chaos, and cure all the ills of Italy. The Ghibellines believed in the Emperor as Mohammedans believed in Mohammed; if he should return, exiles (like Dante) would be restored, peace would bloom, and Rome again become the head of a just and universal empire. Dante, in the "De Monarchia," first contends that universal empire is necessary to the well-being of the world; having established that proposition, he argues that this universal empire rightly belongs to the Roman people, and proves his point by appeals to Virgil and the New Testament; then he proceeds to show that the authority of the Empire is derived directly from God. "Some say," he says, "that Constantine when he was cleansed of the leprosy by the prayers of Silvester, then Pope, gave the seat of the Empire, to wit Rome, to the Church, together with many other dignities appertaining to the Empire. Therefore, they argue, since then no one can receive those dignities, except he shall receive them from the Church, to whom they belong.... This proposition I deny; and when they put forth their proof, I say it proves nothing, because Constantine could not alienate the dignities of the Empire, nor the Church receive them.... No man has a right to do things by means of an office entrusted to him, which go directly counter to that office.... Therefore an Emperor has no right to divide the Empire ... and the Church in no wise is able to receive temporal things because the precept expressly forbids it, as we have it in Matthew 'Provide neither gold, nor silver, nor brass in your purses, nor scrip for your journey,' etc."

This Ghibelline theory was in flat contradiction to Boniface's theory, just as the Imperial creed had always contradicted the papal creed. In Dante's time the two conflicting theories seemed to have become mere ghosts; when of a sudden the Imperial theory started up in reality. A new king of the Romans, Henry VII, announced that he was coming into Italy to take his Imperial crown. The Ghibellines welcomed him with boundless enthusiasm. Dante, in undeserved exile from Florence, flushed with the hope of return to his dearly beloved city, wrote a circular letter to all the princes of Italy:—

"Behold now is the acceptable time, in which arise signs of consolation and peace. For a new day begins to shine, showing the dawn that shall dissipate the darkness of long calamity. Now the breezes of the East begin to blow, the lips of heaven redden, and with serenity comfort the hopes of the peoples. And we who have passed a long night in the desert shall see the expected joy.

"Rejoice, O Italy, pitied even by the heathen, now shalt thou be the envy of the earth, because thy bridegroom, the comfort of the world and the glory of the people, the most merciful Henry, Divus, Augustus, Cæsar, hastens to thy espousals. Dry thine eyes, put off the trappings of woe, O thou Fairest; for he is at hand who shall free thee from the prison of the ungodly, who shall smite the malignant, and destroy them with the edge of the sword, and shall give his vineyard to other husbandmen, who will render the fruits of justice in the time of harvest."

The hope that Henry would restore peace and establish order warmed even the Guelfs; and almost all the Italian cities, excepting stubborn Florence, sent envoys to greet him as he came to take the Imperial crown. The French Pope was greatly perplexed as to what to do. On the one hand, he had begun to wish for an Emperor to subdue the Roman barons and to be a counterweight to the French king, whom he found too masterful a protector; on the other hand, he was afraid to displease the French king, and to do anything that might set the Ghibellines on their feet again. So he played a double game: he encouraged Henry in the North, and in the South he strengthened the Angevin King of Naples, the leader of the Guelfs. Henry VII crossed the Alps in October, 1310. He was brave, honest, and just; he believed devoutly in his Imperial mission, desired peace, and wished to be Emperor of Guelf and Ghibelline alike. At first all went well; many cities opened their gates and received Imperial vicars; Milan lowered her flags as Henry entered, and her Guelf archbishop put the iron crown of Lombardy upon his head. But this happy calm could not last long. Henry was poor, he asked Milan for a great deal of money, and then demanded, ostensibly as a guard of honour for his journey to Rome but really as hostages, fifty noblemen from each of the two parties. The Ghibellines assented: but the Guelfs suspected treachery and refused: their leaders fled and their houses were sacked and burned. This was the end of peace. Henry attempted to enforce obedience. He sacked Cremona, razed her walls to the ground, and laid siege to Brescia. The horrors of the siege were fearful; the citizens fought with desperation, but yielded at last to famine and pestilence. The unfortunate Henry had now been forced into the old position of German tyrant and Ghibelline party chief; and, instead of marching directly on Rome, or on rich Florence which was the head and front of the Guelf cause in the North, he had wasted valuable time in taking unimportant cities. The Ghibellines were in a fever of impatience. Dante wrote:—

"To the most holy Conqueror, and only lord, our lord Henry, by divine providence King of the Romans, ever Augustus, your Dante Alighieri, a Florentine and undeserving exile, and all Tuscans everywhere, who wish for peace on earth, kiss your feet.

"For a long time have we wept by the rivers of confusion, and have incessantly prayed for the protection of a just king, who should ... put us back in our just rights. When you, successor of Cæsar and Augustus, crossing the ridges of the Apennines, brought back the venerable insignia of Rome ... like the sun suddenly uprising, new hope of better time for Italy shone out. But now men think you delay, or surmise that you are going back ... and we are constrained by doubt to stand uncertain and to cry, like John the Baptist, Art thou he that should come, or do we look for another?... Do you not know, most excellent of Princes, do you not see from the watch-tower of your exalted height, where the stinking little fox lurks, safe from the hunters? In truth, the evil beast does not drink of the headlong Po, nor of your Tiber, but its wickedness pollutes the rushing waters of the Arno, and the name of this dire, pernicious creature (do you not know?) is Florence. She is the viper turned against the breast of its mother; she is the sick sheep that contaminates the whole herd of her master. Indeed with the fierceness of a viper she strives to tear her mother; she sharpens the horns of rebellion against Rome, who made her in her own image and likeness....

"Up, then, break this delay, take confidence from the eyes of the Lord God of Hosts, in whose sight you act, and lay low this Goliath with the sling of your wisdom and the stone of your strength; for with his death the dark night of fear shall cover the camp of the Philistines, and they shall flee, and Israel shall be set free. And just as now, exiles in Babylon, we mourn remembering holy Jerusalem, so, then, citizens and at home, we shall breathe in peace and turn the miseries of confusion into joy.

"Written in Tuscany ... fourteen days before the kalends of May, 1311, in the first year of the coming into Italy of the divine and most happy Henry."

Henry did go south, but there were greater obstacles in his way than Dante imagined. The spirit of the age was against him. It was vain to try to bring back the past. Florence shut her gates, manned her walls, sent more money to his enemies, and headed a league of the Guelf cities in Tuscany and Umbria. Even Rome was half against him. The Ghibelline nobles received him and took him to their part of the town; but the Guelfs held St. Peter's, and though there was fierce fighting in the streets, the Guelfs stood their ground, and Henry was forced to receive the Imperial crown from the papal legate (the Pope was too prudent to leave Avignon) in the basilica of St. John Lateran. Here the luckless Emperor stayed for a time in the midst of ruin, material, political, and moral. Then he attempted to crush Florence, the ringleader of disobedience, but her walls were too strong; the impotent Emperor could do no more than harry the country-side. He fell back upon Ghibelline Pisa, and set patiently to work to gather together a new army. The Ghibellines gallantly responded to his call, and Henry actually set forth on his way to Naples, to punish the House of Anjou and avenge the Hohenstaufens, but death cut short his lofty plans. He died in a little town near Siena (1313), and the hopes of Dante and the Ghibellines were ruined forever. The last flicker of the Empire had gone out.

Other Emperors, it is true, crossed the Alps, but not as masters. The connection of Italy with the Holy Roman Empire ends with the death of the gallant Henry. The mediæval Papacy and the mediæval Empire had passed away, for the Middle Ages themselves had come to an end.

CHAPTER XVII: A REVIEW OF THE STATES OF ITALY (ABOUT 1300)

Now that the two great actors, whose long-drawn quarrel has been the main thread of Italian history, have made their exits, and left us, as it were, with a sense of emptiness, it becomes necessary to call the roll and make a better acquaintance with the lesser dramatis personæ, who step to the front of the stage and carry on the plot of history. The programme reads as follows:—

In the South, the kingdom of the Two Sicilies has already been torn in two. Charles of Anjou, the conqueror of the Hohenstaufens, clever, shrewd, and capable as he was, had overreached himself. He entertained great ambitions, and was dreaming of Constantinople and its imperial crown, when a rebellion known as the Sicilian Vespers broke out in Sicily. The country had been overrun with French office-holders and French soldiers, and the Sicilians, who regretted the Hohenstaufens, had reached the utmost limit of endurance. The whole island had become a powder-box; it was a mere matter of accident where and how the powder would ignite. A French soldier insulted a woman on her way to church. In a moment he was killed and his fellow soldiers massacred to a man. "Death to the French!" resounded over the island, and the infuriated Sicilians put all to the sword. The revolutionists needed a leader, and, as the old Norman blood royal still survived in Manfred's daughter, they invited her husband, King Pedro of Aragon, to be their king. Pedro accepted, and he and his descendants, the House of Aragon, made good their claim to the throne of Sicily against all the attempts of the House of Anjou and of the lords suzerain, the Popes, to oust them. By this revolution, Sicily was separated from the Kingdom of Naples for more than a hundred years.

In the centre of Italy there was great disorder. The lords of the Papal States remained at Avignon, and attempted to govern their dominions by legates; but though their sovereignty nominally extended from the Tyrrhene Sea to the Adriatic, they were impotent to enforce it. There was no unity; each town was governed separately by a papal legate, by a powerful baron, or by a communal government. Rome itself, which in the absence of the Popes had dwindled to a little city of ruins, towers, churches, vineyards, and vegetable gardens, was in constant disorder. The towns near by were often faithful to their allegiance, but across the Apennines the obstinate little cities between the mountains and the sea were almost always independent. At present there is nothing of sufficient interest to prevent us from treating Rome as carelessly as the Popes did, and passing hurriedly through to Florence and the independent communes of Northern Italy where we must pause.

Prior to the wars between the Empire and the Papacy feudal institutions had prevailed there, though with less vigour in Northern Italy than elsewhere in Europe, and all the land had been divided up into various fiefs, in which counts and marquesses held sway. During those wars the cities shook off Imperial dominion and got rid of Imperial rulers, and began their careers as independent Italian communes. Most of these cities were of old Roman foundation, but the time of Hildebrand and Henry IV may be deemed their nativity, as then they first appear in Italian history as individuals. All these towns were little republics, each with its own character, but all conforming more or less to a general type. Within massive walls the city clustered round two main points, the cathedral, which was flanked by belfry and baptistery, and the piazza (public square), on which fronted the Palazzo Pubblico, the city hall, where the magistrates had their offices. Round about and radiating off, houses and palaces, grim and heavy, stood high above the narrow streets. Scattered here and there scores of private fortresses raised their great towers thirty yards and more into the air. Street, palace, tower, all were obviously ready for street warfare, waiting on tiptoe for the bells to ring.

The citizens were divided into three classes. The upper class included the old nobility, the high clergy, the large merchants, the rich bankers; the middle class included the petty merchants, the tradesfolk, the master artisans; and below them came the miscellaneous many. In some cities the nobility, allying itself with the proletariat, held the political power. But in the more democratic cities, like Florence, the trades and crafts controlled the government. In Florence there were seven greater guilds,—judges and notaries, wool-merchants, refiners and dyers of foreign wool, silk-dealers, money-changers, physicians and apothecaries, furriers; and fourteen lesser guilds,— butchers, shoemakers, masons, carpenters, blacksmiths, and so on. Every freeman was obliged to belong to one of the guilds; Dante was enrolled in the guild of physicians and apothecaries. Trades and crafts descended from father to son, and each guild was divided into masters, journeymen, and apprentices.

In the government, executive, legislative, and judicial powers were distinguished, but not strictly separated. The executive power was vested in one man, or in several men, who were assisted by a kind of privy council. This council superintended various matters of public concern, such as weights, measures, highways, and fines. There was also a larger council, to which, as well as to public office generally, only the enfranchised citizens were eligible. These privileged persons were never more than a small fraction of the population; in Florence, for instance, barely three thousand, even in her populous days. Finally, there was a parliament or assembly of all the free citizens, which met on the piazza, and shouted approval or disapproval to such questions as were submitted to it.

In the earlier days the joint executives were called consuls. Their places were not easy. If they were fair to all, they displeased their own party; if unfair to the opposite party, they were liable to retaliation. The difficulties of partisanship led to the appointment of a new officer, the podestà. The name and idea came from the governors put in the Imperial cities by Barbarossa. The podestà, who was elected by the citizens, supplanted the consuls in all their more important functions; he became the head of both the civil and the military service, a kind of governor. He was a nobleman, chosen, in the hope of avoiding local partisanship, from some other Italian city. The citizens, if Guelf, of course chose a Guelf; if Ghibelline, a Ghibelline. When the podestà's term of office, which was usually six months or a year, began, he came to the city bringing two knights, several judges, councillors, and notaries, a seneschal and attendants, and in the piazza took his oath of office,—to observe the laws, to do justice, and to wrong no man. His duties, and often his movements, were carefully prescribed; sometimes he was not allowed to enter any house in the city other than the palace prepared for him. At the end of his term he was obliged to linger for a time, in order to give anybody who might be aggrieved an opportunity to lodge a complaint against him and obtain redress. Such was the ordinary form of communal government; but the constitutions varied in different cities, and in each city shifted every few years, as class feeling, partisan enmity, or new men suggested changes.

The prosperity and power of these communes came from trade, and show how trade prospered and riches accumulated. Some merchant guilds carried on a very extensive business. Take the wool guild of Florence. Tuscany yielded a poor quality of wool, and as it was impossible to weave good cloth from poor wool, these Florentine merchants imported raw wool from Tunis, Barbary, Spain, Flanders, and England, wove it into cloth so deftly that foreigners could not compete with them, and exported it to the principal markets of Europe. Trade with the North, however, was less important than trade with the East. Merchandise was carried over the seas more easily than over the Alps, and in many respects the products of the East were better and more varied than those of northern Europe. The Italians loaded the galleys of Venice, Genoa, and Pisa with silken and woollen stuffs, oil, wine, pitch, tar, and common metals, and brought back from Alexandria, Constantinople, and the ports of Asia Minor and Syria, pearls, gold, spices, sugar, Eastern silk, wool and cotton, goatskins and dyes, and sometimes Eastern slaves. Such a wide commerce outstripped the capacity of barter and cash, and gave rise to a system of banking, with its attendant credits and bills of exchange. The quick-witted Florentines excelled at this business, and great banking houses, like the Bardi and the Peruzzi, had branches or correspondents in all the chief cities.

This large commerce in face of the obstacles that barred its way seems extraordinary. A city like Florence, for instance, especially in the earlier days, was greatly hampered by the conditions about her. Outside her walls, within the radius of a dozen or twenty miles, were castles manned by arrogant nobles, who made traffic unsafe. They would not conform to the new economic condition of society except upon compulsion. Rival cities refused to let Florentine wares pass through their territories without payment of ruinous tolls. Wars were waged to moderate these exactions. Or, again, war was necessary to enforce the rights of Florentine citizens in other cities. Moreover, each city had its own system of weights and measures, its own coinage; each imposed customs on all wares entering its gates, in earlier days so much a cart-load, afterwards a percentage of the value. On all highways, at all bridges and fords, there were tolls to be paid. From city to city a merchant had to change his money, until in later times certain coins, like the Florentine florin, passed current everywhere; and sometimes, on entering the gates, he was obliged to adopt a distinguishing badge, as, for instance, according to the usage at Bologna, putting a piece of red wax on his thumb-nail. These were the fetters placed on trade in time of peace; but peace itself was transitory and uncertain. Apart from the wars with the Emperor, the cities periodically fought the feudal nobility, or one another. Venice made war on Ravenna, Pisa on Lucca, Vicenza on Treviso, Fano on Pesaro, Verona on Padua, Modena on Bologna, and the greater cities, like Milan and Florence, on any or all of their respective neighbours. When a city had no absorbing war abroad, factions fought at home. Burghers and nobles barricaded the streets, manned the towers, rang the bells, shot and hacked one another with spasmodic fury. The burghers generally won. They then banished hundreds of their adversaries, and made laws against them. In some cities a register was kept to record the names of the nobles whose democracy was suspected; in others, as in Lucca, nobles were excluded from all share in the government, and were not allowed to testify against burghers. In Pisa, if there was disquiet in the streets, the nobles were obliged to stay indoors.

These factions called themselves Guelfs and Ghibellines. At first Guelfs were the burghers of the communes and partisans of the Papacy, and Ghibellines partisans of the Empire and the feudal system; but subsequently the terms merely served to distinguish political parties, whose platforms, as we should say, shifted with questions of the hour. Even when these two factions were at peace, they distinguished themselves by different badges and fashions. The merlons of the Guelf battlements were square, those of the Ghibelline swallow-tailed. Good party men wore caps of diverse pattern, did their hair differently, cut their bread and folded their napkins in different ways. It was enough that one side should bow, take an oath, harness a horse, in one mode, for the other side to start a contrary fashion.

The growth of population, of property, of commerce, however, shows that history may easily dwell too much upon fighting and war. In these petty wars and street frays, the numbers engaged were few, and but little blood was shed. Most of the fighting was a consequence of economic difficulties. It was the mediæval equivalent of strikes, lock-outs, boycotts, undersellings, rivalries, riots, and other phenomena of modern industry.

The maritime cities were in a very different position from the inland cities, and had a different history. They enjoyed great advantages for trade. No feudal barons could bar the sea, and pirates and infidels were not serious impediments. Greater commercial prosperity, however, begot more bitter commercial jealousy. Genoa hated Pisa; no Genoese sailor could endure the cut of a Pisan sail. Both cities had a large trade in the Levant, and being so near each other became deadly rivals. They fought spasmodically for years, from the Gulf of Genoa to the Black Sea, and at last came to the death grapple. The time was unfortunate for Ghibelline Pisa, as a Guelf league had been attacking her on land. The decisive battle was fought off the island of Meloria, a few miles from the mouth of the Arno. The Genoese, who outnumbered the Pisans, won a great victory, destroyed or captured many galleys, and took ten thousand prisoners (1284). Pisa never recovered from this blow. Florence and Lucca took immediate advantage of it to unite with Genoa, and force Pisa to submit to a Guelf government; and from this time on greedy Florence, like a hawk, kept her eyes fixed on poor Pisa, impatient for the time when she should seize her prey.

Genoa remained a republic, active, eager, impetuous, torn by factions and subject to many vicissitudes, but lack of space compels us to leave her and pass on to where "Venice sits in state, throned on her hundred isles." She, queen of the sea, had even a more lavish portion of individuality than her sister cities, individual as they all were, and hardly belonged to Italy, so completely did she hold herself aloof from the two great interests of mediæval Italy, the Empire and the Papacy. No cries of Pope's men and king's men, of Guelf and Ghibelline, disturbed the Grand Canal or the Piazza of St. Mark's; no feudal incumbrances hampered her mercantile spirit, nor did papal anathemas cause a single Venetian ship to shift her course. Venice had long remained loyal to Constantinople, and even after all political dependence had ceased, was, in character and aspect, more a Constantinople of the West than an Italian city, a grown-up daughter, more beautiful than her beautiful mother, who, living her own triumphant and unfilial life, still retained many of her mother's traits. Untroubled by sentiment, even in the Crusades, Venice always kept steadily in view her fixed purpose of increasing her commerce and of securing foreign markets; and this purpose shaped her political actions, and also, indirectly, the form of her government.

Originally the citizens, assembled in public meeting, elected the Doge, and exercised a right to vote on important political matters; but the great families soon acquired control, and little by little turned the government into an oligarchy. The first great step was taken in Barbarossa's time, just when the Lombard cities were struggling to free themselves from Imperial dominion. A Great Council of four hundred and eighty members was established, to which were given the powers of legislation, appointment, electing the Doge, and filling vacancies in itself. The franchises of the people were all taken away and the oligarchy left supreme. This oligarchy of merchant princes, in whom patriotism, pride of place, and love of gain harmoniously accorded, was an exceedingly competent body of men. The greatness of Venice was their greatness, and they pursued it devotedly. Beginning early in life these patricians were trained for their duties by service in the navy and in the merchant marine, or by employment in the government of the various cities, islands, and territories included in the long stretch of coastwise empire. Knowing that Venice lived by commerce they made every effort by war, diplomacy, and private enterprise, to extend that commerce. After the conquest and division of the Eastern Empire (1204) they became more eager than ever for a monopoly of trade with the Levant, and inevitably came into deadly rivalry with Genoa, also passionately eager to hold the gorgeous East in fee.

The wars with Genoa, destructive though they were for the time being, were of service to the aristocracy, for they made the Venetians appreciate the value of a compact governing body; and the aristocracy took advantage of that appreciation to tighten its hold on the government.

Throughout the thirteenth century the Great Council, though it consisted entirely, or almost entirely, of patricians and elected its own members, had been open to all classes. Any citizen, however unlikely to be elected, was eligible. At the close of the century the patricians secured the enactment of a series of measures, which in substance divided the citizens into two classes, those whose ancestors had sat in the Great Council, and those whose ancestors had not, and decreed that only members of the first class should be eligible. This legislation is known as the closing of the Great Council. As all those who were eligible naturally wished to become members, the Council gradually increased until it finally numbered over fifteen hundred. The patricians also further curtailed the powers of the Doge, divided the various functions of government among the main subdivisions of the Council,—the Senate, the Council of Forty, the Doge's cabinet, and the Council of Ten,—and gave to the State the definite form of government which it maintained to its end.

From Venice we must pass by Milan and the cities of the Po, to where in the extreme Northwest the Counts of Savoy, perched on the Alps, maintained a precarious sovereignty over both slopes, with no resources except the muscles of their mountaineers and the possession of Alpine passes. Little did the proud maritime cities, Genoa and Venice, the great inland cities, Milan and Florence, and Rome least of all, suspect that these poor counts would one day consolidate all the territory from the foot of the mountains to the Riviera in a compact little kingdom (Piedmont), and from that as a pedestal, step to still higher honours. The House of Savoy runs aristocratically back into legend; but about the year 1000, a certain Humbert of the White Hand, emerging from historic obscurity, obtained the city of Turin and part of Piedmont, as a marriage portion for his son, and thereby secured to his house a footing in Italy (1045). In the course of another century or so these Savoyards in a succession of Humberts and Amedeos, brave, shrewd, and usually successful men, extended their dominions by war, by marriage, and by bargains. They made the most of their position as door-keepers to Italy, and exacted various privileges from needy Emperors, as the price of passing the Alps. They fought rival counts, waged innumerable petty wars, and rightly or wrongly acquired territories which are now parts of France, Switzerland, and Italy. The succession of counts reads like any other mediæval genealogy; and their exploits, raids, and sieges viewed from this cold distance have a somewhat monotonous similarity; but survival proves the worth and valour of the stock, and when after long centuries the people of Italy had need of princes, the House of Savoy was the only noble house that had retained power and respect. It is a brilliant example of the truth of the saying that those who have been faithful over a few things shall be masters over many.

Such were the political divisions of Italy in this transition period which intervenes between the departing Middle Ages and the incoming Modern World.

CHAPTER XVIII: THE TRANSITION FROM THE MIDDLE AGES TO THE RENAISSANCE

This intervening period—the twilight between the Middle Ages and the dawn of the Modern World—needs a little further emphasis, from the very fact that it is a period of transition and sheds light both on the time before and the time after. On its emotional side it belonged to the Middle Ages, on its intellectual side it belonged to the Modern World.

Its religion was essentially mediæval. For instance, a religious wave arose in Perugia, spread through Italy, and crossed the Alps. Hosts of penitents, hundreds and thousands, lamenting, praying, scourging themselves, went from city to city. Men, women, and children, barefoot, walked by night over the winter's snow, carrying tapers, to find relief for their emotional frenzy. These Flagellants were like a primitive Salvation Army, and gave unconscious expression to the profound and widespread discontent with the Church. Their actions, however, so clearly exhibited religious mania that governments took alarm; the hard-headed rulers of Milan erected six hundred gallows on their borders and threatened to hang every Flagellant who came that way.

Other forms of religious sentiment were more rational, and expressed themselves in passionate calls for peace between neighbours and countrymen. Priests adjured the fighting cities to be friends: "Oh, when will the day come that Pavia shall say to Milan, Thy people are my people, and Crema to Cremona, Thy city is my city?" In Genoa, one morning before daybreak, the church bells rang, and the astonished citizens, huddling on their clothes, beheld their archbishop, surrounded by his clergy with lighted candles, making the factional leaders swear on the bones of St. John Baptist to lay aside their mutual hate. Gregory X (1271-76) pleaded with the Florentine Guelfs to take back the banished Ghibellines. "A Ghibelline is a Christian, a citizen, a neighbour; then, shall these great names, all joined, yield to that one word, Ghibelline? And shall that single word—an idle term for none know what it means—have greater power for hate than all those three, which are so clear and strong, for love and charity? And since you say that you have taken up this factional strife for the sake of the Popes of Rome, now, I, Pope of Rome, have taken back to my bosom these prodigal citizens of yours, however far they may have offended, and putting behind me all past wrongs, hold them to be my sons." In consequence of Gregory's passionate entreaty, one hundred and fifty leaders of each party met and embraced on the sandy flats of the Arno.

The most famous of these emotional peace-makings was the work of a Dominican monk of Vicenza. On a great plain just outside Verona, a vast congregation assembled (a contemporary said 400,000 people), from all the warring cities far and near, bishops, barons, burghers, artisans, serfs, women, and children. The monk preached upon the text, "My peace I give unto you." The great company beat their breasts, wept for repentance and joy, and embraced one another. Then the friar raised the crucifix and cried, "Blessed be he who shall keep this peace, and cursed be he who shall violate it;" and the audience answered "Amen." It is hardly necessary to say that these emotional peace-makings were soon followed by martial emotions; freed prisoners were hurried back to prison, the recalled were banished again, and sword and halberd were picked up with appetites whetted by abstinence.

The intellectual side of this period is best represented by the universities, which had sprung up in many of the North Italian cities in the preceding century. The term university signified a guild of students, and possessed many of the characteristics of our colleges. The university was composed of students and professors, and governed itself. It owned neither lands nor buildings, and in case of need could shift its abode with little trouble. The students, at least in a great university like that of Bologna whither young men flocked by thousands from all Europe, were divided into two bodies, those from beyond the Alps and Italians. These two bodies were subdivided into groups according to their state or city. Each group elected representatives, and these, together with special electors, elected the rector. This representative body made a formal treaty with the town authorities, and secured good terms, because the presence of a university, bringing money and fame, was of great consequence to the town. The professors were appointed by the students. At Bologna Roman law was the chief study, and very famous jurists lectured there. We may remember that Barbarossa had recourse to Bologna when he was in need of lawyers to determine his Imperial rights. It was Roman law that attracted the great concourse of students, for the growing needs of civilization made a constant demand for men learned in the law; but other branches of knowledge were also taught, theology, canon law, medicine, and astrology, as well as the so-called quadrivium, music, arithmetic, geometry, and astronomy.

The universities, although theology and canon law were taught in them, distinctly represented the secular side of intellectual life. The religious, at least the theological side, was represented by the Church, and more particularly by those philosophers who devoted themselves to that mixture of theology and philosophy known as scholasticism. The greatest of them was Thomas Aquinas (1227-74), whose surname is derived from a little village, Aquino, once existing near Monte Cassino in Neapolitan territory. Aquinas lectured at various universities. His great work, "Summa Theologiæ," was a justification of the Roman Catholic faith by an appeal to the reason and to science as then accepted. He started on premises laid down by the Church, and justified all the derivative doctrines by close logic and clear reasoning, as well as by appeals to the Bible, to Aristotle, then deemed the possessor of all knowledge, and to the Church fathers. His work is a complete exposition of God, nature, and man, as conceived by mediæval theology, and is still taught by the Catholic Church as the true exposition of its doctrines. The grateful Church canonized him, his treatise being the miracles he had performed, and named him the Angelic Doctor. Those of us whose minds have no natural aptitude for scholasticism, find his views on purely earthly matters much easier to understand, and not uninteresting, as they throw light on the democratic character of the Church. Speaking of positive law, Aquinas says that it should consist of "reasonable commands for the common good, promulgated by him who has charge of the public weal;" and of kings, that "a prince who makes personal gratification instead of the general happiness his aim, ceases to be legitimate, and it is not rebellion to depose him, provided the attempt shall not cause greater ills than his tyranny;" and, of the nobility, that "many men make a mistake and deem themselves noble, because they come of a noble house.... This inherited nobility deserves no envy, except that noblemen are bound to virtue for shame of being unworthy of their stocks; true nobility is only of the soul." St. Thomas Aquinas is also interesting because his theology inspires Dante throughout the "Divine Comedy."

These diverse traits, emotional and intellectual, were natural to a period of transition, when society was passing from an age in which the chief interests were emotional to one in which the chief interests were intellectual; and it is interesting to notice that at the same time social life was passing from a stage of extreme simplicity to one of comparative luxury. The accumulation of wealth had its effect in every department of life; it gave people time and opportunity for intellectual interests, and also for luxury and more delicate needs. The advance in wealth was very rapid. By the year 1300 men had already begun to blame the luxurious habits of their time, and to look back to the simplicity of their grandfathers as to an age of primitive innocence. Dante gives full expression to these sentiments through the mouth of his ancestor, Cacciaguida, in the "Paradiso." Others speak in the same way. One of them, referring to the time of Frederick II, says: "In those times the manners of the Italians were rude. A man and his wife ate off the same plate. There were no wooden-handled knives, nor more than one or two drinking-cups in a house. Candles of wax or tallow were unknown; a servant held a torch during supper. The clothes of men were of leather unlined; scarcely any gold or silver was seen on their dress. The common people ate flesh but three times a week, and kept their cold meat for supper. Many did not drink wine in summer. A small stock of corn seemed riches. The portions of women were small; their dress, even after marriage, was simple. The pride of men was to be well provided with arms and horses; that of the nobility to have lofty towers, of which all the cities in Italy were full. But now frugality has been changed for sumptuousness; everything exquisite is sought after in dress,— gold, silver, pearls, silks, and rich furs. Foreign wines and rich meats are required. Hence usury, rapine, fraud, tyranny," etc.

To us to-day this period of transition, with its mediæval mixture of commerce, religion, and war, of emotion and logic, of admiration for St. Augustine and belief in the infallibility of Aristotle, looks extremely odd. We forget that our generation may be in danger of similar criticism. Odd or not, this was the state of Italy in the period preceding that great burst of the arts and intellectual life known as the Renaissance.

CHAPTER XIX: THE INTELLECTUAL DAWN AFTER THE MIDDLE AGES (1260-1336)

Though the beginning of the Modern World manifested itself in every department of life, political, social, and intellectual, it is best known to us through the arts, because in them it embodied itself in permanent forms. Italy suddenly leaped forward, as if she had drained a beaker of champagne. To explain and illustrate this burst of passion, the books generally use such phrases as emphasis upon individuality, imitation of the classic, observation of nature, wider range of interest, the awakening of spiritual energy, etc. No doubt the phrases are just, but one must remember that underneath these manifestations of an eager interest in life, there actually was a larger, happier life, due in great measure to security, ease, and the accumulation of property, which set men free from the bondage of continuous daily labour to satisfy corporal needs. Of that happier life, with its gayety and luxury, Villani, the historian of Florence, has given us a description. He himself was a boy at the time. "In the year of Our Lord 1283 the city of Florence, chiefly on account of the Guelfs who were in power, was prosperous and at peace, and in a state of great tranquillity, which was very advantageous to the merchants and artisans. In June, at the Feast of St. John, in the quarter across the Arno, where the Rossi and their neighbours were the principal people, the nobility and the rich organized themselves into a company, and adopted a dress all white, and chose a master called the Lord of Love. The object of the company was to have feasts, games, and dances for the ladies and gentlemen of the city, and other persons of quality. They used to parade the town with trumpets and other musical instruments, and had great dinners and suppers and all kinds of jollity. The festivities lasted nearly two months, and were the finest and most celebrated that were ever held in Florence or all Tuscany. Gentlemen and troubadours came from far and near, and all were received and entertained with distinction. And it is worth remembering that the city and its citizens were better off then than they had ever been, and this prosperity continued till the division into Burghers and Grandi. There were then in Florence three hundred knights, and there were many companies of gentlemen and ladies, who morning and evening kept open table richly spread, and had buffoons in attendance, so that from Lombardy and all Italy jesters, players, and jugglers came to Florence, and all were welcome; and whenever a stranger of distinction passed through the city there was rivalry between the companies to get him as their guest, and then he was accompanied, on foot or on horseback, all through the city and the country round, most politely."

This was the light and careless side of the general awakening of interest in life, which showed itself in so many nobler forms.

In literature Dante (1265-1321) is the first great figure. But, owing to his disproportional importance, we are liable to forget that he has his orderly place in the revival of poetry and literature which began in the brilliant court of Frederick II in Sicily. On the destruction of the Hohenstaufens, the poetic primacy passed to Bologna, where Guido Guinicelli and others composed poetry in a somewhat learned fashion, as befitted a university town, and then passed on to Tuscany, and in particular to Florence, where Dante was preceded by his friend Guido

Cavalcanti. Dante, although distinctly mediæval by his theology, his appeals to the authority of Virgil and Aristotle, and by his political views, has the characteristics of the new spiritual energy. He lays immense stress on individuality, and delineates real life with wonderful vividness. These traits mark him as belonging to the new world coming in rather than to the old world going out.

From the point of view of history, Dante's most marked achievement, perhaps, was to raise the Tuscan (or more strictly speaking the Florentine) idiom, from among many competitors, to the dignity of being the Italian language. This was the consequence of writing the "Divine Comedy" in Tuscan, instead of in Latin. Dante's Tuscan verses were recited in the tavern and on the piazza, and were greeted with loud applause by apprentices and artisans, shopmen and tavern-keepers. He excited the enthusiasm of both educated and ignorant. At that time the spoken dialects were very numerous. A friend remonstrating with Dante for writing in an Italian dialect instead of in Latin, said that there were a thousand. Dante himself in his treatise "On the Vernacular Speech" enumerates Sicilian, Calabrian, Apulian, Roman, Tuscan, Genoese, Sardinian, Romagnol, Lombard, Venetian, and others. These dialects of the provinces were further subdivided among themselves. In Tuscany the people of Siena spoke one idiom, those of Arezzo another. In Lombardy the citizens of Ferrara spoke in one way, the citizens of Piacenza in another. Even in one city, as in Bologna, the dwellers in St. Felix Street and those in Greater Street did not speak alike. Besides the difficulties of many dialects, besides the immense prestige of Latin as the language of learning, of law, of the Church, French appeared as a possible literary language for Italy. Authors in Florence, Venice, Siena, and Pisa wrote books in French, "because the French language goes over the world, and is more delectable to read and to hear than any other." But Dante made the Florentine tongue immortal, and not only wrote the "Divine Comedy" in Florentine, but also "The New Life" and "The Banquet." Prior to his time the divers idioms had stood on an equality; after his time Tuscan became the language of polite speech and of literature, the real Italian language, and the others were degraded to the position of mere dialects. Petrarch and Boccaccio, both Florentines, also deserve their share of praise. Petrarch's sonnets and Boccaccio's stories firmly established the primacy to which Dante had raised the Tuscan idiom.

The revival of sculpture also began before the middle of the thirteenth century. Here the great leader is Niccolò Pisano (1206-78?). There has been a dispute as to his birthplace. Some say he came from Southern Italy and learned his art there. If this theory is true, Frederick's kingdom has the honour of having revived sculpture as well as literature; but it is more likely that Niccolò came from some village in Tuscany, and early went to Pisa, where he got his designation Pisano. The first certain record of his work is an inscription on the pulpit in the Baptistery at Pisa, which states that he completed the pulpit in 1260. Pisa was then at the height of her glory, in the happy years before her fatal conflict with Genoa; she had built the Cathedral, the Leaning Tower, and the Baptistery, and now wished to beautify them within. Niccolò's pulpit shows both imitation of the classic and observation of nature. He had before him bits of ancient sarcophagi, which had been built into the wall of the Cathedral: his Madonna bears traces of the Phædra of the sarcophagus, one of his three Wise Men resembles a young Greek, and his modelling in general has a touch of classic freedom, dignity, and repose. In his conception of the scenes Niccolò adhered to ecclesiastical tradition, just as Dante did to ecclesiastical theology, but in his figures, in the drapery and various details, his faithfulness to reality is striking, at least when compared with the Byzantine style theretofore prevailing. The success of this pulpit was so great that a few years later he was asked to carve another for the cathedral in Siena. An envoy came on purpose, and in the Baptistery of Pisa a contract was drawn up in which it was agreed that Niccolò should go to Siena and stay till the work was done, taking three assistants, and also his young son Giovanni, at half pay, if he wished. This contract was made in 1265, the year of Dante's birth. Niccolò also worked at Bologna, Perugia, Pistoia, probably at Lucca and almost certainly in many other places. This was the period of the free development of the communes after the death of Frederick II, and Niccolò's popularity is proof of widespread prosperity and interest in art. Niccolò's son Giovanni (1250-1328?) inherited his father's genius; and his work, especially his masterpiece, a pulpit at Pistoia, shows how fast art was developing. Giovanni, in his eagerness to express the animation and passion of life, neglected the classic and went directly to nature, at least in desire if not in execution. This passionate interest in life is the very quality that gives Dante's "Inferno" its intense vividness. These two Pisani founded the great Tuscan school of sculpture, and influenced both painting and architecture as well.

Italian architecture at this time does not show one great figure like Niccolò Pisano, nor does it show a definite beginning of a new period. On the contrary, throughout the Middle Ages building held its own surprisingly well in comparison with the other arts. In the days of Theodoric the Ostrogoth, it carried on the Byzantine tradition at Ravenna, and for centuries the churches in Rome were built on the old basilican principle. Over a hundred years before Dante was born, and before Niccolò carved his pulpit, the Lombard style flourished in Lombardy, Tuscan Romanesque in Tuscany, and Norman Sicilian in Sicily. Before the Empire had received its coup de grâce the Gothic style came down from the North, and its struggle with the Romanesque seemed to typify the conflict between the German Empire and the Italian people. Nevertheless, if we confine ourselves to Tuscany, as perhaps is fair in view of the very great influence of Tuscany on all the arts, there is one man who stands out conspicuous. Arnolfo di Cambio (1232-1300?) began life as one of Niccolò's assistants at Pisa, and did so well that he was included by name in the contract for the pulpit at Siena. In Florence he built the church of Santa Croce for the Franciscans, designed the Palazzo Vecchio, and made the first plans for the Duomo; and so left a deep impress on Florence and through Florence on the world.

In painting, more than in any other art or department of life, perhaps, authority had reigned supreme throughout the Middle Ages. The decadent Greek painters of Constantinople had made a series of rules, which were as autocratic as the edicts of the Emperors. Every Madonna was painted in one attitude, with her eyes opening wide in the same way, arms, legs, and body in the same constrained position, with the same wooden child in her wooden lap, and the same wooden saints about her. But gradually, side by side with the art of authority, another style, at first very simple and primitive, developed. The older style dominated mosaic work, and as mosaics were most intimately associated with the symbolic representation of sacred things, it was strongly intrenched behind all the beliefs and prejudices of the Middle Ages. Nevertheless, the revolutionary spirit in Tuscany, for the leaders of the revolution which threw off the authority of the Middle Ages came from among the free men of Tuscany, prevailed in painting as well as elsewhere. The last of the masters who employed the Byzantine manner was Cimabue (1240-1302); yet Cimabue had a sense of the coming change, and showed a desire to break through the enveloping shell of Byzantine authority and portray the grace and beauty of living human beings. However mediæval his manner seems to us, his contemporaries, eager as the Athenians for new things, perceived the novelty in it. When he was painting a Madonna for the Dominican monks in Florence, Charles of Anjou, fresh from his triumph over Manfred, visited his studio for the honour of a first view, and crowds pressed about hoping to get a glimpse of the picture. When the picture was carried through the streets to its destination in the church of Santa Maria Novella, a great procession followed, as if it were a hero returned from the wars. Poor Cimabue, however, is seldom mentioned except as a dull background against which the conquering Giotto stands in brilliant relief.

Giotto (1267?-1336) is the master revolutionist of painting. He was a contemporary of Dante, a few years younger, born at the time when Niccolò and Giovanni were working at the pulpit in Siena, and Charles of Anjou was posing as an admirer of the fine arts in Cimabue's studio. He painted Dante in a fresco on the wall of the Bargello (a palace in Florence), at least so tradition says; and Dante in the "Divine Comedy" speaks of him as outstripping the once renowned Cimabue. Giotto was an ugly little man, of great character and quick wit. Various stories are told of his repartees. Once, when he was painting for the King of Naples and working with great diligence, the king, who used to watch him, said, "Giotto, if I were you, I should not work so hard." "I shouldn't,—if I were you," retorted Giotto. He studied under Giovanni Pisano, and learned so much that it has been said that "Giotto is the greatest work of the Pisani." Giotto was also the successor to Arnolfo as the leading architect in Florence, and built the Campanile of the Duomo, and, being likewise a sculptor, modelled some of the bas-reliefs that ornament the panels of the base. His great art was painting, and especially the painting of figures. Giotto was in demand to paint frescoes on the walls of churches and chapels at Florence, Arezzo, Assisi, Padua, Ravenna, Rome, and Naples; and other painters came from far and near to study under him. He dominated Italian painting, and his school was the only school for a hundred years. After the world had adopted Raphael's frescoes as the type of excellence his fame was dimmed for a time, but since Mr. Ruskin's enthusiastic admiration it has regained its ancient lustre.

These instances of revolution in the arts show that a new intellectual life had begun, that the Middle Ages had really ended. In fact, the passing away of the Holy Roman Empire and of the European suzerainty of the Papacy was merely an episode in the general intellectual revolution.

CHAPTER XX: THE DESPOTISMS (1250-1350)

Perhaps the quality which strikes us most in this dawn of our Modern World is its suddenness; Niccolò Pisano gets up, as it were, out of the ground, Giotto follows Cimabue, Dante is born while Guido Guinicelli is still a young man. We are amazed and bewildered, and it is not in the arts alone that the change is so startling. The political structure shifts with equal quickness, and while we are trying to connect and coördinate this outburst of art with the democratic triumph of the communes, the democratic communes disappear under our eyes. At first as we look we are a little puzzled, for the outward form of the commune remains unchanged; the podestà is still there, the Great Council and the inner council are still there, the committees and the sub-committees superintending and directing the affairs of the commonwealth; but further observation discloses a lack of spontaneity. The motive power does not seem the resultant of the debate and argument of numerous discordant wills, but to proceed from some one definite inner source. More careful observation shows that these outward committees are but registering boards that record an inner will, that their members go to one particular palace to have their minds made up, at first privily, but soon openly, and at last confessedly and ostentatiously. This is the regular course. The commune is, as it were, a political chrysalis out of which a full-blown tyrant bursts. The tyrants were men of capacity, who gathered the various functions of the government into their own hands, and by a course of adroitness and fraud, or by a coup d'état, reduced the city to obedience, and then, after having exercised sovereign rights during their lives, bequeathed the principality to their heirs. The reason of their success is plain. It was impossible for trade to flourish, for property to collect its income, for luxury to enjoy itself, under the political confusion that attended the democratic endeavours for self-government. The uncertainty in government, law, and trade, was too high a price to pay for liberty. Men of property, men of business, men of pleasure, preferred the comparative stability of a tyranny.

Before we look at this process in individual states we must eliminate the exceptions. The kingdom of Sicily under the House of Aragon, and that of Naples under the House of Anjou, had become, in great measure, absolute monarchies, for the gifted Emperor Frederick, who was no lover of democracy, had crushed or circumvented the communal spirit in his kingdom. The suppression of popular liberties did not result in the strict enforcement of order in either kingdom, particularly not in Sicily where feudal anarchy was rampant; but we must leave those Southerners to their oranges and lemons, to their flowers and azure skies, to their churches and cloisters, where Romanesque, Byzantine, and Arab influences met and combined in arch and dome and sculptured trimming, and go northward to find the main historical current of the century.

Florence, too, we must except from the tyrannic system, for a democratic government prevailed there for many years to come, and also Rome, where the Papacy prevented Colonna and Orsini from establishing a despotism.

Verona shall serve as the paradigm for the despotic form of government. In this ancient city on the banks of the Adige, where the amphitheatre of Augustus still stood though the churches built by Theodoric the Ostrogoth had crumbled away, the spirit of material and intellectual activity had been busily at work. The stately church of San Zeno (eleventh century), most beautiful of Romanesque churches, coloured with the hues of early dawn and rich with bronze doors and sculptured front, stood proudly apart outside the walls; but within, the cathedral had been begun, and the great Ghibelline tower already lifted its crenellated top high over the market-place. Rushing through the city the headlong Adige turned innumerable mill-wheels, and Veronese girls washed the clothes of the Capulets and Montagues in its waters. Altogether the city was a very desirable signory. This fact had been discovered in Frederick's time, and Ezzelino da Romano, one of the Ghibelline nobles of the North, had made good his power there and distinguished himself by his cruelty, for which he is still remembered. On his most satisfactory death, not long after Frederick's, the Scaligers succeeded to the dominion of the city (1259). These Scaligers were of the best type of tyrant, especially Can Grande (1311-1329), the fifth in possession of the signory, who presents the type in its noblest and most attractive form. Nevertheless, despite his brilliance, his success and magnificence, his chief renown is as host to the exiled Dante, who in gratitude for "my first refuge and first hostelry" dedicated the "Paradiso" to him, and celebrated his carelessness of hardship and of gold, and his doughty deeds from which even enemies could not withhold their praise.

Can Grande, like other despots, had two objects,—to make his signory secure, and to enlarge it. As he was secure of Verona, he cast his covetous glances abroad and fixed them on Vicenza, a little town some thirty miles to the northeast. Vicenza was, so to speak, no longer in the market, as she had been snapped up by her neighbour, Padua, which had had the advantage of being less than twenty miles away. But Can Grande played his cards well, and by help of the Emperor Henry VII, who appointed him Imperial vicar, got possession of the prize. Padua, a rich and prosperous Guelf city, with subject towns round about, and a famous university within, refused to acquiesce in a surrender of Vicenza to a Ghibelline lord. A long war ensued. The fair fields in the forty miles between Verona and Padua were laid waste, the poor peasants were dragged to one city or the other and held for ransom, and the Guelfs in Verona and the Ghibellines in Padua were persecuted, imprisoned, and tortured. At last Padua, her signory over, her neighbours lost, her population fallen away, her citizens fighting among themselves, her nobles destroying one another in the hope of becoming lords of the city, gave way and surrendered to Can Grande. Other cities shared Padua's fate, and Can Grande, by virtue of his conquests as well as of his character, became one of the chief powers in Italy. Can Grande was brave even to recklessness, covetous of dominion, steadfast in his political aims, true to his promises, generous to his enemies. On his death he bequeathed his signory to his nephew; and his body was buried in the churchyard of a little Gothic chapel, where stone effigies of armoured Scaligers on caparisoned steeds surmount Gothic tombs, and the pride of life and conquest strives to overcrow death.

The story of the Scaligers must be continued somewhat further, for they exhibit the phenomenon, so frequent in Northern Italy at this time, of a despotism that begins in vigour, continues in energy and success, and then dies down under degenerate heirs to go out at last like a candle. Can Grande's nephew, Mastino (1329-51),—the family had a fondness for canine appellations. Great Dog and Mastiff,—began his career with ability and courage; he conquered Brescia to the west, halfway to Milan, and Parma, which lies beyond Mantua. These particular acts of aggression helped his ruin, for Milan and Mantua took alarm and joined a league against him. But that was not till later. In the days of his prosperity Mastino was very magnificent. Soldiers, horse and foot, attended him; his palace was thronged with lords, gentlemen, and buffoons; his stables were full of chargers and palfreys, his bird-sheds of falcons. At his court there were innumerable fashionable devices for driving care away, dancing, singing, jousting; everything was luxurious; men and furniture were decked with embroidery, cloth of gold, cloth from France, and cloth from Tartary. When Mastino rode forth all Verona rushed to the windows; when he was angry all Verona trembled. He was a dark-skinned, bearded man, with heavy features and a great belly; in later life he ate grossly, and sank into dissipation. Seldom on a Friday or Saturday, or even in Lent, would he refrain from meat; and he did not care a rap for excommunication. He became arrogant and vainglorious. His dissipation and lack of piety, however, were less direct causes of his fall than his ambition; he coveted, rumour said, a kingdom of Lombardy or even of all Italy. But at last he overreached himself in dealing with the Florentines. They wished to get possession of Lucca, and he undertook to buy it for them,—it was a fourteenth-century custom to sell a city,—but when he got possession of Lucca he kept it for himself. The Florentines declared war, and induced all his rival despots, the Visconti of Milan, the Gonzaga of Mantua, the Estensi of Ferrara, to join a league against him. Venice also joined, being indignant with the Scaligers for levying tolls upon merchandise that went up the Po, and for interference with the Venetian monopoly of salt. The league was victorious and forced the Scaligers to hard terms. Venice took the towns near her, thus acquiring her first territory on the Italian mainland; the great Paduan family, the Carrara, took back Padua; the Visconti of Milan took Brescia (1338). The Scaligers were shorn of their power, and from this time on the house dwindled; assassinations of brother by brother darkened its close, and at the end of the century it lost Verona and all.

What the Scaligers did at Verona other great families were doing elsewhere. The Gonzaga established themselves in Mantua, the Estensi in Ferrara, the Bentivogli in Bologna, the da Polenta in Ravenna, the Malatesta in Rimini, the Montefeltri in Urbino, the Baglioni in Perugia, and greatest of all the Visconti in Milan. The city of Milan has so important a place in the history of Italy, that we must pause over the Visconti. This family succeeded in dispossessing its rivals and in becoming masters of the city in 1295, about the time that the oligarchy was clinching its hold on Venice, and the democracy becoming all powerful in Florence. In fact, one may accept this date as the point at which Florence, Venice, and Milan start on their upward careers towards becoming three of the six chief divisions of Italy. Convenience has its rights, and it is eminently convenient to start the Renaissance, politically as well as intellectually, in this eager, passionate last quarter of the thirteenth century.

The Visconti, however, were not firm in their seats till the gallant Henry VII, Dante's hope, came down into Italy to revive the Empire. We have seen that Henry did not revive the Empire, but he did strengthen Can Grande, his loyal lieutenant in Verona, and also the Visconti, his loyal friends in Milan. It is pathetic, even now, to think of that high-aspiring Henry, with his noble, old-fashioned ideas concerning the Roman Empire and universal brotherhood under the shelter of the Roman eagle, and of the great Dante fastening all his hopes on those same old-fashioned ideas, while the crafty lords of Milan and Verona, laughing in their sleeves, professed the most devout Imperial creed and feathered their own nests. On the Emperor's death (1313) the Visconti were firmly seated. The signory descended from one generation to the next. Their sway was extended over the cities round about, until it included most of Lombardy. Ambition, growing by what it fed on, aimed at the cities of Pisa, Bologna, and Genoa. Such plans aroused both jealousy and fear. The ambition of the Visconti to take Pisa alarmed Florence, who had marked Pisa as her own; that to take Bologna stirred the absentee Popes, who went through the old forms of excommunication, interdict, and crusade; but Genoa, crippled by her wars with Venice, rent asunder by internal factions, wearily gave herself to Milan, in the vain hope of winning peace and security. In spite of checks here and there, the state of Milan became more and more powerful, and the signory of the Visconti by far the greatest of the tyrannies in Italy.

There were, of course, many men who attempted to become despots and failed; and others who succeeded for their lifetimes, but were not able to make their signories so strong as to become family possessions to be enjoyed by their heirs after them. Of the latter kind one must be mentioned. In Lucca Castruccio Castracane (died 1328), a very brilliant politician and soldier, became so powerful that he reduced to subjection much of the country round and nearly succeeded in conquering Florence, with whom he was long at war. Like other successful tyrants he called himself a Ghibelline, and drew what advantage he could from his profession of faith, but really only aimed to acquire a principality for himself. He died in the prime of life (to the great relief of the Florentines), and left so brilliant a reputation for the qualities which achieve success by fair means or foul, that two centuries later Machiavelli held him up as an example for princes to follow.

CHAPTER XXI: THE CLASSICAL REVIVAL (1350)

We are now well started on the fourteenth century, and it will be well to glance at the chief Italian states in order to get our bearings.

Sicily was in a state of hopeless despondency. The island was nominally subject to the House of Aragon, but its kings were not men of sufficient character to impose their authority, and the unfortunate kingdom was beginning to go down hill. The Kingdom of Naples was, for the time being, much better off, for its king, Robert, grandson of Charles of Anjou, was a man of unusual gifts and capacity, but he was succeeded by a foolish, frivolous, light-minded, light-mannered granddaughter, Joan (1343-81), who brought forty years of trouble to her kingdom, and under her Naples started rolling down that same incline on which Sicily was rolling somewhat ahead of her. The failure of Sicily and Naples to take part in the great career in matters intellectual now opening before Northern Italy is partly due to the race that populated them, a miscellaneous mixture of bloods (at least it is customary to explain unknown causes of success and failure by saying good blood and bad blood), and partly to the autocratic will of the brilliant Frederick II, who crushed out independence in his kingdom, and so deprived it of that communal life which is the only obvious factor, except "good blood," in the intellectual success of Northern Italy.

The whole pontifical state, from the fortresses of the Colonna on the Tiber to the strongholds of the Malatesta in Rimini, was in the vortex of confusion.

Florence was well off, for though the foreigners whom she had invited to be protectors against Castruccio Castracane and others were rather detrimental than useful, and though there were signs of a new struggle between the Grandi and the Burghers, her commerce prospered, her dominion spread over the towns round about, and her luxury grew so fast that the troubled elders passed all sorts of sumptuary laws to prescribe what should be worn and what not, by both fashionable and simple.

In the northwest, now Piedmont, there were, besides the Counts of Savoy, several struggling claimants who severally asserted titles to their own and other strips of territory. In the northeast, Venice, which had acquired a footing on the mainland destined to grow into the province of Venetia, was prosperous. And between Piedmont and Venice the successful Visconti of Milan, soon to receive the keys of Genoa, were likewise well satisfied. The political situation may now be dismissed, and we may turn to the distinguishing mark of the century, the classical revival.

The distinction which Italy enjoys as the most famous country in Europe is due to three ages,— first, the ancient epoch of Augustus Cæsar and Trajan, when the Roman Empire imposed the pax romana on a grateful world; second, the mediæval epoch of Hildebrand and Innocent III, when the Papacy, following its great prototype with unequal steps, imposed its pax romana on both troubled souls and angry hands; and third, the epoch of the Renaissance, when Italy took the lead in the intellectual development of modern Europe. It would be as absurd to subordinate intellectual life to politics in the period of the Renaissance as it would be to subordinate the religion of the era of Hildebrand to its art, or the politics of the Augustan age to its religion. The highest life of Italy, the life which gives importance to the history of this coming period, is its intellectual life, and, though we must not forget politics entirely, we should lay the chief stress on intellectual rather than on political matters.

Since the date of the Pisan pulpit, prosperity had increased fast, and curiosity, the desire to investigate, the wish to know, had grown lustily. There were still the same two stores of knowledge,—nature and the classics,—but the first, for many reasons, seemed vague, intangible, when compared to the second, in which the demi-gods (so they appeared then) of the ancient world had garnered the rich harvest of their thoughts. The classical heritage, the record of a higher civilization, seemed a lay Bible, the revelation of truth, the means of salvation; and the young generation emerging in the dawn of intellectual light turned thirstily to this newly found inheritance. The leader of this pilgrimage to the land flowing with intellectual milk and honey was Francis Petrarch (1304-74).

Petrarch was a Florentine, but he lived in exile. His father had been banished at the same time with Dante, and after a few wandering years had settled at Avignon. Petrarch studied law at the University of Bologna and became a confirmed Ghibelline. This item of biography is important, because it reminds us that Petrarch's passion for the classic world, though it had its roots in the traditional admiration for Rome, received strength and justification not only from Latin literature, but also from the Civil law. Men who grasped the complexity and richness of the Roman law necessarily admired Roman civilization, and inferred that all other manifestations of that civilization must be as admirable as the law, and perhaps less dry. Petrarch found the law dry, but he left Bologna with a passion for the classic world; and when he went back to Avignon he met all the most cultivated men of Europe. Learning still attended the papal court, and Avignon served to make this charming young scholar of genius known to the world. He flung up the law and devoted himself to literature. Cicero was his hero. Petrarch was the first of the humanists, the herald of the Renaissance, and, if we look farther forward still, the harbinger of the Reformation. Petrarch's importance was very great because he was not too far ahead of his generation. He shouted aloud the glory of Rome, of Roman literature and Roman thought, and the echo resounded throughout Europe. In the year 1341, in Rome, upon the Capitoline Hill, Petrarch received the crown of laurel, as scholar and poet, from the Senate and People of Rome. The King of Naples was his sponsor, and the tyrants of the North applauded. This ceremony was the conspicuous recognition that a new period was opening before Italy; and Petrarch's laurel crown may be put beside the Imperial wreath of Augustus and the tiara of Hildebrand, as the starting-point of Italy's third great period of triumph.

After his coronation, Petrarch went about Italy spreading the seeds of the new enthusiasm. He lived or made visits at Parma, Bologna, Verona, Florence, Arezzo, Naples, Rome, Milan, Padua, and Venice. He became tremendously fashionable. The Pope invited him to be papal secretary, the King of France extended the hospitality of Paris to him, the Emperor bade him to Prague, the Visconti wanted him at Milan, the Scaligers at Verona, the Cararresi at Padua, the lord high Seneschal at Naples; the Florentines asked him to accept a chair in their new university, the Venetians offered him a house. All this honour ostensibly shown to Petrarch was really the salutation to the new dawn.

The strength of this classic revival, though most effective in literature and the arts, is perhaps still more noticeable in the political career of another young man of genius who had as passionate a love of classic Rome as Petrarch himself. Cola di Rienzo (1314-54) was an imaginative, poetical dreamer, who fed his youth on Livy, Cicero, Seneca, and delighted to muse on the glories of Julius Cæsar and to study the antique monuments of Rome. His public career began as envoy on one of the unsuccessful embassies which used to entreat the Popes to return to the deserted city. Cola was handsome, eloquent, ardent, a sort of Don Quixote, and roused the Roman populace to share his dreams and to believe in the possible restoration of the Senate and People of Rome to their ancient grandeur. He led the people against the nobility, forced the riotous barons to submit to his rule as tribune of the people, and established a government of law in the city; but his ambition flew far beyond the city walls. He dreamed of the confederation of all Italy under the lead of Rome. He would have smiled at limiting imitation of the great days of old to the arts or to literature; he intended to restore the Roman Republic as it had been in its high and palmy days. His wild aspirations throw a backward light over the history of the city of Rome throughout the Middle Ages, and over that republicanism which played so important a part in the struggle between Empire and Papacy, and light up the old theories under which the Roman people claimed the right to elect both Emperor and Pope; just as Boniface's bulls portray the outworn papal theories, and Dante's "De Monarchia" the dead Imperial beliefs.

Cola's first step was to invite all the princes and communes of Italy to attend a general meeting in Rome; and as all Italy had responded to Petrarch's appeal in behalf of the classic past, so did she, for the moment, respond to Cola's appeal. Milan, Genoa, Lucca, Florence, Siena, and the smaller cities nearer by, answered with apparent sympathy. Petrarch was mad with delight, and hailed Cola as Camillus, Brutus, Romulus. For the moment, such was the strength of classical illusion, the dream seemed to be real. Cola wrote to the Florentines (September, 1347), "We have made all citizens of the states of Holy Italy Roman citizens, and we admit them to the right of election. The affairs of Empire have naturally devolved upon the Holy Roman People. We desire to renew and strengthen the old union with all the principalities and states of Holy Italy, and to deliver Holy Italy itself from its condition of abject subjection and to restore it to its old state and to its ancient glory. We mean to exalt to the position of Emperor some Italian whom zeal for the union of his race shall stir to high efforts for Italy."

Cola's great idea was destined to wait five hundred years for fulfilment. The time was not ripe, and he himself not a suitable instrument. His career was brief. He became not only vainglorious but also very cruel. He grew fat, and lost the charm of youth and novelty. The nobles and the upper classes of Rome hated him; and when, in need of money, he increased the taxes, the Roman populace turned upon him, stormed the Capitol, captured him as he tried to slink away in disguise, and murdered him on the steps leading down from the palace. His head was cut off, his body was dragged through the streets and burned, and the ashes scattered to the winds.

The mad dream had been, in its nature, evanescent. The classical heritage was too purely intellectual, too remote from existing needs, to be able to shape politics. But that fourteen hundred years after the death of Julius Cæsar, Cola should have been able to establish himself as

Roman tribune on the Capitoline Hill, and to act as if the Republic of the days of the Gracchi had been but temporarily superseded, shows the immense influence of Rome over the mediæval imagination, and helps us to understand the autocratic power of the classical heritage in shaping and directing the intellectual revolution in Italy.

CHAPTER XXII: THE ILLS OF THE FOURTEENTH CENTURY

The fourteenth century undoubtedly felt itself emancipated from the limitations of the Middle Ages, and with justice, so far as the classical revival was concerned, but it did little or nothing to free itself from ills that were distinctly of a mediæval character,—plague, lawlessness, and tyranny. In that respect, the transition from the Middle Ages to the Modern World was slow and made a striking contrast with the rapid evolution of art.

The chief of these ills was the plague. Only in remote places of the East, if at all, does the scourge of disease now fall as it then did in the most civilized cities of the world, and it was from the East that these plagues came, brought by sailors. One blasted Tuscany in 1340, one Lombardy in 1361; but the worst was the awful Black Death of 1348, which wrought havoc in various parts of Italy and then swept northward across the Alps on its destructive path. It was this plague which Boccaccio describes in the beginning of the "Decameron." It spread like fire among dry wood which has been sprinkled with oil. At first swellings appeared the size of an egg or an apple, then black and hard spots; on the third day came death. Even animals caught the disease. Boccaccio saw two pigs which had chewed the garment of a plague-stricken man die in convulsions. Medicine was useless. Some thought the wisest course was to live on the daintiest food and drink, and never speak of the plague; others believed in carousing and jollity, and went about from tavern to tavern seeking diversion, but always keeping sober enough to avoid the sick. Private houses were deserted and lay open to anybody. Loyalty disappeared. All who could fled into the country. Thousands fell sick daily. In place of decent burial, dead bodies were tossed huggermugger into trenches. Between March and July, Boccaccio says, more than 100,000 people died within the walls of Florence.

Florence was not singular. In Siena 80,000 people, three quarters of the population, died; in Genoa, 40,000; in Pisa, seven out of ten, and so on in Venice, Rome, Naples, and Sicily. These figures seem incredible; but Petrarch says: "Posterity will not believe that there ever was a period in which the world remained almost entirely depopulated, houses empty of families, cities of inhabitants, the country of peasants. How will the future believe it, when we ourselves can hardly credit our eyes? We go outdoors, walk through street after street, and find them full of dead and dying; when we get home again we find no live thing within the house, all having perished within the brief interval of absence. Happy posterity, to whom such calamities will seem imaginings and dreams." Poor Petrarch! The lovely Laura, of whom he wrote so many perfect sonnets, died of the Black Death in Avignon. Giovanni Villani, the historian, died in Florence. This terrible calamity throws into high relief the great classical impulse, to which the last chapter was devoted. In earlier times men would have turned to religion and the Church; but now Petrarch, a most devout Christian, and his disciples continued to worship Cicero and the heroes of the Augustan age, and to talk of Cæsar and Pompey, Scylla and Charybdis, as the most important and interesting of things.

Another great evil which rivalled the plague as a curse, was the host of mercenary soldiers who swarmed over Italy like locusts. In the days of Barbarossa, battles like that of Legnano had been fought between the train-bands of the communes on one side and the feudal chivalry and men-at-arms on the other. But since then a great change had come over the methods of raising soldiers. Under the feudal system the term of service in the field for the liegemen of the Emperor had been forty days; but that time was too short for an effective campaign. When the Emperor wished to cross the Alps and go to Rome in order to receive the Imperial crown, he was obliged to hire soldiers; and, as years went on and these Imperial descents became mere adventurous expeditions, the character of the soldiers degenerated, until in Petrarch's time the Imperial armies were made up of ruffians recruited anywhere. There were also other reasons for establishing mercenaries in place of militia. The despots of Northern Italy did not wish their subjects trained to arms. The burghers of mercantile cities did not wish to leave their counting-rooms, nor to have their employees mustered out, so they too preferred hired soldiers to a native militia. Moreover, warfare had changed; cavalry needed frequent man[oe]uvres, bowmen and pikemen required drill and continuous discipline. Thus the old train-band system of the communes, under which the militia hurried to their appointed posts on the ringing of the bells, gave way to the system of mercenary troops led by soldiers of fortune, condottieri, as the Italians call them.

These soldiers, who had come down from the North to serve Emperors, or despots like the Visconti, or perhaps had sailed from Spain to fight under the House of Aragon in Sicily, as soon as the immediate war was ended, having been left unpaid or having taken a liking to a trade in which the labor was congenial, the risk small and booty enormous, decided not to disband, but to continue to try their luck together. They sold their services to whatever city or despot would pay them most, or wandered about in a nomadic fashion, capturing a city if they could, if not, living on the country-side. One can imagine these rogues among unwarlike peasants, or in a pleasant little city like Lucca or Cremona. They were very fickle, fought one another only upon compulsion, and then most reluctantly and gently, and were very nearly as terrible to their employers as to their adversaries. They were organized, sometimes very well, in bands under a general or a council of officers, and had such names as The Company of St. George, or The Great Company. Some of their leaders became very famous, like Duke Werner, who proclaimed himself "Lord of the Great Company, enemy to God, to Pity, and to Mercy." The most interesting of these leaders, at least for us, is John Hawkwood, an English adventurer, who began life as a London tailor, but dropped scissors and needle to enlist for Edward III's French campaign, and then, seeing fortune smile most sweetly from distraught Italy, crossed the Alps and led his company all over the peninsula. There is a full length fresco of him on horseback in the Duomo at Florence, painted in gratitude for his deeds in life or merely for his death.

For a hundred years and more these ruffians swaggered about Italy. Petrarch finds in them one cause the more to hold out his arms toward the mighty past. He writes in a letter: "Oh, would that you were alive, Brutus, Great-heart, that I might turn to you. O Manlius—O Great Pompey—O Julius Cæsar [etc., etc., etc.], O Jesus, Lord of the world, what has happened? Why do I moan and groan for grief? Oh! a vile handful of robbers, spewed out of their nasty dens, walks and rides over the ancient queen of the world, Italy. Christ Jesus, in tears and supplication I turn to Thee. Oh, if we have abused Thy goodness more than was right, if we have shown ourselves too proud in Thy aid and favour, if we have borne ourselves ill towards Thee, well mayst Thou not permit us to be free; but let not this slaughter, these sacrileges, these robberies, these deeds of violence, these ravishings of wives and maidens, find mercy in Thine eyes. Put an end to this evil. To the wicked who have said in their hearts 'There is no God,' show that Thou art; and to us however unworthy, show that we are Thy children. O Almighty Father, help us; in Thee alone we put our hope, and in supplication we invoke Thy name, weeping and confessing that there is none who shall fight for us, unless Thou, our Lord, be he."

This strange mixture of classic enthusiasm and Christian piety, this odd idea that the triumphant cause of the Roman Republic was due to the favour of Christ, shows us that Petrarch had not yet got wholly clear of mediæval beliefs. But, as with Cola di Rienzo, everything Petrarch says testifies to the power of the Roman tradition.

A third evil, yet not to be compared with the plague and the condottieri, was the tyranny of the despots. The founders of despotisms were men of vigour and political capacity, and gave to their subjects in lieu of liberty greater security and order than they had enjoyed before. Their descendants, like proverbial heirs, finding hard work both distasteful and unnecessary, gave themselves up to dissipation and cruelty; they dropped their ancestors' attitude of leading citizens and treated the principalities as private property, intended for their amusement. The Visconti, though they retained their family ability and force of character longer than most princely houses, shall serve to illustrate the general dynastic development, more especially as the history of Milan, which had become the chief power in Italy, will be the best thread to carry us to the end of the century.

Towards the middle of the century Archbishop Giovanni Visconti had become the lord of Milan (1349-54). He was a clever, cultivated man, interested in letters. He employed scholars to prepare a commentary on the "Divine Comedy," and by urgent persuasion induced Petrarch to take up his abode at Milan. On the archbishop's death his three nephews succeeded jointly to the signory. As one of these three nephews, Bernabò (1354-85), illustrates the moral degeneracy of the tyrant we will glance at his habits. Bernabò was addicted to the chase. Nobody else was allowed to keep a dog, but he kept five thousand. These he billeted on the citizens of Milan. Every fortnight the masters of his kennels made their rounds; if the dogs were too thin, a fine was imposed; if dead, a general confiscation. If a man killed a wild boar or a hare, he was maimed or hanged, or sometimes, in mercy, merely obliged to eat the quarry raw. Bernabò was afraid of conspiracies and rebellion. No man might go out into the street after dark for any cause whatever, under pain of having a foot cut off. No man might utter the words "Guelf" or "Ghibelline," under penalty of having his tongue cut out. Once Bernabò shut up his two secretaries in a cage with a wild boar. On another occasion a young man who had pulled a policeman's beard was condemned to pay a small fine, but Bernabò ordered his right hand cut off. The podestà delayed execution of the sentence, so that the lad's parents might have time to ask mercy. For this Bernabò caused the lad's two hands to be cut off and also the podestà's right hand. A sexton who demanded too much for digging a grave was buried alive side by side with the dead body. Two monks who came to remonstrate with Bernabò for his cruelty were burnt alive. Nevertheless, Bernabò protested himself devout; he fasted, built churches and monasteries. This amiable man had thirty-two children. His brother, joint heir of the principality, Galeazzo II, was of the same stuff, except that in place of piety he substituted an interest in letters; he founded the University of Pavia, and exchanged figs, flowers, and flattery with Petrarch. Galeazzo's son, Gian Galeazzo (1378-1402), rose still higher in the world; he gave 300,000 sequins to the King of France, and in return received the king's daughter in marriage. For a second wife he married his cousin, daughter of his amiable uncle Bernabò, who thought that this marriage would bind his nephew to him by bonds of filial affection. Gian Galeazzo however, by means of a trick, got his father-in-law within his reach, arrested him, accused him of witchcraft, put him in prison and poisoned him, and so became sole lord of Milan. This worthy lord converted his principality into a dukedom and became duke (1395); but as we have followed the family to the end of the century, and long enough to make ourselves acquainted with the habits of tyrants, we must leave them.

Poor Italy suffering from these three evils, plagues, condottieri, and tyrants, naturally sought for a cure, and, with what seems to us a singular lack of imagination, turned to the old remedies, Emperor and Pope. From time to time Emperors came into Italy, but the Hapsburgs were very different from the Hohenstaufens, and their trips to Rome were mere money-getting excursions. They sold privileges and honours, imposed what taxes they could collect, and sneaked back to Germany. Obviously there was no hope from Emperors. Then rose the cry for the return of the Papacy. Every Italian, however he might hate or despise the Popes, felt proud that the Papacy was an Italian institution, and believed that every Pope, good or bad, should live in Rome and sit on his throne at St. Peter's. Sentiment grew strong, especially among the women; Petrarch thundered, St. Catherine of Siena pleaded. Moreover, the sharper argument was urged with great practical effect, that the Papal State might shake off the papal dominion if the Pontiffs did not look after it themselves. The Popes began to stir uneasily. The cardinals indeed, accustomed to the safe city of Avignon, did not care to go to turbulent Rome, or perhaps, as Petrarch said, they could not bear to leave their Burgundian wines. But finally Gregory XI (1370-78) raised his courage to the sticking point. He returned to Rome in 1377, and the Babylonish Captivity of seventy years ended.

CHAPTER XXIII: A BIRD'S-EYE VIEW (1350-1450)

The return of the Papacy to Rome was an event of importance both for Italy and the Catholic Church. Had it remained in France, it must have dwindled and shrunk, like Antæus, kept away from its source of strength. Nevertheless, the Papacy was no longer what it once had been; it cannot serve us now as a central channel for the course of Italian history, and will rank no higher than the first of half-a-dozen little channels, which we must pursue separately.

The returning Pope found his territory in greater obedience than he deserved; for a brilliant Spanish cardinal, Albornoz who had been sent some time before had reduced almost all the cities to subjection (1353-67); even Bologna, successfully disputed with the Visconti, acknowledged papal dominion. But there was neither peace nor tranquillity. Everywhere turbulence and murmurous threatenings rumbled; and worse was to come. The very year after the return from the Babylonish Captivity the Great Schism rent the Church asunder for forty years. There were two parties in the College of Cardinals, the French and the Italian, with little love lost between them. The Italians were in control and elected Urban VI (1378-89), a domineering, cruel, most unpastoral person, who insulted the foreign cardinals, and so angered them that they left Rome, declared his election illegal, and elected one of themselves as Pope in his stead. This anti-pope, attended by his troop of cardinals, returned to Avignon. Christian Europe divided in two: some countries recognized Urban, others recognized the anti-pope. Thus the schism began, and prepared the way for the next great split of Christian Europe into Catholics and Protestants. There were now two sources of apostolic succession, two supreme rulers, and two systems of taxation. Misbehaviour and confusion at the top lowered the moral tone of the whole Church. The Curia in Rome was scandalously venal. Indulgences were sold; offices were bestowed for money. Nobody in Rome respected the Pope, hardly anybody respected the clergy.

All Christendom felt that reformation was necessary, and that, first of all, the schism must be closed. Thereupon some outward deference was paid to public opinion; the Roman Pope went so far as to make ostensible overtures to his rival at Avignon, and he of Avignon bowed and smiled most politely in return. Friendly greetings went to and fro, and a meeting was talked of. It became obvious, however, after a time, that neither Pope had the slightest intention of abdicating in the other's favour. Christendom remained insistent, and the two batches of cardinals took the matter into their own hands. They held a Council at Pisa, which deposed both Popes, and elected a third (1409), but, as the other two Popes refused to acknowledge their deposition, matters were worse than before. The situation recalled the old days when a German Emperor had come down to Rome and had deposed three rival Popes together. The need seemed to revive the past. The Emperor Sigismund (1410-37) assumed to speak as the head of Christendom. He summoned an Ecumenical Council to meet at the city of Constance, on the Lake of Constance, to judge the schismatic quarrel and to consider the general state of the Church. Other troubles besides schism had begun to appear. The failure of Rome to satisfy the conscience of Europe had borne fruit. Heresy had appeared. In England, Wyclif (1327-84) had denounced the higher clergy for greed and arrogance; he had disavowed allegiance to the divided Papacy, and had opposed the doctrine of transubstantiation. In Bohemia, Jerome of Prague rejected the temporal jurisdiction of priests, and John Huss asserted that Constantine had done great wrong when he endowed Pope Silvester with lands and temporal power.

Christendom responded to the Emperor's call. Prelates and scholars of the highest character and standing assembled at Constance (1414). It was a great occasion, and belongs to the history of Europe. This Council, the seventeenth Ecumenical Council of the Christian Church (1414-18), deposed all three Popes, and elected a Roman, of the House of Colonna, Martin V (1417-31), and so closed the schism and restored unity to the Church. The more difficult matter of crushing heresy was not so readily dealt with. The two reformers, Jerome of Prague and John Huss, refused to recant or modify their views. They were condemned and handed over to the secular arm for punishment; and the Emperor, heedless of the safe-conduct he had given, burnt them at the stake (1415-16).

To follow the proceedings of this interesting Council more fully would take us too far into papal affairs. It must suffice to say that the Reformation can be sniffed in the air. Rome had not done its elementary duties as head of Christendom, and Christendom insisted on a change and on reform; but Rome was powerful and would not submit. Two parties appear, the reformers and the papists. The former wished to purify the Roman Curia and the whole Church, and to give the Papacy a republican character,—to make the Pope a president, as it were, and the College of Cardinals a senate. The latter liked the old easy ways and wished the Pope to be absolute monarch. The papal party by dexterous politics foiled the plans of the reformers and prevented change of any kind, although no doubt it acted less from desire to obstruct reform than to prevent the anti-monarchical party from getting control of the Church and using the prestige of reform to attack the papal autocracy. From this time on the papal party consistently pursued this course, and therefore reformation came not from Rome, but from Germany, and instead of being a reform from within, came practically as an attack from without, and caused the permanent schism of the Reformation. We must now leave the Papacy, which follows its wilful course—via Babylonish Absenteeism, Schism, and refusal to reform—and steers directly towards the rocks of the Reformation, and betake ourselves to the other parts of Italy.

The Kingdom of Naples would have been badly off at best under its light-mannered queen, Joan I (1343-81), but it became involved in the papal schism, and got into a wretched plight. The queen rashly took sides with the Avignon Pope, and the irascible Roman Pope vowed vengeance. He set her cousin, Charles, who belonged to the Durazzo branch of the House of Anjou, on the throne in her stead. The story is a miserable mixture of treasons, battles, and vulgar crimes. Charles got possession of the unfortunate queen and strangled her, and he and his heirs fought her adopted heirs for years. Each side hired mercenaries. John Hawkwood was there, and other notable leaders. Poor Naples, taxed, robbed, and ravaged by rival kings, their favourites, and mistresses, rolled rapidly from bad to worse. Exception must be made in favour of Charles's son Ladislaus (1390-1414), a bold, enterprising soldier, who played a part in the affairs of Italy like that of his ancestor, Charles of Anjou. But he failed in not leaving a son to inherit the crown, and was succeeded by his sister, another Queen Joan (1414-35), likewise light-mannered. There is nothing memorable to grace her career, except the presence of a soldier of fortune, once a Romagnol peasant, Muzio Attendolo, better known as Attendolo Sforza (strength). His son was Francesco Sforza, destined to a brilliant career in Milan. The queen did one thing, however, for which we, who clutch at any unification of Italian history, must thank her. She adopted, not wholly of her free will, Alfonso of Aragon, King of Sicily, and so brought about, though for a few years only, the reunion of the Two Sicilies.

With regard to Sicily we need say nothing except that the royal House, which still had a strain of Hohenstaufen-Norman blood, died out, and that Sicily passed as a marriage portion to the crown of Aragon, and became a mere appanage of that kingdom (1409). Finally, as I have said, King Alfonso was adopted as heir to the second Queen Joan, and took part in the civil wars that devastated Naples. Then began the long struggle of Spaniard against Frenchman (the Neapolitan House of Anjou was still French), which was destined to be so disastrous to Italy. Alfonso conquered and was acknowledged King of the Two Sicilies by his suzerain the Pope (1443). Thus for a time the Southern Kingdom was united and at peace. It is a happy moment to leave it and go northward, in the hope of finding greater moral and intellectual activity, if not greater tranquillity and order.

To the northeast, Venice had been growing in power; but with the growth of her power the number of her enemies and their bitterness towards her had grown. Her possessions on the mainland, wrested from Verona, brought her into hostility with Padua; her Adriatic possessions, Istria and Dalmatia, made her an enemy of Hungary; her coastwise empire and trade in the Levant made Genoa her deadly rival; and her imperial expansion entangled her in war after war. Both the war with Padua and that with Hungary told upon her, but the struggle with Genoa was far worse. During the last grapple, known as the war of Chioggia (1378-81), Venice was reduced to narrow straits, and but for her great admirals, Vettor Pisani and Carlo Zeno, would have been defeated. Genoa never recovered from the losses she sustained; but Venice regained her strength, and renewed her conquests on the mainland. She conquered Padua (1404) and strangled the last heirs of the House of Carrara, though they were prisoners of war; she seized Verona, and set a price on the heads of the last of the Scaligers, though they had been her allies. Her chief expansion on the mainland of Italy was under the Doge Francesco Foscari (1423-57), when she annexed Bergamo and Brescia, and carried her western boundary to the river Adda. For the sake of convenience we may divide the life of Venice into four stages: first, her lusty youth, which closed with the profligate capture of Constantinople and the piratical dismemberment of the Byzantine Empire (1204); second, her vigorous prime, which lasted till she annexed Italian territory, threw in her lot with Italy, and from being almost an Oriental outsider became an Italian state (1338); third, her glorious maturity, which continued till the League of Cambrai, when almost all Europe united to destroy her (1508); and fourth, her long period of ebbing fortune, during which she slipped slowly into decrepitude. In the present chapter we deal with the earlier part of her maturity, when Venice was contesting with Milan for primacy in power and importance.

During all this period the oligarchy had been tightening its hold on the government, and was now absolute and secure. One last attempt had been made to overthrow it, but had easily been put down. No one knows exactly what led to the conspiracy, or what was the exact purpose of the conspirators. The ringleader was the Doge himself, Marino Faliero, one of the old nobility. The story is that he wished to revenge himself for a gross insult from a young nobleman, and it seems likely that a personal quarrel had some connection with a general plot which aimed to overthrow the oligarchy, and substitute a government of the old nobility supported by the people. The plot was betrayed. Nine of the conspirators were hanged from the windows of the Ducal Palace. Faliero's head was cut off, his portrait in the hall of the Ducal Palace was painted out, and in the blank space was written: "This is the place of Marino Faliero, beheaded for his crimes."

The oligarchy did not fail in its duty to itself, but neither did it fail in its duty to the state. Commerce was the life of Venice; and the oligarchy tended it with the utmost care. The famous Venetian arsenal was the foster-mother of that commerce. There the money-getting ships were built and equipped: caracks with three decks and great depth of hold, galleasses with high forecastle and poop, galleys with long rows of oars and lateen sails, all of different builds to suit the rough Atlantic Ocean, the Mediterranean Sea, or the safer Adriatic.

Riches, a firm rule, and the security of an island home, showed visibly in Venice. Instead of fortresses with massive walls and solid towers, light, elegant palaces, decked with gay balconies and incrusting marbles, lined the canals. All revealed tranquillity and prosperity; and the adoption of Gothic architecture in place of Byzantine, and in especial the long Gothic arcades of the Ducal Palace (1300-40), testified how Venice had turned her face from the East to the West. In contrast with Sicily and Naples, rolling down hill separately or together, and with the troubled Papal States, Venice appears altogether happy and successful as she passes from the fourteenth into the fifteenth century.

Milan we have brought to the dignity of a dukedom, for which Gian Galeazzo Visconti (1378-1402), the amiable nephew of the too-confiding Bernabò, paid the price of 100,000 sequins to the fount of honour, the ultramontane Emperor. This nephew, despite a moral inadequacy in his family relations, was in many respects an excellent ruler. He reduced the more burdensome taxes (in one city, it is said, he cut them down from 12,000 florins to 400), and abolished others altogether. He corrected abuses, reorganized the administration of justice, and enacted wise laws. He understood the pride of the Milanese in their city, and laid the foundations of the great Gothic cathedral on a scale to gratify that pride; he began the beautiful church of the Cistercian monks, the Certosa, at Pavia; he completed the palace at Pavia, whither he transported his famous collection of books and an equally famous collection of holy bones. He had the family ambition, and annexed Vicenza, Verona, Padua, Siena, Assisi, Perugia, Pisa, and Bologna. Rumour said that he aspired to a kingdom of Lombardy, and even of all Italy. But Venice and Florence were too powerful for the success of his plans. Venice, perhaps, might have regarded herself as still too much detached from Italy to care to oppose him single-handed; but the doughty burghers of Florence were zealously democratic and would not endure any suggestion of foreign dominion. They had fought the Pope, when they suspected him of designs on their city, and now they organized a league against Gian Galeazzo. Perhaps it would have been a most fortunate thing for

Italy if the Duke of Milan had been able to consolidate all Italy, or even all the North, in one kingdom. Centuries of suffering, of ignominy, of foreign domination might have been avoided; but then, perhaps, the great intellectual harvest, that gave Italy for the third time primacy over Europe, would not have attained its full growth. These are idle speculations, for Gian Galeazzo died in his prime (1402), and the universal dominion of Milan became an academic question. Nevertheless, one cannot withhold a sensation of regret. There was undoubted brilliance in Gian Galeazzo; whatever he did was done royally. His ambitions were high, planned always on a large scale. His purchases of the French king's daughter and of the ducal title were splendidly prodigal. The design of the cathedral was noble and bold. It was an endeavour to give the Gothic style an Italian character. In this it is easy to find symbolism. The Gothic style represented the Ghibelline cause, as well as Teutonic blood and influence, whereas the Italian represented the Guelf cause and also Latin blood. The high-aspiring Gian Galeazzo wished to use both Teutonic and Italian elements as the materials for his kingdom. In view of his intellectual gifts, one readily slurs over his moral inadequacy, if that term may be applied to traits which would have done honour to Iago; in fact, prior to Cæsar Borgia, he was the most distinguished example of the type of intellectual, murderous Italian, which exercised so powerful an attraction over the wild fancy of the Elizabethan dramatists.

Gian Galeazzo's death left his dukedom in a chaotic condition. A widow, a regent committee, and three boys were left to see the state, built up with so much care and astuteness, fall away piecemeal into the hands of the petty despots, who had been dispossessed during the process of integration. Venice took Verona, Padua, and other cities near by; the Papacy got back Bologna, Florence managed to secure Pisa. Thus the dukedom was carved up. The eldest son died soon, leaving behind him a memory of the pleasure he took in watching mastiffs tear his prisoners to pieces; but the second son, Filippo Maria (1412-47), inherited his father's craft and much of his ability. By means of two famous condottieri, Carmagnola, best remembered as the victim of Venetian anger, and Francesco Sforza, of whom we have heard in the Neapolitan service, he gradually restored the dukedom very nearly to its boundaries under his father. Filippo Maria was the last of his race, and we will leave him, engaged in speculation as to the best political use of his marriageable daughter Bianca Maria.

We must pass over the Counts of Savoy, now become dukes (1416), the marquesses of Monferrat and Saluzzo, and the lords of other petty territories, and turn our attention to Florence. Florence was always in a state of struggle, always engaged in exiling, deposing, or in some way suppressing aristocrats. Forced, in days of peril, to receive foreign lords as military leaders, she had managed to expel the last of them, one Walter of Brienne, a clever knave, who bore the odd title of Duke of Athens, which he had inherited from his grandfather, one of the gentlemen adventurers who had gone to the East. His father had been expelled from Athens, and the son was happily driven out of Florence. The burghers followed up their victory (1343) with new laws against the aristocrats, and held the government for a generation. Then first appears the name of Medici. One Salvestro dei Medici, as Gonfaloniere of Justice, the supreme officer in Florence under the existing constitution, proposed further laws in favour of the people. The lower classes, with whetted appetites, wanted more. The mechanics and artisans of the lower guilds, and more particularly the wool carders and combers (the Ciompi) of the great wool guilds, rose in riot, overturned the government, and put a wool-carder, Michele di Lando, at the head of the city (1378). Florence was democratic, but not so democratic as to submit to the rule of a wool-carder. The rich burghers would not stomach a plebeian any more than they would a king. A reaction set in, and the government passed into the very competent hands of an oligarchy of distinguished citizens. This oligarchy governed well. Its leaders, Maso degli Albizzi, and Niccolò da Uzzano, acted patriotically and wisely. They resisted the aggressions of Milan from the north, and of Naples (under that exceptional king Ladislaus) from the south, and made it their policy to maintain the balance of power in Italy. Under this oligarchy began the great development of art, known as the Renaissance, or, to be more exact in quoting the textbooks, the First or Early Renaissance. To that subject, which shall give us for a time at least a centre, and save us from these puzzling political subdivisions, we joyfully proceed; only remembering that at this period Italy has these main political divisions,—the Kingdom of Sicily, the Kingdom of Naples (the two temporarily reunited), the Papal States, the city of Florence, the duchy of Milan, and the city of Venice.

CHAPTER XXIV: THE EARLY RENAISSANCE (1400-1450)

By Renaissance, new birth, we mean the rapid, many-sided, intellectual development which started forward in Italy at this time. It was really a stage in the movement which began a hundred years earlier, but the textbooks confine the term Renaissance to the period which began at the opening of the fifteenth century; and just as the first beginning took place in Florence, so this fresh start, like a stream of energy issuing at a divine touch, also burst out of the city of Florence. The simplest way to get an idea of this period, known as the Early Renaissance, will be to notice a few of the men, leaders in their several spheres, in whom that energy became incarnate.

We must not let ourselves think that the Renaissance was a merely artistic movement. A few men are known to us, and we think of them as wandering about in artistic isolation, as if they were hermits in a Thebaid. But, in reality, only a slight fraction of even the deeper feelings and interests take artistic or literary form; the great majority are put into life. The celebrated Florentine artists of those days were merely representative of their fellows; they were surrounded by crowds of neighbours, all crammed full with ardour for living, for expression, for discussion, for money-making, for glorifying their city. In recognition of this fact, and of the great service rendered to the arts throughout the Renaissance by men who were not artists, but potent signors of wealth and cultivation, whether merchants, dukes, or cardinals, I take Cosimo dei Medici (1389-1464) as the first figure in this brief account of the Early Renaissance.

Cosimo's father, the richest banker in Italy, and one of the chief citizens of Florence, had been active in politics, and chief of the party which was opposed to the ruling oligarchy. Cosimo succeeded to his father's position, and when the oligarchy fell became the actual head of the city, though he always affected the rôle of private citizen. His quick intelligence and his broad cultivation gave him keen sympathy with the fermenting intellectual life about him, and his great wealth enabled him to express that sympathy in most substantial ways. He got his first schooling from a Florentine humanist, and then went abroad, travelled in Germany and France, and visited the Council of Constance then in session. After that his attention was devoted to business and to political affairs. His position in Florence during early manhood was always precarious, for the sharp-witted Florentines were not easily hoodwinked and saw whither Cosimo's masterfulness was tending. For a time he was in exile, but after a tussle he won his place and banished his enemies. Wealth was his great instrument. He lent and gave lavishly. In later life he used to say that his chief error had been that he had not begun to spend money ten years sooner than he did. He was a serious man, given to intellectual matters, and averse to buffoons and strolling players, so popular then; by virtue of wide experience in the conduct of large affairs, of extensive reading, of a retentive memory, and a natural gift for language, he was both an interesting talker and good company. He talked literature with men of letters, but he was equally ready to talk divinity, in which he was well read, or philosophy, or astrology in which he believed although some men did not. He liked gardening, and enjoyed going out of town to his country-place; there he would prune the vines for two hours in the morning, and then go indoors to read. His connection with the arts of the Renaissance, however, is our chief concern. He employed the famous architect Michelozzo to build his palace, now known as Palazzo Riccardi, his villa, and also the Dominican convent of San Marco. He employed the still more famous Brunelleschi to rebuild the abbey of Fiesole. He was fond of sculptors, especially of Donatello, and had statues by the best masters of the day in his palace. He employed Fra Angelico to paint in the convent of San Marco, and Benozzo Gozzoli in his private chapel. Benozzo painted a procession of the Three Wise Men, with Cosimo, his son, and his grandson, young Lorenzo the Magnificent, riding in their train. Cosimo's greatest interest, however, was in the humanities. He built several buildings for libraries in Florence, and one in Venice, and interested himself greatly in the preservation and increase of the libraries themselves. For the library in the abbey at Fiesole he employed a man of letters (Vespasiano da Bisticci, his biographer), who hired forty-five copyists, and in twenty-two months finished the two hundred volumes deemed necessary for a good library. His list included the Bible and concordances and commentaries, beginning with that by Origen; the works of St. Ignatius, St. Basil, St. Gregory Nazianzen, St. John Chrysostom, and all the works of the Greek fathers which had been translated into Latin; St. Cyprian, Tertullian, and the four doctors of the Latin Church; the mediæval masters St. Bernard, Hugo of St. Victor, St. Anselm, St. Isidore of Spain; the scholastic philosophers, Albertus Magnus, Alexander of Hales, Thomas Aquinas, Bonaventura; Aristotle, and commentaries; books of canon law; the Latin prose classics, Livy, Cæsar, Suetonius, Plutarch, Sallust, Quintus Curtius, Valerius Maximus, Cicero, Seneca; the Latin poets, Virgil, Terence, Ovid, Lucan, Statius, Plautus; and "all the other books necessary to a library." One wonders if this clause includes Dante, Petrarch, and Boccaccio, or whether the humanists did not regard them as necessary or appropriate to culture.

Taken altogether Cosimo may stand as an heroic model of the Florentine burgher, such as one sees in the frescoes of the time, shrewd, prudent, thoughtful, cautious in plan and prompt in action, interested in the best things of this world, and in a measure generous, but wholly without romance, chivalry, or idealism. At the close of his life he used to stay hours at a time, wrapt in thought, without speaking a word. One of the women of the house asked him the reason of this. He answered: "When you have to go out of town, you spend a fortnight all agog to prepare for going; and now that I have to go from this life to another, doesn't it seem to you that I have something to think about?" The last book he is reported by his biographer to have read was the "Ethics" of Aristotle.

Cosimo was named Pater Patriæ, though his real work was the foundation of the House of the Medici, which ruled in Tuscany for centuries and mingled its blood with the royalties of Europe; but for us he is the patron of the arts, the friend of artists, and serves as the central figure round which to group the men of artistic genius.

In architecture the greatest name is that of Brunelleschi (1377-1446). His biography by Vasari opens with these words: "Many men are created by nature little in person and features, who have their souls so full of greatness and their hearts so full of the inordinate fury of genius, that, unless they are at work on things difficult to impossibility, and unless they finish them to the astonishment of the spectator, they never give themselves any rest all their lives; and whatever things chance puts into their hands, no matter how mean and cheap, they bring to worth and dignity.... Such was Brunelleschi, no less insignificant in person than Giotto, but of so lofty genius, that it may be said he was endowed by heaven to give new form to architecture, which for hundreds of years had gone astray [such was the Renaissance view of the Gothic and Romanesque]. Moreover, Brunelleschi was adorned with the greatest virtues; among which was friendship to such a degree, that there never was a man more kind or more loving than he. His judgment was wholly free from passion; wherever he saw the worth of another man's merits, he totally disregarded any advantage to himself or to his friends. He knew himself; he inspired others with his own noble qualities, and he always succoured his neighbour in time of need. He declared himself a deadly enemy of the vices, and a lover of those who practised virtue. He never wasted time, for he was always busy with his own affairs or with the affairs of others when they had need of him, and when out walking he used to stop and see his friends and always lent them a hand." Brunelleschi was no scholar, but, being a Florentine, he was very fond of talking, and did not hesitate to take part in conversation with learned men, especially when the talk ran on Holy Writ, and then, as a friend said, he talked like a second St. Paul.

He began life, as most architects did, as a member of the guild of goldsmiths, and learned to model, but he had a bent towards physics and mechanics, and developed naturally into an architect. A great event in his life was a trip to Rome with Donatello; there the two examined all the classical remains in the city and in the country round about, taking measurements and learning all they could.

In Florence besides the abbey of Fiesole, built for Cosimo, Brunelleschi built the church of San Lorenzo for Cosimo's father, and he designed and began the lordly Pitti palace across the Arno, but his great achievement was the dome of the cathedral. The cathedral, first begun by Arnolfo di Cambio, had been in charge of a succession of famous architects, and was nearing completion; but the gap at the intersection of the nave and transepts presented a most difficult architectural problem. The diameter of this gap was about one hundred and thirty-five feet, and the height above the ground was about one hundred and forty-five feet. No such span had been vaulted since the building of the Pantheon. A public competition for a dome was held in which Brunelleschi took part. After long discussion, for Florence was "a city where every one speaks his mind," and after much consideration, Brunelleschi was chosen architect. His great dome, though no copy of Roman forms, was thoroughly classic in its simplicity and its spirit, and is the great achievement of the Early Renaissance in architecture.

Brunelleschi and his fellow architects, no doubt, wished to revive the old Roman art, and did so as far as they could, but their problems were new and their models few, so they were forced, in the main, to follow their own principles of construction and limit their use of Roman forms to ornament and detail. Other famous men seconded Brunelleschi; and Florentine, or at least Tuscan, architects spread the ideas of the new art. To them is really due the foundation of the various schools of Renaissance architecture which sprang up in Milan, Venice, Pavia, Bologna, Rimini, Brescia, Siena, Lucca, Perugia, and in almost every city of Northern Italy.

In sculpture, the puissant Donatello (1386-1466) is the greatest figure. It has been said, that

Michelangelo's soul first worked in Donatello's body or that Donatello's soul lived again in Michelangelo. Donatello was a realist; he shows classic influence at times, in technique and in sundry bits of detail, but his instinct was to imitate what he could see and touch. His vigour, his energy and variety produced a profound effect on sculpture and also on painting. His earlier works were statues for the outside of the Campanile and of the church of Orsanmichele, of which the most famous are that known as Zuccone, Baldhead, and the splendid St. George. Afterwards he modelled a young David, the first nude bronze since the Romans, and the statue of Gattamelata at Padua, the first equestrian statue since that of Marcus Aurelius in Rome. The spectator who examines the collection of Donatello's works in the Bargello is chiefly struck by his intellectual power, and by the immense variety of his style, from the simple outline of the lovely St. Cecilia in low relief, to the passionate dramas carved in altars and pulpits.

Donatello was a great friend of Brunelleschi, and Vasari tells this anecdote about them. Donatello modelled a Crucifix for Santa Croce, and thinking he had done something unusually good, asked Brunelleschi what he thought of it. Brunelleschi, with his unswerving artistic rectitude, answered that Donatello had put a peasant on the cross, and not Jesus Christ. Donatello, piqued more than he had anticipated, said: "If it were as easy to model as it is to criticise, my Christ would seem to you a Christ and not a peasant; but let's see you take a piece of wood and go and make one." Brunelleschi did so secretly, and when he had at last finished his Crucifix, asked Donatello to come home and dine with him. They walked to Brunelleschi's house together, stopping at the market to buy eggs, cheese, and other things for the dinner. Then Brunelleschi said, "Donatello, you take these things and go to my house, and I will come after in a minute or two." So Donatello caught them up in his apron, went to Brunelleschi's, opened the door, and saw the Crucifix. He was so dumbfounded that he dropped the dinner on the floor, and when Brunelleschi, coming in, said, "Why, Donatello, what shall we have for dinner?" Donatello answered, "For my part I have had my share to-day. If you want yours, pick it up. No more of that. It is my lot to model peasants, and yours to model Christs."

Donatello was also a great friend of Cosimo's, modelled many things for him, and inspired Cosimo with a taste for collecting antiques. He loved Cosimo so much that he did whatever he wanted, except when it interfered with his personal idiosyncrasies. One day Cosimo gave Donatello, who used to go about in his workman's blouse, a cloak and a fine suit of clothes, the costume of a gentleman. Donatello wore them for a day or two, and then said he could not wear them, they were too fashionable. He was buried, at his own request, near Cosimo, in the church of San Lorenzo, which Brunelleschi had designed, and he had adorned with his sculpture.

Donatello worked in Venice, Mantua, Modena, Ferrara, and Prato, spent several years in Siena, and nine in Padua, and introduced the Renaissance into the sculpture of Northern Italy. He was a man of strong character and poetic spirit, striving in his statues to be true to nature and to the beautiful, to mingle pagan and Christian notions, tradition, and freedom. He and his pupils affected the whole plastic art of Italy.

In painting, Masaccio (1401-28) stands conspicuous, even among many painters of rare gifts. Modern critics call him Giotto reincarnate. Masaccio is an unflattering nickname for Tommaso, and recalls the only personal trait we know of him. Vasari says: "He was a most absent-minded person and very casual, like a man who has fixed his will and his whole mind on art only, and cares little about himself and less about others. He never wanted to think in any way about the things or the cares of this world, even of his own clothes, and he never went to get the money due him from his debtors except when he was in extreme need. Instead of Thomas, everybody called him Masaccio; not because he was bad, being good nature itself, but because of his great absent-mindedness. Nevertheless, he was as affectionate in doing useful and amiable acts for other people as could possibly be wished." This "marvellous boy" died at the age of twenty-seven, but left an ineffaceable mark on Italian painting. Across the Arno, in the ugly church of Santa Maria del Carmine, is a chapel on the right, in which, mingled with the work of contemporaries and continuers, are Masaccio's frescoes, figures of St. Peter and St. John, of a shivering boy, and a few others. Leonardo da Vinci said: "After Giotto, the art of painting declined again, because every one imitated the pictures that were already done; thus it went on till Tommaso of Florence, nicknamed Masaccio, showed by his perfect works how those who take for their standard any one but Nature—the mistress of all masters—weary themselves in vain." In that little chapel, Leonardo, Michelangelo, Raphael, and scores of the greatest painters of Italy have admired, studied, and copied.

Brunelleschi, Donatello, Masaccio are but the greater names in the fine arts. Well might Leon Battista Alberti, himself a great architect and humanist, on return from exile to his native city, say to Brunelleschi: "I have been accustomed both to wonder and to grieve that so many divine arts and sciences which we see to have abounded in those most highly endowed ancients were now lacking and utterly lost ... but since I have been restored to this our native land that surpasseth all others in her adornment, I have recognized in many but chiefly in thee, Philip [Brunelleschi], and in our near friend Donato [Donatello] the sculptor, and in those others, Nencio [Ghiberti], and Luca [della Robbia], and Masaccio, genius capable for every praiseworthy work, not inferior to that of any ancient and famous master in the arts."

CHAPTER XXV: THE RENAISSANCE (1450-1492)

The last chapter confined itself to the fine arts and omitted the main element, humanism, which gave volume and impetus to the stream, and, though not memorable for conspicuous achievements as the fine arts were, flowed more directly from the classic impulse and produced the greatest immediate effect. The humanists played a part analogous to that which men of science play in our own time; they devoted themselves heart and soul to the classics, as men of science do to Nature. For some time they had had access to the Latin past through Italy, and now they also found their way to the far greater classic world of Greece. The one uninterrupted communication with that world was through Constantinople, which, like a long, ill-lighted and ill-repaired corridor, led back to the great pleasure domes of Plato and Homer, and all the wonderland of Greek literature and thought. Aristotle, indeed, had come by way of the Arabs, and had long been a lay Bible, but for the other Greek classics the rising humanism of Italy was indebted to Constantinople. The glowing young city of Florence lit its torch at the expiring embers of the imperial city. A few Italians went to Constantinople and learned Greek, then stray Byzantines came to Italy. The doom which hung over Constantinople frightened scholars and drove them westward, and the fall itself (1453) dispersed the last of them. These Greeks brought invaluable manuscripts and firmly established Hellenic culture in the kindred soil of Tuscany. In the list of books in Cosimo's library, there was no mention of any Greek classic except Aristotle; but after the immigration of Greek scholars all intellectual Florence went mad over Plato, and Cosimo founded a Platonic Academy. The study of Greek brought with it examination, comparison, criticism; it brought new knowledge; it gave new ideas to all the arts, new impulses to the creative imagination, and general intellectual freedom. Interest in the humanities became so widespread throughout the peninsula that we get a feeling of Italian unity stronger than any we have experienced since the days of Theodoric.

The importance of the humanists, however, was merely as an intellectual leaven. They need not be spoken of apart from the general intellectual movement which expressed itself so much more fully and freely in art than in any other way. That movement kindled enthusiasm from Lombardy to Calabria; and Florence still maintained her primacy. All the other cities of Italy lagged far behind her. We must therefore keep Florence as our paradigm, only remembering that at her heels a score of cities toil and pant in artistic eagerness to make themselves as beautiful and famous as Florence.

There Cosimo, Pater Patriæ, had died in fulness of years and was succeeded by his grandson, Lorenzo the Magnificent, though not immediately, for there was a short-lived Piero in between. Lorenzo took his grandfather's place, became lord of Florence in all but name, and stood the centre of a brilliant group of artists, sculptors, poets, and scholars. His reign, for it must be so called, lasted from 1469 to 1492, a most notable span of time. The mere names of the famous Florentines would fill pages. A few must be mentioned: Benedetto da Maiano, sculptor and architect, who carved the beautiful pulpit in Santa Croce, and drew the designs for the palace-fortress of the Strozzi; Giuliano da San Gallo, sculptor and architect, who made the plans for

Lorenzo's villa at Poggio a Caiano; Andrea della Robbia, nephew to Luca, and almost his equal in the tender charm of his blue and white Madonnas; Mino da Fiesole, who made a bust of Lorenzo's father, and carved in marble the sweetness of young mothers; Antonio Rossellino, who wrought the famous tomb for a great Portuguese prelate in the church of San Miniato; Andrea Verrocchio, who painted the Uffizi Annunciation, so beautiful that it was long attributed to Leonardo, modelled the lady dalle belle mani in the Bargello, and the Colleoni at Venice, greatest of equestrian statues; Benozzo Gozzoli, who painted the three generations of Medici in the Riccardi palace, and in the Campo Santo at Pisa the enchanting frescoes which turn the Old Testament into a kind of Arabian Nights; Antonio Pollaiuolo, sculptor and painter, a leader in the new school of realism, and notable for the feeling of movement which he conveys; Filippino Lippi, Lippo Lippi's son, who completed the frescoes in the chapel in Santa Maria del Carmine left unfinished by Masaccio; Botticelli, the greatest of all the Florentine painters, except Leonardo and Michelangelo; Domenico Ghirlandaio, whose frescoes in Santa Maria Novella tell us more about those shrewd, capable, quick-witted Florentines than any historian; Pulci, the poet, who wrote "Morgante Maggiore," a gay epic, which Savonarola thought ought to be burned; Poliziano, great embodiment of culture, who wrote the first lyrical tragedy, and led the way towards the opera; Marsilio Ficino, the philosopher who helped Cosimo found the Platonic Academy; Pico della Mirandola, the charming scholar, whom Machiavelli called "a man almost divine."

Perhaps none of these men were equal to the leaders in the group which surrounded Cosimo, but they are more interesting to us, and touch our sympathy more readily. They are nearer to us. The earlier problems in architecture, sculpture, and painting were more difficult, but they had been successfully solved; and the fresh problems, which confronted the younger generation, though less adventurous, were more refined. The sons have entered into a hard-earned inheritance, and live more freely. They have more spiritual alertness than their fathers though less vigour, more sensitiveness to passing moods though less robustness, greater mastery of technique though less genius for principles. Less great themselves, they have created greater works. Benedetto's Palazzo Strozzi is more majestic and splendid than Michelozzo's Palazzo Riccardi; Verrocchio's statue of Colleoni surpasses Donatello's Gattamelata; Botticelli's poetry is more interesting, at least to the unlearned, than Masaccio's puissant drawing. Nevertheless, the greater intimacy of sympathy and interest which we feel for the later men is not accounted for by their greater command of their crafts. There is some new element less readily discovered. We perceive a change of attitude toward life, a new conception of human existence. The readiest explanation and perhaps the best, if we do not treat it as completely adequate, lies in the new Greek thought (or rather Greek thought as the Florentines understood it), which the humanists contributed to Italian culture; and indeed not so much in Greek thought itself, as in the impulse it gave to a subtler and more complicated conception of life.

Direct Greek influence is most conspicuous in Botticelli. This rare spirit wandered about half in the world of reality which he ill understood and depicted badly, and half in a world of fantasy which he knew better than any other painter. The secret of this world of fantasy, as he discovered, was motion. If a vision tarries, it becomes touched by the blight of familiarity, soiled by the comradeship of life. The fairy spirit of imagination must be ever on the wing. No artist ever let Sweet Fancy loose as Botticelli did in his two great pictures, The Primavera (Spring) and The Birth of Venus. In them this Greek influence finds its fullest direct expression. The glory of dawn, the first unveiled fresh beauty of the world, which the Greeks saw, Botticelli saw also. But besides the childlike joy in pure beauty is another, more complicated, element. Into the rapturous Greek world, beautiful with sensuous charm, the bewildering idea of a moral order presents itself. On the countenance of Venus and in the figure of Primavera there is a wistfulness, as if they had a presentiment that they must leave the rose-strewn ocean and the magic wood in which they found themselves. The consequence is a sadness as of beholding an antagonism between two beautiful things.

The subtler and more complicated conception of life is best expressed by Verrocchio, the other master spirit of this generation, who displays in his paintings and statues the joy he takes in pure beauty, but always adds some other element. The little boy who hugs a dolphin in the court of the Palazzo Vecchio is the incarnation of the grace and happiness of childhood, but he has an impish, Puck-like expression. The young bronze David, who has just conquered Goliath, has an odd, mischievous sprightliness. Both statues intimate a sceptical attitude towards the fine seriousness of life which had marked Puritan Florence of the older days. His painting of the Annunciation shows a magic background, beautiful and mystical, with enchanted cities, rivers, mountains, like the part of Xanadu where Kubla Khan decreed his pleasure dome, or the strange land where La belle Dame sans Merci left her knight-at-arms alone and palely loitering. Subtle thoughts play over his statues and paintings, and he taught his pupil Leonardo that strange and beautiful fascination of face which expresses one knows not what. The earlier simplicity of the quattrocento has passed, the artist's attitude to life has become complicated, although the love of beauty for beauty's sake remains abundantly.

The lord of Florence, Lorenzo the Magnificent, the centre and patron of this glittering ring, is the best exponent of the late quattrocento taken as a whole. He touched life on every side, public and private, intellectual and frivolous, religious and cynical, artistic, literary, philosophical. Lorenzo had a striking, indeed a fascinating, personality. His figure was strong and lithe, and his face among a thousand caught the eye. His big jaws, under his lean, furrowed cheeks, were square and grim. His long irregular nose and curving lips gave him a somewhat sardonic expression, but his broad forehead was grave and thoughtful, and "princely counsel" shone in his face. His whole aspect was full of character and dignity. Every one felt his fascination. He was a poet and wrote poems of many kinds, grave and gay, some of which are of acknowledged merit:

Di doman non v'è certezza. Chi vuol essere lieto, sia, Che si fugge tuttavia,Quant'è bella giovinezza

He was a scholar, and full of the fashionable admiration for Plato, though he probably shared the current confusion between Plato's own thoughts and those of the Alexandrian Neoplatonists. He was a statesman of foresight and shrewdness, and contributed more than any one else to preserve the peace of Italy, by maintaining the balance of power among the greater states. He was also a very charming person, and endeavoured to make life in Florence a happy mixture of mirth and intellectual pleasure; and it must be remembered in appreciation of the general sobriety of his life, that a gifted company of men did all they could to spoil him.

Lorenzo was the most remarkable prince of the quattrocento, but there were many others who patronized scholars and artists as generously as he. Alfonso of Aragon, the king who temporarily united the Two Sicilies, was devoted to the humanities. He was wont to hear Terence and Virgil read aloud at dinner, and took Livy with him on his campaigns. But Naples and Sicily had almost no share in the achievements and glory of the Italian Renaissance. Lawless, ignorant, poor, unsuccessful, they responded feebly to the efforts of individuals, who, here and there, strove to emulate the great Florentines. But in the North all the world was mad for art, and its princes led the fashion. Federigo da Montefeltro, Duke of Urbino (1422-1482), was the foremost scholar among soldiers and the foremost soldier among scholars; he gathered together a noble library, now lodged in the Vatican; he built a palace, unmatched in Italy; and collected about him artists of all kinds. Yet Federigo was a soldier by nature as well as by profession, as one may see from the great portrait of him in the Uffizi, painted by Piero della Francesca. His strong profile, with firm mouth and big, broken, aquiline nose, testifies far more forcibly to his character as a warrior than as a virtuoso. His near neighbour, the tyrant of Pesaro (a little city by the Adriatic coast), Alessandro Sforza, passed the intervals between his battles in buying books. Duke Ercole of Ferrara was likewise a patron of art, and adorned his capital as well as his palaces and villas with all sorts of beautiful things. The dukes of Milan were somewhat eclipsed, but only for a time, by their less powerful rivals of Ferrara and Urbino. The old ducal line of the Visconti had died out with Filippo Maria, and Francesco Sforza (husband of Filippo's daughter), who succeeded to the duchy (1450), was busy making good his very defective title, and had little time to attend to art or letters. Even he kept humanists in his pay, and continued work on the glorious Certosa of Pavia.

Not only princes but private citizens were lovers and patrons of art. In almost every city of the North—excepting Piedmont—there was some artist of whom the whole city was proud. Nevertheless, throughout the reign of Lorenzo the Magnificent Florence continued to be the most intellectual of Italian cities, as she had been for many generations; but on Lorenzo's death the primacy in the arts and in matters of the mind passed from Florence to Rome. By a flattering chance that primacy seemed to follow the fortunes of a single family. Under Cosimo, Piero, and Lorenzo dei Medici, the Renaissance may be said to have made Florence its home; in the later period it found its fullest expression in Rome, and even there took its name, the Age of Leo, from another Medici, Lorenzo's son. It was not to Pope Leo, however, but to his predecessors, that Rome was indebted for preëminence. At the summons of the Papacy men of genius went to Rome from all Italy, but chiefly from Florence; and a distinguished Tuscan, almost a Florentine, who went from Florence to Rome at the culmination of a brilliant career, fairly serves as the personification of this intellectual migration. Tommaso Parentucelli, who was born in a little town near Lucca, was educated in Florence and Bologna. He took holy orders early, and, going back to Florence, quickly became intimate with the clever set of humanists who surrounded

Cosimo. He was a great student, and won so high a reputation for learning that it was to him Cosimo applied for advice, when he wanted the right books for the library at Fiesole. This collection became famous and was copied both at Rimini and Urbino. Parentucelli was a very capable and attractive man, and embodied in its best form the essence of Florentine humanistic culture. His character, talents, and accomplishments were recognized in the Church; he became bishop, cardinal, and finally Pope, as Nicholas V (1447-55).

At Rome Nicholas showed the well-marked characteristics of the Renaissance. He fostered learning, art, and general culture, not only because of his interest in them, but because he thought that by their means he could overcome that rumbling spirit of reform, which was making trouble in Bohemia and Germany, and that by giving the reformers intellectual interests he could occupy their minds and quell their discontent. He entertained lofty imaginings of a Papacy, resting on learning and culture, housed in a nonpareil city, which should be the acknowledged and admired head of Christendom. He gathered together scholars of all kinds, collected a library of five thousand volumes, and founded the Vatican library. He rebuilt or restored numerous churches and other buildings in Rome, he began the new Vatican palace, and planned a new cathedral in place of the old basilica of St. Peter's, to be the greatest church in Christendom. He brought to Rome architects, painters, goldsmiths, artists, and artisans of all sorts. With him began the brilliant period of the Papacy as a secular power devoted to art and culture, which culminated in what is known as the Age of Leo X.

CHAPTER XXVI: THE BARBARIAN INVASIONS (1494-1537)

We must now leave the great intellectual progress of the Renaissance on its way from its home in Florence to its culmination in Rome, and look over the political condition of the principal divisions of Italy. A complete change comes during this period, that can only be likened to the change wrought by the invasions of the Barbarians in ancient times. In fact, it is a period of fresh invasions by Barbarians, as the Italians, and not without some justice, still called foreigners. The year 1494 was the fatal date of the first invasion of the French. From that year onward there was a series of invasions of French, Austrians, and Spaniards, until Italy was finally parcelled out according to the pleasure of the invaders. Before that time Italy was in a peaceful and prosperous condition. The famous Florentine historian Guicciardini (1483-1540) thus records the time of his boyhood: "Since the fall of the Roman Empire Italy had never known such great prosperity, nor had experienced so desirable a condition as in the year 1490 and the years just before and after. The country had been brought to profound peace and tranquillity, agriculture spread over the roughest and most sterile hills no less than over the most fertile plains, and Italy, subject to no dominion but her own, abounded in men, merchandise, and wealth. She was embellished to the utmost by the magnificence of many princes, by the splendour of many most noble and beautiful cities, by the seat and majesty of Religion; she was rich in men most apt in public affairs, and in minds most noble for all sorts of knowledge. She was industrious and excellent in every art, and, according to the standard of those days, not without military glory."

In these happy years, and in the decades that preceded them, Italian politics was a domestic game between the five principal powers, Papacy, Naples, Florence, Venice, and Milan, who treated one another's border cities as stakes. They made leagues and counter-leagues, waged innumerable little wars, fought bloodless skirmishes, flourished their swords, blew their trumpets, and made a good deal of commotion; but they were all Italians, they all knew the rules of the game, however irregular and complicated those rules might appear to an outsider, and if there were bloody heads, they were all in the family. With 1494 came the change. History seemed to turn back a thousand years; the French poured over the Alps from the northwest, the Imperial soldiers of the House of Hapsburg from the northeast, and the Spaniards from their province of Sicily to the south.

Milan, 1466-1535

Our chronicle had better begin with the duchy of Milan. There, on the death of Francesco Sforza (1466), his son, Galeazzo Maria, succeeded to the throne. This duke was a typical Italian ruler, brilliant in display, liberal in giving, harsh in taxing, interested in art and scholarship, crafty and cruel in politics, and shamelessly dissolute in private life. Fearful stories of his brutality are told. He was literally insufferable, and was assassinated (1476). It is interesting to see the great classical influence, which stimulated the arts and the humanities, quickening the spirits of young men and giving an antique lustre to murder. The story goes that a schoolmaster of Milan, who had drilled his boys in Plutarch, till Plutarch's world seemed to live again, burst out in his lecture, "Will none among my pupils rise up like Brutus and Cassius to free his country from this vile yoke and merit eternal renown?" Three of his pupils, stimulated by private wrongs to emulate the classical example, murdered the duke in a church. All three were put to death. The last to die was skewered on iron hooks and cut to pieces alive. "I know," he said, "that for my wrongdoings I have deserved these tortures and more besides, could my poor flesh endure them; but as for the noble act for which I die, that comforts my soul. Instead of repenting it, were I to live my life ten times again, ten times again to perish in these tortures, none the less would I consecrate all my life's blood, and all my might, to that noble purpose."

The results of the murder were unimportant. In politics, even more than in the arts, the classic impulse only affected details. Lodovico Sforza, nicknamed Il Moro, the late duke's brother, seized the government and supplanted the lawful heir, his young nephew, in every ducal prerogative except the title. Lodovico was a brilliant, intellectual man, devoid of moral sense; and for a time flourished in the full sunshine of the opening High Renaissance. He patronized Bramante, he employed familiarly Leonardo da Vinci. But his political talents were suited to the earlier period of domestic Italian politics. Had he lived then, his abilities, inherited from both the Sforzas and Visconti, would have kept him secure on his ducal throne; but he did not understand the larger forces of European politics.

Milan being at odds with Naples, and the other Italian powers as usual either taking part, or biding a more favourable time, Lodovico Sforza thought it would be a brilliant play, in the little Italian game, to use a foreign piece to checkmate Naples. He invited the French king, Charles VIII, who represented the claims of the House of Anjou to the Neapolitan crown, to come into Italy and take possession of his own. Other Italian politicians, with no more knowledge of European politics than Lodovico, joined in the petition. Charles VIII, an ugly little man, of scant intelligence, strong in a compact and vigorous kingdom, believing that he could play the part of a Charlemagne, accepted the suggestion with alacrity, got together an admirable army, and crossed the Alps, in the memorable year 1494. He received the respects of Lodovico and swept triumphantly down through Italy. No resistance to speak of was attempted. Florence made a treaty with him, the Pope was delighted to be able to do the like, and Naples watched her king run away and the French march in, with blended indifference and pleasure. This brilliant success, however, was a mere blaze of straw. The powers of Europe took alarm, and while the puny Charles was rioting in Naples, made a league, in which Venice, the Pope, and the double-dealing Sforza joined. Charles hurried north as fast as he could, and barely escaped across the Alps. But the episode was full of portent for Italy. The Barbarians had once again broken through the barrier which nature had set up to protect Italy; they had rediscovered what a delightful place Italy was; and the second period of Barbarian invasion had begun. We cannot dally over Milan. Sforza's treachery overreached itself. The succeeding King of France, Louis XII, a prince of Orleans, was a grandson of Gian Galeazzo Visconti's eldest daughter, and had as good a legal title to the inheritance of the Visconti as his second cousin Lodovico; though in strictness neither title had any legal value. Revenge lent strength to Louis's claim. In a few years (1499), the French again descended into the pleasant plains of Lombardy, captured Milan, took Sforza prisoner, and locked him up in a French prison for the rest of his life.

It is useless to follow the shifting ownership of Milan, tossed about in the great struggle between Francis I of France and the Emperor Charles V. The Empire espoused the cause of the Sforza heirs and put them back on the throne. Then France gained the battle of Marignano (1515) and recovered Milan, but the Empire conquered at Pavia (1525), and finally won. The male line of the Sforzas became extinct in 1535; and the dukedom of Milan, though it continued to be a nominal fief of the Empire, was annexed to the Spanish crown by Charles V (who was King of Spain as well as Emperor), and passed as a part of the Spanish inheritance to a line of Spanish kings. The Barbarian occupation of Milan was destined to last for three hundred years.

Florence, 1492-1537

Now that we have followed Milan into the service of Spanish masters, we must do a somewhat similar office for Florence. But Florence's liberty was put out in glory. The politic statesman, Lorenzo dei Medici, whose sagacity had contributed so much to the pleasant state of Italy prior to the French invasion, died in 1492. The great period of Florentine intellectual primacy ended with him, for, though Florence continued to pour forth genius, that genius no longer was gathered together at home but emigrated to honour other places. Nevertheless, she again challenges our admiration; the ancient republican city once more asserted its preëminence by a burst of moral enthusiasm. Nowhere else in Italy throughout the Renaissance was such a spectacle seen, and though the leader, Girolamo Savonarola (1452-98), was a native of Ferrara, yet it was in Florence, and among Florentines, that he kindled enthusiasm and ran his brilliant career. Savonarola was the reincarnation of a Hebrew prophet, a Florentine Habakkuk, passionately sure of the moral government of God, passionately convinced that the wickedness of Italy must bring its own punishment and purification. Shortly before Lorenzo's death he became a distinguished preacher, spoke in the cathedral, and won the ear of the people. He preached righteousness and judgment to come. He proclaimed spiritual evils and political punishments, and foretold that God would stretch forth His hand and send His avenger to punish Italy. The prophecies were so definite, and fitted the invasion of Charles VIII so accurately, that Savonarola was hailed as a prophet. In the excitement over the French invasion Lorenzo's sons were driven out, the former republican constitution reëstablished, and Savonarola raised by a burst of popular enthusiasm practically to the position of guiding and governing the city. The best way to understand Savonarola's influence is to read a few extracts from the diary of Luca Landucci, a Florentine apothecary:—

"December 14, 1494. On this day Fra Girolamo greatly laboured in the pulpit that Florence should adopt a good form of government; he has been preaching in Santa Maria del Fiore [the Duomo] every day, and this day, Sunday, he preached, and he did not want women but men, and he wanted the officers of the city, and nobody stayed in the Palace [Palazzo Vecchio, the City Hall] except the Gonfaloniere and one other; all the officials in Florence were there, and he preached about matters of state, that we ought to love and fear God and love the common weal, and that no man henceforth should wish to hold his head high or wish himself great. He always inclined to the people's side, and insisted that no blood should be shed, but that punishment should be made in some other way; and he preached like this every day....

"April, 1495. Fra Girolamo preached and said that the Virgin Mary had revealed to him how the city of Florence would become richer, more glorious, and more powerful than she had ever been, but not till after many troubles; and he spoke all this as if he were a prophet, and most of the people believed him, especially the better sort who had no political or partisan passions....

"June 17, 1495. The Frate nowadays is held in such esteem and devotion in Florence that there are many men and women who would obey him implicitly, if he should say 'walk into the fire.' Many believe him to be a prophet, and he said so himself....

"February 16 [1496], the Carnival. Fra Girolamo preached a few days ago that the children, instead of foolish pranks, throwing stones, etc., should collect alms and distribute them to the worthy poor; and, thanks to divine grace, such a change was wrought, that in place of tomfoolery the children collected alms for days beforehand, [and to-day six thousand of them or more, carrying olive branches and singing hymns, marched to the Duomo where they offered up their alms] so that good sensible men wept from tenderness and said, 'Truly this new change is the work of God.' ... I have written this because it is the fact and I saw it, and I felt the greatest happiness to have my children among those blessed innocent bands....

"August 15, 1496. Fra Girolamo preached in Santa Maria del Fiore [the Duomo, where great scaffolds had been erected which were filled with children singing], and there was so much holiness in the church, and it was so sweet to hear the children sing, above, below, and on every side, singing so simply and so modestly, that they did not seem like children. I write this because I was there and saw it and felt so much spiritual sweetness. In truth the Church was full of angels."

The friar's political enemies were strong, and the Pope, the very notable Borgia, Alexander VI, in anger and in fear, excommunicated him, and bade the Signory of Florence forbid him to preach. There was great disturbance over this action, and feeling ran to a passionate height. One of Savonarola's disciples, a foolish Dominican, challenged an adversary to the ordeal by fire; the challenge was accepted, and on the appointed day all Florence, in great excitement, flocked to the piazza. The Dominican and his adversary were there, and their respective partisans, but nothing was done. One delay followed another; there was nothing but hesitancy, disagreement as to conditions, backing and filling. The disappointed populace turned on Savonarola. They had believed him a prophet and expected to see a judgment of God. The Pope took advantage of this resentment, and demanded his trial. Savonarola was tried, and tortured. During the torture a confession was extorted from him, which was undoubtedly pieced out by forgery. Our apothecary says:—

"April 19, 1498. The confession of Fra Girolamo was read before the Council in the Great Hall, which he had written with his own hand,—he whom we held to be a prophet,—and he confessed that he was not a prophet, and had not received from God the things he preached, and he confessed to many things in the course of his preaching which were the opposite of what he had given us to understand. I was there to hear the confession read, and was bewildered and stood astonished and stupefied. My soul was in pain to see such an edifice tumble to earth because it all rested on a lie. I expected Florence to be a new Jerusalem from which should proceed laws, glory, and the example of a good life and to behold the restoration of the Church, the conversion of the infidels, and the comfort of good men, and now I behold the opposite,— and I took the medicine. In Thy will, O God, stand all things."

Savonarola was condemned to death for heresy; he was hanged, his body burned, and his ashes flung into the Arno. So ended the one moral effort of the Italian Renaissance.

After his death the Republican government endured for a time; but the Medicean faction was powerful and forced its way back in 1512. Then Lorenzo's second son, Giovanni (1475-1521), following the steps of Florentine art and humanism, went to Rome and became Pope Leo X. As Pope, he was able to strengthen his family in Florence and to extend its dominion. But Republicanism, quickened by the events then happening in Rome, flared up once more in 1527; but it was helpless before the hostile spirit of the time. Another Medici had become Pope, Clement VII, and the requirements of policy induced the calculating Emperor, Charles V, to suppress what he deemed a rebellion. Florence made a gallant defence; Michelangelo strengthened her walls, and the courage of the defenders threw a dying glory over the city. A great grandson of Lorenzo, Alessandro dei Medici, was put into power, and married to a daughter of Charles V. He was succeeded by a distant cousin, Cosimo (1537), who was honoured by His Holiness the Pope with the title of Grand Duke of Tuscany. Thus Florentine liberty was extinguished, and the Medici were established as dukes in name as well as in fact.

The Two Sicilies, 1494-1516

In the south, it will be remembered, Alfonso the Magnanimous, as the grateful humanists dubbed him, had united Sicily and the mainland; but on his death (1458) the kingdom fell asunder. Sicily, as a part of the Kingdom of Aragon, devolved on a legitimate brother, whereas Naples, claimed as a conquest, was bequeathed to a bastard son, Ferdinand the Cruel. The two kingdoms followed their respective dynasties for nearly fifty years, when Sicily came by inheritance to Ferdinand of Aragon. That crafty and eminently successful monarch, not satisfied with Castile, Granada, Sicily, and a transatlantic realm, but coveting the Kingdom of Naples, conspired with Louis XII of France, who now represented the traditional Angevin claim; the two invaded the coveted kingdom, and divided it between them (1500-1). Naturally, the rogues disagreed over the division of the spoils, and fell foul of each other. The Spaniards were triumphant, and the Kingdom of Naples was annexed to the crown of Spain. Thus the Two Sicilies were reunited under the Spanish crown, and on Ferdinand's death (1516) descended to his grandson, the Emperor Charles V. The unfortunate kingdom remained an appanage of Spain for two hundred years.

Venice, 1453-1508

In the northeast Venice still led a brilliant career, like a charming woman who has received some fatal hurt and does not know it, but instinctively lives more brilliantly than ever. Her fatal hurt was the conquest of Constantinople by the Turks (1453). At first the only obvious ill consequence was war. Venice, willy-nilly, stepped into the place of Constantinople, and became "the bulwark of the West." She waged war after war with the Turks and maintained her reputation for valour and resolution, but Turkey was too strong for her, and little by little stripped her of her long-drawn-out empire of coast and island. A far worse blow than direct war was the cutting of the great trade routes with the East, which damaged all the maritime cities of Italy, but Venice most. Turkey stopped the supplies of Venetian greatness, and slowly but surely sapped Venetian strength. On the stoppage of the straight road to Asia, the blocked current of commerce poked about for a new way, and discovered that it could reach the East by doubling the Cape of Good Hope. Commerce thus avoided Turkey, but it also abandoned the Mediterranean, great centre and source of ancient civilization, and left the maritime cities of Italy stranded, as it were, on the shores of a forsaken sea.

This doom, however, was still hidden in the obscurity of the future, and Venice appeared to be at the height of prosperity. The French ambassador, Philippe de Commines, called her "the most triumphant city I have ever seen." The Venetians were a people apart from other Italians; they never suffered from foreign invasion, or domestic revolt; they lived in isolation, maintained their own customs and usages, and enjoyed a sumptuous, opulent life, in proud security. Venice was the richest, the most comfortable, the best governed city in the world. In military strength she was commonly reckoned the first power in Italy, with the Papacy, the Kingdom of Naples, and the Duchy of Milan about equal in second rank. Venice entertained no suspicion of any seeds of decadence, and continued her greedy career of annexation on the mainland, with a haughtiness worthy of ancient Rome. She laid hands on part of Romagna, and angered the Popes who had a title thereto, which, however imperfect, was much better than the Venetian title. She provoked the Emperor Maximilian, of the House of Hapsburg, who claimed Verona as an Imperial city; and to the west she came into dangerous competition with the French invaders. These enemies, taking their cue from the piratical seizure of Naples by the French and Spanish, agreed together to partition the Venetian territory on the mainland, and invited all the powers of Europe to join them and take a share of the booty. The coalition planned a kind of joint-stock piracy. This was the League of Cambrai (1508), which stripped Venice of all her Italian territory, and threatened the city herself. The allies, however, fell out among themselves; and Venice, by biding her opportunity, in the course of time managed to recover most of her lost territory. Thus, though for a season the Barbarians brought the haughty city to her knees, she weathered the storms better than the rest of Italy, and continued to maintain her independence for three centuries to come.

The Papacy deserves a chapter to itself.

CHAPTER XXVII: THE PAPAL MONARCHY (1471-1527)

The Papacy found itself in an exceedingly difficult situation. It had to adapt an ecclesiastical system, matured in the Middle Ages, to new political systems, to new knowledge, to new thought, in short, to a new world. During its struggle with the Empire, the course before it, however arduous, had been plain, namely, to abase the Emperors; during its captivity at Avignon, its duty to return to Rome (though individual Popes were blind or indifferent) likewise had been plain; during the schism, the one end to be aimed at was union. But now everything was new, and a new policy had to be devised. There were three matters which required particular consideration: the demand for reform which came from across the Alps; the great intellectual awakening of the Renaissance; and the ambitions of the other Italian powers. For these problems the solution which the Papacy tried was twofold: to establish a firm pontifical principality, and to use the new intellectual forces as a motive power to keep itself at the head of Christendom. By a strong pontifical principality the Papacy hoped to secure itself against the covetousness of the other Italian states. By using the new intellectual forces it hoped to range them on its side, and so to choke, or at least to overcrow, the ultramontane cry for reform. One need not suppose that such a plan was consciously thought out in detail from the beginning; rather it was the course which the Papacy gradually took, partly from theory, partly under the stress of passing circumstances.

We remember that the Council of Constance closed the Great Schism, and sent Martin V (1417-31) back to Rome as sole Pope. His pontificate marks the end of the old Republican commune, which had made so much trouble for Popes and Emperors in days past, and therefore marks the first definite stage in the transformation of the Papacy into a local secular power. Rome, although she did not deny herself an occasional outbreak in memory, as it were, of good old days, settled down into a papal city.

The most interesting part of the papal story is the process that went on within the Church. The intolerable burden of ecclesiastical taxation, the growth of heresy, and the degeneration of the clergy, as well as the Great Schism, had roused Europe to a sense that something must be done, and Europe attempted the old remedy of Ecumenical Councils. At Constance the question of general reform had come up, but the papal party had managed to prevent action. At the next Council, held at Basel, internal difficulties appeared still more plainly. Party lines were sharply drawn; the ultramontanes, as before, wished to subject the Popes to the supremacy of Councils, to substitute an ecclesiastical aristocracy of bishops in place of a papal monarchy, and, as it were, transfer the centre of ecclesiastical gravity from Rome across the Alps. Feeling ran so high that the Council split in two. Part followed the Pope to Italy, and part stayed in Basel and elected an anti-pope (1439). It looked as if schism had come again, but the danger passed. The anti-pope resigned; unity was restored and lasted for seventy years.

Nicholas V, as we have seen, hoped to maintain the Papacy at the head of Christendom by means of the new intellectual forces. Such a conception was purely Italian, and showed plainly enough that the Papacy had ceased to represent Christendom, had ceased to be the real head of a

Universal Church, and had become a purely Italian institution. While Nicholas and his successors were thinking of culture and of becoming Italian princes, the pious ultramontanes, comparatively indifferent to the intellectual excitement of the Renaissance, were thinking of sin and of the remedy for sin. The papal Curia was clever, but did not foresee that to subordinate the old conception of the Papacy as the head of the religious and ecclesiastical organization of Europe to the new conception of it as an Italian principality would surely alienate the Teutonic peoples; it did not foresee that the Renaissance, with its spirit of examination, investigation, criticism, with its encouragement of the free play of the human mind, was necessarily preparing the way for the Reformation. But the Curia perceived the opposite difficulties, to which we are generally blind, that unless the Papacy did establish itself as a temporal power, it might well be reduced to another Babylonish Captivity by a king of Naples, a duke of Milan, or even by some condottiere. And it perceived that other difficulty as well, that if the Papacy turned against the intellectual movement, the intellectual movement would, in self-defence, turn against the Papacy.

The Popes did indeed seek to revive the old rôle of the Papacy in one respect. They tried to arouse the sentiment of Christendom against the invading Turks, and to lead a crusade themselves. But the time for such a course had passed. The kings and princes of Europe were busy with their own kingdoms and principalities and would not budge; and the Papacy was obliged to give up the plan. Discouraged by this failure it naturally turned to the new theory of a little papal kingdom and vigorously put the theory into practice. The three Popes who accomplished this task were Francesco della Rovere, Sixtus IV (1471-84), Rodrigo Borgia, Alexander VI (1493-1503), and Giuliano della Rovere, Julius II (1503-13). Their careers must be looked at more closely.

Sixtus IV was the son of a peasant. Educated by the Franciscans, he became distinguished as a scholar in theology, philosophy, and ecclesiastical affairs, and was chosen general of the order. When Pope, after a last futile attempt to start a crusade, Sixtus openly abandoned the rôle of Pontiff of Christendom and became an Italian prince. Energetic and masterful, he set to work to consolidate the loose and insubordinate papal territories into a compact state. The task was not easy, and one of the obstacles in his way was lack of men whom he could trust. It was of little advantage to gather together an army, or to capture a city, if the papal general or governor found his own interests opposed to papal interests. Loyalty was held in scant esteem by Italians of the Renaissance. Sixtus met the difficulty by employing his nephews. This policy was by no means the beginning of papal nepotism, but these nephews happened to be young men with marked tastes for greed, ferocity, and dissipation, and brought the system into especial notoriety. To one nephew the Pope gave a cardinal's hat, four bishoprics, an abbey, a patriarchate, as well as free access to the papal treasury. When this young man had died of dissipation, the post of chief favourite descended to his brother. For him the Pope procured a wife from the ducal house of Sforza, and began to carve a dukedom in Romagna, with the intention of adding slices cut from the neighbouring states. This young man was arrogant, ignorant, and brutal, with no interests except ambition and the chase. In due course he was murdered. Whatever effect nepotism of this character produced across the Alps, it served certain purposes in Italy. Sixtus made himself feared, and advanced the project of a papal kingdom to a point where his successors were able to take it up and complete it.

Sixtus also pursued Nicholas's plan of making Rome the first city of the world in art and magnificence. He brought together architects and artists, and patronized art and literature. But this aspect of the plan to maintain the Papacy at the head of Christian Europe belongs rather to the story of the high Renaissance, and must be postponed to the next chapter.

We may pass over the next Pope, who was not distinguished except for a frank recognition of his illegitimate children, and for what then appeared a whimsical desire to maintain peace, and proceed to the notorious Rodrigo Borgia, Alexander VI. It was in Borgia's pontificate that the French invasion of 1494 took place. This introduction of a new and terrible element into Italian politics frightened him as well as other Italian rulers, for he knew that the Papal State would never be strong enough to resist single-handed such an army as that of Charles VIII, and he tried to form a union of the Italian powers for common defence. His policy met little success, especially as he himself, seeing advantages to be gained from a French alliance, whirled about, granted to the French king a dispensation for divorce, to the French favourite a cardinal's hat, and made a separate treaty for himself (1499). Borgia did no more than any other Italian prince would have done, but he must bear his share of the responsibility. It was a deliberate sacrifice of Italian for papal interests. Whether that was justifiable or not is another matter. The Pope wished to establish a Pontifical State, and acted in the manner which he thought would be most likely to achieve success.

Borgia also followed the example set by Sixtus, and raised his family to power and rank, partly, of course, from affection, but partly in order to strengthen the Papacy. His task was to reduce the papal vassals in the Pontifical States to obedience and so to create a strong central government. The instrument he employed was his son Cæsar Borgia. This brilliant young man has won a great reputation, owing in large measure to Machiavelli's admiration. He was an athletic, handsome, taciturn man, quick, cunning, and cruel. He began his career in the Church, but at the time of his father's reconciliation with France, gave up his cardinal's hat, and was created duke by the French king. Cæsar made an excellent instrument for rooting out the disobedient vassals of the Papal State. They were crafty, greedy, and false; he was craftier, greedier, and falser than they. He dispossessed them with ruthless vigour, and established himself in their stead. His energy and success were extraordinary, and frightened other Italian rulers. None knew how far his ambition might stretch, or how far the Papacy might be able to push him. The direct military power of the Pontifical State was not very great and could readily be measured, but the indirect power of the Papacy as head of the Christian Church was vague and alarming. Nevertheless, Cæsar's principality, which rested wholly on the Papacy, fell to pieces when his father died.

Borgia's attitude towards the arts belongs to the next chapter; but in respect to them as well as to the Pontifical State, he followed what I have called the twofold policy of the Popes of the Renaissance. That policy undoubtedly had its advantages; but it also had its disadvantages, and these appear more conspicuous in Borgia's pontificate than in any other. The establishment of papal dominion, as we have seen, encouraged, if it did not necessitate, nepotism; and nepotism involved prodigality and dissipation. The Popes used their families to strengthen their position; and the upstart families, giddy with sudden wealth and power, misbehaved. The nephews of Sixtus rendered some service to the Papacy, but they caused scandal. Cæsar Borgia rendered greater services, and caused still greater scandal. The other branch of the twofold policy, by a different path, led to the same result. Patronage of arts and letters involved great expense and encouraged luxurious tastes; luxury led to idleness, and idleness to vice. The Roman atmosphere had never been favourable to spiritual life, and now, surcharged with the classical spirit of the Renaissance, practically extinguished religion.

For centuries the Roman Curia had been a butt for the arrows of satire. The minnesingers of Germany, the troubadours of Provence, had paused in their amorous ditties to compose bitter gibes against the greed and luxurious life of the great Roman prelates. Taunts such as this became household phrases: Curia Romana non quaerit ovem sine lana. Dante had put priest, prelate, and Pope into hell. Petrarch had written scathing verses:—

Slaves to wine, debauch, and gluttony, All evil that besets the world to-day,Nest of treachery, wherein is hatched

School of false thought, temple of heresy, etc.Well-head of woe, and baiting place of wrath,

One of the best tales in the "Decameron" turns on the conversion of a Jew, who goes to Rome, sees the conduct of Pope and cardinals, and becomes convinced that only a Divine Church can support so staggering a burden. In Borgia's time the Curia outdid itself, and Borgia led the way. He acknowledged his children, and lavished papal revenues upon them; he bestowed a cardinal's hat on Alexander Farnese, founder of the Farnese family, for the sake of Giulia Farnese, his frail sister; he sanctioned ballets and theatricals of a scandalous nature in the Vatican palace, and encouraged his sons and his cardinals in a dissolute life. Vice was not all; the odour of crime infected the air. The Pope's son, the Duke of Gandia, was murdered, so was his son-in-law, husband of his daughter Lucrezia. Cardinals died mysteriously. The common voice, whispering low in Rome and loud elsewhere, ascribed these murders to Cæsar Borgia. It appeared as if the Pope believed the charges himself. "Cæsar," he said, "is a good-natured man, but he cannot tolerate affronts." Lucrezia, too, became the object of the grossest slanders. No doubt common gossip then, as always, raised a tree of falsehood from a mustard grain of truth; but credulity accepted every accusation as true. North of the Alps the simple-minded Germans shuddered and crossed themselves. Even the Romans were shocked. When the Pope died, no man would touch his body; it was dragged by a rope fastened to its foot from the bed to the grave, and there tumbled in. No one doubted that his soul had gone to hell.

Alexander VI violated every rule of domestic morality; nevertheless, Pope Julius II (1503-13) violated the sacred character of priest as fundamentally, though in a much less repulsive way. Julius, a nephew of Sixtus IV, was a fiery soldier, a high-aspiring prince, a man of great qualities, impatient and magnificent. Had he been duke of Milan or King of Naples, he would have presented a noble figure; but a Pope armed cap-à-pie, entering a conquered city through the breach battered by his cannon, was as clear a defiance of the evangelical spirit of the reformers as the private profligacy of Pope Borgia.

Julius pursued the twofold policy of the Papacy with greater zeal and greater success than any of his predecessors. His furious energy completed the work of making the incohesive states of the Church into a compact principality; and he is the real founder of the absolute Papal State, the first real Pope-king. He achieved equal success in the other branch of the policy, and revelled in the kindred spirit of the High Renaissance. Julius exalted Rome to the place of first city in the world; and if the world had asked for art from the Papacy instead of asking for religion, it would have been abundantly satisfied. But Germany was thinking of sin, of vice, of simony, of taxation, and was becoming conscious of an extreme national antipathy to Italian rule; and when a young German monk, like Martin Luther, went to Rome, instead of taking pleasure in the architecture, painting, and sculpture that adorned the city, he was horrified at the lack of religion.

Julius, however, was entitled to a sense of accomplishment at his death. He left to his successors a little kingdom in the middle of Italy, and he had made Rome the centre of the arts. Not till the days of his successors did the failure of that policy appear. By a kind of poetic justice the utter failure of art to satisfy the demand for reform, for purity, for religion, was proved during the pontificates of the two Medici, Leo X and Clement VII. The Medici had patronized the arts, both in Florence and in Rome, and the arts repaid the Medici with enjoyment and renown. But the Medici had done nothing for the spirit of reform; on the contrary, they had helped crush Savonarola, and the spirit of reform turned upon them. Germany hoisted the standard of secession during the pontificate of Leo, and an army of the unfaithful sacked Rome during that of Clement.

Leo X was a fat, clever, cultivated man, with no great virtues and no real vices. "Let us enjoy the Papacy since God has given it to us," is the sentiment put into his mouth, and serves to characterize his reign. Bred in his father's intellectual circle, and a member of the luxurious Roman society, Leo shared the tastes of both. He was a connoisseur of works of art, and derived genuine æsthetic pleasure from them; he was also fond of agreeable company, good cookery, the chase, and most forms of social amusement. His political conduct was not of much real consequence, as matters had gone too far. In the interminable struggle between Charles V and Francis I, the Papacy tried to hold a balance of power, and bargained with both sides; but, as the Spaniards, in possession of both Milan and Naples, were the stronger, the Papacy generally found its advantage on that side. As to the larger matter of the ecclesiastical unity of Christendom there was practically nothing to be done. The causes which split the Teutonic world from the Latin were already matured. It was too late to stop the Reformation. Luther might have been dealt with more shrewdly, but the forces behind him could not have been kept in check. Leo excommunicated Luther (1520), and the Imperial Diet at Worms condemned him and his doctrine, but the unity of the Church was doomed.

To Leo succeeded his cousin Clement VII, after a brief pontificate by the last foreign Pope. Clement was incompetent, and failed to realize the gravity of his situation; neither he nor Rome understood the crisis they had reached. The prevailing state of mind may be inferred from this extract from the diary of a young Roman burgher: "I saw this Pope the first day of May, 1525, come in the morning of the Feast of SS. Philip and James to the Church of the Holy Apostles, and after celebrating high mass, remain all day and night in the palace of the Colonna.... That day it was an old and foolish custom in the Colonna palace (which connects with the church and has windows looking in it), to throw various kinds of fowls and animals into the church to the people who were there, all of the lowest sort. They also put a pig in the middle of the church up high, and whoever was able to climb up and take it, won it; and on top of the roof were kegs and pots of water, which they poured on the persons who climbed up. The amusement of those gentlemen, and of the rest who looked on, was to see the crowd in a mess, battling, shrieking, pushing, shoving, like beasts,—a merrymaking not becoming in a church or any sacred edifice." The diary adds: "Now let people learn to know the souls of the great and especially of priests, how wicked, deceitful, and false they are, how full of fraud and knavery." There were plenty of other facts to prove this conclusion. The merrymaking was doomed to cease.

The incompetent Pope was totally at a loss what policy to follow, not knowing whether it was better to incline towards the Empire or to France. He shifted at the wrong time, joined a league against the Empire, then wriggled and shuffled, and so drew upon himself and the devoted city the punishment due to a long course of wickedness. The Imperial army, a ruffian host of Germans (many of them Lutherans), Spaniards, and Italians, under the command of the traitor Bourbon, was encamped in the north; the unpaid soldiers clamoured for plunder, and Bourbon led them to Rome, carried the neglected walls by assault, and put the city to sack. Rome was a little city, with perhaps 90,000 inhabitants, but rich in the oblations and tribute money of Christendom; the churches were decked with gold and silver, the palaces stuffed with precious paintings, tapestries, and ornaments of every kind. Popes, cardinals, and princes had rivalled one another in accumulations of works of art and articles of luxury. Though license, profligacy, and crime had then shut out Rome from the sympathy of the world, it is impossible to read to-day of the horrors of the sack—men murdered, mothers, daughters, nuns outraged, old men and priests brutally insulted, churches and sacred relics defiled—without the sharpest pity. For eight days the devilish work went on, and but 30,000 inhabitants were left, so many had fled, or been killed, or made prisoners (1527).

Terrible was the punishment that Clement witnessed,—Rome sacked, the liberty of Italy taken away, the Roman Catholic Church rent in two.

CHAPTER XXVIII: THE HIGH RENAISSANCE (1499-1521)

We are now at liberty to return to the great intellectual and artistic movement that lifted Italy to the primacy in Europe, and reached its zenith in the period of time to which the last two chapters have been devoted. This is the culminating period, in which the greatest masters did their work, and separates the earlier and more experimental stage that preceded it from the later stage of exaggeration and decadence which followed. The movement swept all the arts along with it. It produced the greatest men in literature since Petrarch, the greatest architects since the Gothic masters of the Ile de France, the greatest sculptors since Praxiteles, the greatest painters that ever were.

Italian literature cannot compare with English literature or French in compass, variety, richness, or delicacy. Indeed, except for Dante, it would have rather a thin and tinkling sound. Nevertheless, in the High Renaissance it roused itself brilliantly. Niccolò Machiavelli was the ablest writer on the policy of government between Aristotle and Burke. Guicciardini was the first modern historian. Count Baldassare Castiglione's "Book of the Courtier" is as singularly excellent in its way as Boswell's "Life of Johnson." Of this book, which portrays fashionable society at the elegant court of Urbino, Tasso says: "So long as there shall be princes and courts, so long as ladies and gentlemen shall meet in society, so long as virtue and courtesy shall abide in our hearts, the name of Castiglione will be held in honour." The book purports to be a series of conversations between the duchess and her guests concerning the proper qualities of a perfect gentleman. This society, no doubt, is a little affected, stilted, and conceited, but it is dignified, well-behaved, and high-minded. These people discuss deportment, athletics, propriety of speech, whether one must keep within the Tuscan vocabulary of Petrarch and Boccaccio or may make use of the vernacular spoken elsewhere, whether painting or sculpture is the nobler art, what a gentleman's dress should be, and so on. The discussion proceeds to the proper behaviour of a lady, and by natural steps to love. Bembo, a famous littérateur, here takes the floor, plunges into Platonic ideas, and argues that the higher love, governed by reason, is better than lower love, and will lead to contemplation of universal beauty; but that even this stage of love is imperfect, and the lover must mount higher still, until his soul, purified by philosophy and spiritual life, sees the light of angelic beauty and, ravished by the splendour of that light, becomes intoxicated and beside itself from passion to lose itself in the light. "Let us, then, direct all the thoughts and forces of our soul to this most sacred light, which shows us the way that leads to heaven; and following after it, let us lay aside the passions wherewith we were clothed at our fall, and by the stairway that bears the shadow of sensual beauty on its lowest step, let us mount to the lofty mansion where dwells the heavenly, lovely, and true beauty, which lies hidden in the inmost secret recesses of God, so that profane eyes cannot behold it," etc. This may savour somewhat too much of Platonic rhetoric, but such feelings were genuine, emotionally genuine, even if they proved evanescent in practice; they were familiar to Lorenzo dei Medici and his friends, and to the nobler spirits throughout Italy, and are as characteristic of the period as its cruelty, treachery, or sensuality. The effect of such cultivated circles upon art must have been great; they gave artists encouragement, sympathy, employment, and by the union of fashion and intelligence helped educate the taste of a larger public. It must be remembered that both Bramante and Raphael came from Urbino.

Poetry, with the delightful spontaneity and capriciousness of Italian genius, chose Ferrara, the home of the House of Este, to hang its laurels in. There Matteo Boiardo wrote the "Orlando Innamorato" (Roland in Love). This poem is an epic of chivalry concerning Charlemagne's court, and deals seriously, and yet at times ironically, with the subject of Roland's love for the beautiful Angelica. It was left unfinished, and Lodovico Ariosto (1474-1533) picked up the thread and carried it on, far more brilliantly and far more ironically, under the title "Orlando Furioso" (Roland Crazed). Ariosto's poem, which was immensely popular, was intended to entertain, and it succeeded; its variety, wit, irony, sarcasm, and levity make it entertaining even now. Inferior in moral and sensuous beauty to Spenser's "Faerie Queene," it is far easier to read. Its interest for us lies in the light it sheds on the intellectual state of educated Italians of the Renaissance, especially in regard to religion. Biblical allusions, sacred north of the Alps, are lugged in to give a touch of humour, as, for instance, where one of the knights, Astolfo, goes on a search for Roland's lost wits and meets St. John the Evangelist, who drives him to the moon in Elijah's chariot; or where, in another passage, St. Michael finds that the goddess of Discord has not obeyed his commands, "the angel seized her by the hair, kicked and pounded her incessantly, broke a cross over her head, till Discord embraced the knees of the divine envoy and howled for mercy." Ariosto, himself, conformed to the rites of the Church. Like most educated Italians he accepted them as conventional forms, tinged possibly with supernatural power, and kept ecclesiastical ideas wholly separate from moral ideas. His sceptical, ironical, Epicurean attitude towards non-material things is characteristic of the decadence of this period in which mental activity had outgrown morality.

Ariosto was a gentleman of birth and position. He spent most of his life in the service of his princes, the House of Este. In later life he withdrew from their employment, and lived in his own house, parva sed apta (small but suitable), to which the literary pious still make pilgrimages. He wrote the "Orlando Furioso" between 1505 and 1515, and thereafter devoted most of his leisure to improving and polishing it. Basking in the sunshine of fashionable admiration, he little suspected that another man, who had spent his life in mighty feats of architecture, painting, and sculpture, would in his old age write sonnets that should be read and reread like a breviary by serious men and women who passed his own luxurious rhetoric unheeded. Michelangelo's sonnets (some of which were written to Vittoria Colonna) are the noblest embodiment of those high ideas of love which came down from Plato to the philosophers of the Palazzo Medici in Florence and the courtiers at the ducal palace in Urbino. They are crammed to bursting with passionate intensity, and in that respect have no equals, even in English.

In the fine arts the High Renaissance has a score of famous men. Among them three or four stand head and shoulders above their fellows. Each is marked by extraordinary individuality of talents, character, and disposition: Michelangelo by passionate fury—terribilità; Raphael by sweet serenity; Bramante by his even commingling of poise and ardour; Leonardo by his noble curiosity.

Of Leonardo, Vasari says: "Sometimes according to the course of nature, sometimes beyond and above it, the greatest gifts rain down from heavenly influences upon the bodies of men, and crowd into one individual beauty, grace, and excellence in such superabundance that to whatever that man shall turn, his very act is so divine, that, surpassing the work of all other men, it makes manifest that it is by the special gift of God, and not by human art. This was true of Leonardo da Vinci; who, beside a physical beauty beyond all praise, put an infinite grace into whatever he did, and such was his excellence, that to whatever difficult things his mind turned he easily solved them." Leonardo (1452-1519) was a Florentine. He was trained by the subtle Verrocchio, from whom he learned the smile, if it be a smile, on the faces of his portraits of women. After leaving Verrocchio's workshop he went to Lombardy, where he spent sixteen years at the court of Milan. There he did a hundred different things: he modelled a great equestrian statue of Francesco Sforza (since destroyed), painted portraits, drew architectural designs,—for a cupola, a staircase, a bathroom, a triumphal arch, etc.,—executed hydraulic works, studied the cultivation of the grape, and played on his silver lyre. In the refectory of a Dominican monastery he painted his fresco of The Last Supper. One of the novices, who watched this handsome young painter at work, says that sometimes he would dash up the scaffold, brush in hand, put a few touches and hurry down; sometimes he would paint from sunrise to sunset without stopping even to eat; sometimes he would stand for hours contemplating the different figures. After Sforza's fall, Leonardo left Milan, and for a time took service with Cæsar Borgia as military engineer and architect. He subsequently returned to Florence, and finally went to France, where he died.

Little remains of all that Leonardo planned. A half-destroyed fresco, a few easel pictures, some incomparable drawings, some treatises on his arts, some apothegms, are enough, however, to justify his fame. One of his apothegms, Tu, o Iddio, tutto ci vendi a prezzo di fatica (Thou, O God, sellest us everything at the price of hard work), is but poorly borne out by his own prodigal portion of genius, which rather supports Vasari's view that God makes special gifts. Very rarely has any man received the native endowment of Leonardo da Vinci.

The greatest architect of the High Renaissance was Bramante of Urbino. He, like Leonardo, worked in Milan during the resplendent reign of Lodovico Sforza. There he did much charming work and imposed his personality on Lombard architecture; but his great reputation was made in Rome, whither he went, drawn by the great Romeward flow of art, when the French invasion drove the fine arts from Milan. In Rome, Bramante became the papal architect. He shares with Raphael and Michelangelo the honour of making St. Peter's basilica and the Vatican palace what they are. He also built a little building, whose historical importance is ludicrously out of proportion to its size, it being as little as St. Peter's is big. It is a tiny circular temple in the court of a church on the Janiculum hill across the Tiber. On the ground floor a Doric colonnade encircles the temple, on the second story a balustrade. A dome, capped by a lantern, covers the whole. It is the first building which fully reproduced the style and spirit of antiquity. It set the fashion for the architecture of the sixteenth century, and determined, among other indirect and not altogether happy results, the plan of St. Paul's Cathedral in London and the Capitol in

Washington.

It was not chance which took Bramante, Raphael, and Michelangelo to Rome. They went because the papal court, pursuing its policy of maintaining the Papacy at the head of Christendom by means of culture, summoned them to come. Rome never produced great artists. She never was artistic, any more than she had been spiritual. But just as in earlier times she had drawn spiritual forces to herself and used them, so now she attracted to herself and used the artistic forces of Italy. She had been making ready for years; step by step as she had become more secular, she had also become more artistic, more intellectual. For seventy years every Pope contributed to this end. Eugenius IV employed distinguished humanists as his secretaries, and invited the most notable painters and sculptors to Rome. Nicholas V conceived the splendid scheme of making Rome the mistress of the world's culture. Pius II, Æneas Sylvius Piccolomini, was the most eminent man of letters of his age. Paul II was a virtuoso in objects of art and increased the grandeur of the papal court. Sixtus IV improved the city, built the Sistine Chapel, and employed Botticelli, Perugino, Signorelli, Ghirlandaio, and Rosselli to decorate it. Innocent VIII brought Mantegna from Padua and Pinturicchio from Perugia to embellish the Vatican palace. Pope Borgia made Pinturicchio his court painter; and that charming master decorated the papal apartments in the Vatican with the great bull of the Borgia crest, and with portraits of the Pope's children and (so Vasari says) of the lovely Giulia Farnese as the Virgin with the Pope worshipping her.

Popes and cardinals felt the great movement and many strove to lead it, but the master figure of the Renaissance at Rome was the fiery Julius II, whose plans in the arts were even more grandiose than in politics. He was the centre of this period, as Cosimo and Lorenzo had been in their generations. Less astute than Cosimo, far less subtle and accomplished than Lorenzo, he was a much more heroic leader than either. His hardy, weather-beaten face in Raphael's portrait, with its strong, well-shaped features, shows his imperious, arrogant, irascible, and yet noble, nature. This Pontiff brought to Rome the greatest genius of the Renaissance, Michelangelo, bade him build for him a monumental tomb, more splendid than any tomb ever built, twelve yards high and proportionately wide and deep, and decked with two or three score statues. Such a gigantic monument could not have found room in the old basilica of St. Peter's, and therefore, as St. Peter's was the proper place for it, it became necessary to proceed with the larger plans of Nicholas V. Piecing and patching did not suit Julius. He discussed plans with his architects Bramante and Giuliano da San Gallo, and then resolved to pull down the old basilica, founded by Constantine and Silvester, despite its thousand years of sacred associations, and build a new church in its place. Bramante's fiery enthusiasm for great designs matched the Pope's. Satire suggested that in heaven he would say to St. Peter, "I'll pull down this Paradise of yours and build another, a much finer and pleasanter place for the blessed saints to live in." He designed the new church in the form of a Greek cross with a cupola, proposing, as it were, to lift the dome of the Pantheon on the basilica of Constantine, an enormous ruin in the Roman Forum. This gigantic plan befitted the new papal scheme of making Rome the head of Europe and the Papacy the head of culture. The corner-stone was laid on April 18, 1506, and the old building was demolished piecemeal, the choir first, the nave last; and in its place, as demolition proceeded bit by bit, the cathedral now standing rose, slowly lifting its great bulk in the air, and finally reached completion and consecration in 1626. The greatest architects of Italy succeeded one another as masters of the works, Bramante, Giuliano da San Gallo from Florence, Fra Giocondo from Verona, Raphael, Antonio da San Gallo the younger, Baldassare Peruzzi from Siena, and Michelangelo, who, when an old man, took charge and designed the dome.

The Vatican was altered according to Bramante's plans in order to make it a fit abode for the head of cultured Christendom: Michelangelo painted his frescoes on the ceiling of the Sistine Chapel (1508-12); and Raphael began to paint the stanza della segnatura. Raphael, the most charming figure in the world of art, was equally charming in life. Vasari says: "Among his exceptional gifts I take notice of one of such rare excellence that I marvel within myself. Heaven gave him power in our art to produce an effect most contrary to the humours of us painters, and it is this: the artists and artisans (I do not refer only to those of meaner sort, but to those who are ambitious to be great—and art produces many of this complexion) who worked in his atelier were so united and had such mutual good-will, that all jealousy and crossness were extinguished on seeing him, and every mean and spiteful thought vanished from their minds. Such unity was never seen before. And this was because they were overcome both by his courtesy and his art, but more by the genius of his good nature, which was so full of kindness and overflowing with charity, that not only men, but even the beasts almost worshipped him."

At this time, too, classic art, owing to the discovery of antique statues, had its fullest effect. The Nile, now in the Vatican, had been found in a Roman garden, the Apollo Belvedere in a vineyard near the city, and the Laocoön and many others here and there. Of the discovery of the Laocoön a record remains. "I was at the time a boy in Rome," wrote Francesco, son of Giuliano da San Gallo, the architect, "when one day it was announced to the Pope that some excellent statues had been dug up out of the ground in a grape-patch near the church of Santa Maria Maggiore. The Pope immediately sent a groom to Giuliano da San Gallo to tell him to go directly and see what it was. Michelangelo Buonarroti was often at our house, and at the moment chanced to be there; accordingly my father invited him to accompany us. I rode behind my father on his horse, and thus we went over to the place designated. We had scarcely dismounted and glanced at the figures, when my father cried out, 'It is the Laocoön of which Pliny speaks!' The labourers immediately began digging to get the statue out; after having looked at them very carefully, we went home to supper, talking all the way of antiquity."

Thus these various forces—the discovery of antique statues, the passion for art, the eager Italian intellect, the conception of Rome as the mistress of culture, the character of Julius II and the genius of Bramante, Michelangelo, and Raphael—worked together to cover the Papacy with a pagan glory in its time of religious need. On the other hand, as these monumental works required vast sums of money, the sale of indulgences and the exaction of tribute buzzed on more rapidly than ever.

Leo X (1513-21) has given his name to this age of papal culture, but he was not entitled to the honour; he had the inborn Medicean interest and enjoyment in intellectual matters, a nice taste, and some delicacy of perception, but it needs no more than a look at his fat jowl in Raphael's portrait to see that he could not have been a motive force in a great period. He stands on an historic eminence as the last Pope to wield the Italian sceptre over all Europe, the last to send his tax-collectors from Sicily to England, from Spain to Norway, the last to enjoy the full heritage of Imperial Rome.

CHAPTER XXIX: ITALY AND THE CATHOLIC REVIVAL (1527-1563)

We have now come to the beginning of long centuries of national degradation, and one has a general sense of passing from a glorious garden into a series of gas-lit drawing-rooms, somewhat over-decorated, where naughty princes amuse themselves with bagatelles. We must glance at the political degradation first.

The struggle between the Barbarians of France and Spain for mastery in Italy, of which we spoke in the last political chapter, was practically decided by the battle of Pavia (1525), in which the French king lost all but life and honour. France was most reluctant to acquiesce in defeat, and from time to time marched her troops across the Alps into unfortunate Piedmont, sometimes of her own notion, and sometimes at the invitation of an Italian state; but the Spanish grip was too strong to be shaken off. From this time on Italian politics were determined by the pleasure of foreign kings. Two treaties between France and Spain, that of Cambrai (1529) and that of Cateau-Cambrésis (1559), embodied the results of their bargains and their wars. The sum and substance of them was a practical abandonment by France of her Italian claims, and the map of Italy was drawn to suit Spain.

Milan was governed by Spanish governors, Naples and Sicily by Spanish viceroys. The business of a Spanish viceroy, then as always, was to raise money. Taxes were oppressive. It was said that in Sicily the royal officials nibbled, in Naples they ate, and in Milan they devoured. In addition to regular taxes, special imposts were laid on various occasions,—when a new king succeeded to the throne, when a royal heir was born, when war was waged against the Lutherans in Germany or the pirates in Africa. In the south, where the people were less intelligent and laborious, oppressive taxation and unwise government caused a gradual increase of ignorance and poverty, and left as a legacy to the present day the conditions from which spring the Mafia of Sicily and the Camorra of Naples.

In Florence the sagacious Cosimo I (1537-74) ruled with prudence and severity. He understood that his position depended on his fidelity to Spain and the Papacy, and acted accordingly. He married a Spanish lady, Eleanora of Toledo, daughter to the viceroy of Naples, took up his ducal residence first in the Palazzo Vecchio, where there are many remembrances of his duchess, and afterwards in the great palace, begun by Luca Pitti, across the Arno. He reduced Siena, once Florence's dangerous rival, to subjection, and crushed out the last traces of republican sentiment in his duchy. He employed Vasari to design the Uffizi, completed the edifice that holds the Laurentian library, and led as magnificent a life as a due regard for his purse would allow. In short, he was what one would expect an unrefined member of the Casa Medici to be; and when one recollects that his grandmother was a Sforza of Milan, all expectations based on heredity are amply satisfied. Cosimo I left a long line of descendants to sit upon his grand-ducal throne. Their marble effigies at the head of the stairway in the Uffizi tell their story. The brutal Sforza vigour and the elegant Medicean astuteness could not save them from sharing in the general degeneracy that spread like a blight over all Italy. However, one must remember that they did collect the finest picture gallery in the world and housed it in the Uffizi and Pitti palaces.

North of Tuscany the petty duchies of Ferrara, Urbino, Modena, Parma, and Mantua formed a little ducal coterie, very characteristic of the next two centuries. The Papacy indeed swallowed up Ferrara (1598) and Urbino (1631), but the House of Este of Ferrara moved on to Modena, and remained there till Napoleon's time. In Parma, Pope Paul III (1534-50), our old acquaintance Alexander Farnese, a careful father as well as a lucky brother, established his son as duke. This son was bad, and believed to be worse, so the nobles of Parma murdered him; but his descendants made good their title, and the little duchy of Parma, with its palace, its custom-house, its barracks, and its pictures, stepped forth as one of the petty states of the peninsula, and endured till the Union of Italy. Genoa and Lucca were permitted to remain republics.

Up in the northwest we get our first definite notions of Savoy. This duchy, built up piecemeal, was a composite state, which included a good deal of Piedmont, and portions of what are now France and Switzerland, and, unfortunately, lay directly in the way of the French armies on their marches into Italy. During the wars of Francis I and Charles V, the Duke of Savoy hopefully attempted to maintain neutrality, and, in consequence, lost all. France deemed it more convenient to own her line of march, and annexed Savoy; and for twenty years Piedmont was both camping-ground and battleground for the contending nations. It looked as if Savoy would be blotted from the map of Europe; but Duke Emanuele Filiberto (1553-80), Iron Head, an accomplished soldier, had the sense to take the winning side. He served in the Spanish army, and, in the Peace of Cateau-Cambrésis, as his share secured the restoration of his duchy. That portion of this duke's policy which concerns us especially is that he gave Piedmont precedence over his French and Swiss provinces, established the seat of government at Turin, put the university there and brought men of letters and science, substituted Italian for Latin in public documents, and proclaimed himself an Italian prince and Savoy an Italian state. He gave Savoy the general character which it has always retained. He checked the priests, built up the army, reformed the law, converted the old feudal dominion into an absolute autocracy, and started his dukedom on the course which ultimately enabled it to play its great part in the liberation of Italy in the nineteenth century. Emanuele Filiberto is reputed one of Italy's national heroes.

Venice had already recovered most of the territories on the mainland of Italy wrenched from her by the League of Cambrai, but in the East the Turks steadily took away city, island, and province. After a long period of war, one gallant exploit gilded the fortunes of the losing side. A league against the Turks was effected between Spain, the Papacy, and Venice, and the united fleets, under the supreme command of Don John of Austria, won the renowned sea-fight off Lepanto (1571); but except for chopping off a goodly number of infidel heads and limbs, little was accomplished. In this battle a young Spanish soldier, Miguel de Cervantes, lost an arm. Soon afterwards peace was made on terms hard for the Venetians, but beneficent in that it was destined to last for seventy years.

We now come to the Papacy, and there, in extraordinary contrast to the degeneration and decay all around, we find militant vigour and energy. This phenomenon is so remarkable that we must glance back at the perils through which the Papacy had passed. Ever since the fall of the Empire (when the political union of Italy and Germany broke in two) disruptive forces had been at work to break the ecclesiastical union, until at last, in the pontificate of Leo X, Martin Luther affixed his theses concerning indulgences to the door of the Castle Church at Wittenberg, burnt the papal bull, and threw off his allegiance. The North of Europe followed him. The record of the Papacy had been utter failure and worse. It had smeared itself from head to foot with simony, nepotism, and vice; it had cast religion to the winds. No expression of indignation would have been adequate without the sack of Rome. A statesman might well have predicted that all Europe would dismember and suppress the Papacy and adopt a system of national churches. Nevertheless, at the end of the century the Papacy stood erect and vigorous, shorn indeed of universal empire, but reëstablished, the Order of Jesus at its right, the Holy Inquisition at its left, draped in piety by the Council of Trent, and hobnobbing on even terms with kings. The process which effected this change is called the Counter-reformation, or the Catholic Reaction. That process was a happy blending of virtue, bigotry, and policy. Borne upward and onward by the forces of reform and conservatism, the Modern Papacy rose triumphant on the ruins of the Papacy of the Renaissance.

The same spirit that caused the Reformation in the North started the Catholic Revival in the South. A wave, comparable to the old movement for Church reform in Hildebrand's time, swept over the Catholic Church, and lifted the reformers within the Church into power. The South emulated the North. Catholic zeal rivalled Protestant ardour. Bigotry followed zeal. Moreover, a reformed Papacy found ready allies. The logical consequence of Protestantism was personal independence in religion, and the next logical step was personal independence in politics. Protestant subjects, more especially where their rulers were Catholics, tended to become disobedient; and monarchs, who stood for absolutism and conservatism, found themselves drawn close to an absolute and conservative Pope. The kings of Spain and the Popes of Rome became friends and allies.

Within three years after the sack of Rome, Clement crowned Charles V with the Imperial crown in Bologna, where, for the last time in Italy, proclamation was made of a "Romanorum Imperator semper Augustus, Mundi totius Dominus;" and the Papacy, strengthened at once by its league with Spain, lifted its head. Further strength came from other sources. The brilliant young Spaniard, Ignatius Loyola, founded the Order of Jesus, which vowed itself to poverty, chastity, and obedience to the Papacy (1534). Spain, too, by the moral effect of example, procured the Inquisition for Italy. From the time of Innocent III, the Dominican monks had had charge of preserving the purity of the faith and of punishing heretics, and they had performed this function with what might appear to a sceptic sufficient zeal, but during the great racial and religious struggle in Spain which ended in the capture of Granada, more zeal was deemed necessary and the Spanish Inquisition was established. Its fame spread far and wide. The Spanish viceroys introduced it in a modified form in Naples, and Cardinal Caraffa, a zealous reformer, urged the need of such an institution in Rome. The Holy Office of Rome was established, and Caraffa put at its head (1542). Heretics were frightened into conformity or punished; some were driven out of the country, a few were burned to death. Freedom of thought was vigorously attacked; and the Index Librorum Prohibitorum was decreed. The great and growing power of the reformers may be measured by the fact that the Pope who sanctioned these great bulwarks of the papal system was the once gay Alexander Farnese, Paul III, whom we otherwise know as a brother and a father. The culminating exhibition of the power of the reformers, however, was in the Council of Trent (1545-63).

Europe had been too long accustomed to the idea of ecclesiastical unity to sit still without some attempt at reconciliation between the Catholics and Protestants. It was hoped that a Council would heal all wounds, smooth all difficulties, and bring back the irrevocable past. The Popes, however, had come to regard Councils as inimical bodies with dangerous tendencies towards investigation and with hostile canons, and were inclined to take the risk of losing the tainted parts of Christendom altogether, rather than make use of so perilous an instrument to recover them. But the Emperor, Charles V, was insistent; his Empire, as well as the Church, was cracked, and in great danger of breaking in two. The Council was convoked, and met at Trent. The primary object was reconciliation; but everybody knew that no reconciliation was possible without radical reforms in the Church, so the papal party played its cards with exceeding wariness. The Lutherans did not attend, and the papal party, in order to forestall practical reforms, plunged into the comparatively safe matter of defining dogma, and defined it in such a way as to fence out all the Lutheran schismatics. The reformers, nevertheless, managed to sandwich in between the definitions of dogma various decrees for the reform of Church discipline. In Catholic theory an Ecumenical Council acts under the inspiration of the Holy Ghost; but looking at this Council from a purely secular point of view, it is hard to find other guidance than the quarrelling interests of Pope, bishops, Emperor, Spaniards, French, and Italians. In fact, the Council was twice broken up. The first time the Pope, having taken alarm, declared the Council adjourned to Bologna. The second time the Lutherans, then at war with the Emperor, swooped down near Trent and frightened the Council away. It met again, for the third time. All hope of reconciliation with the Protestants had then passed away, and the Council set to work as a purely Roman Catholic partisan body. A striking change of attitude within the Council showed that since the early sessions the reforming party had won complete control. Paul IV (1555-59), a man of high character, formerly Cardinal Caraffa, head of the Roman Inquisition, had promulgated many edicts concerning reforms; and his successor Pius IV, Giovanni Angelo Medici of Milan (not of the Florentine family) (1559-66), who was Pope during the final sessions of the Council, followed his lead. Pius, a clever man who had received a legal training, instead of wasting efforts in persuading disputatious bishops, first made diplomatic arrangements with the Catholic sovereigns of Spain, France, and Austria, and then secured the embodiment of those arrangements in decrees by the Council. Nothing, however, could have been accomplished without the reforming spirit within the Church; Pius removed obstacles in its way and let it have full play. Stern rules were made against the corrupt practices, which had given Luther his strength. Canons regulated the conduct of the clergy, the duties of bishops, the affairs of monasteries and nunneries, and all matters connected with the great organization of the Roman Church. These reforms came too late to affect Protestant opinion, but they rallied the doubting, confirmed the faithful, and gave the Papacy wide-reaching moral support. The dogmas of the

Church were cast in adamant, and secured the immense advantage of definiteness and fixity. The Council of Trent remains the principal monument of the Catholic Revival, and that Revival is certainly the most important event for Italy in the period immediately following the Renaissance. Pius IV, the clever lawyer, had a great share in the work of the Council, but his most skilful achievement was to maintain and confirm the doctrine of the subordination of Councils to the Papacy. This great stroke, as well as his share in the reforms, has won for him the title of founder of the Modern Papacy.

In this manner the Papacy prospered during the very generations in which the greatness of Italy dwindled away. The fortunes of the two had wholly parted company. The Papacy, indeed, had made itself an Italian institution,—never again would it seat a foreigner on the chair of St. Peter,—but in all other ways it had ceased to have any national affections. Italy, her genius faded, her vigour faint, not only deprived of what might have been a great support, but even pushed down and held under by the help of her own greatest creation, the Church, ceased to be a country. She had become, in Metternich's famous phrase, a mere geographical expression, an aggregate of little states, with no tie between them except that of juxtaposition and of common subservience to foreigners. If we look at a map drawn at the close of the sixteenth century, we shall find the following political divisions:—

The Duchy of Savoy,
The Spanish province of Lombardy,
The Republic of Venice,
The little Duchy of Parma, under the Farnesi,
The little Duchy of Mantua, under the Gonzaga,
The little Duchy of Modena, under the Este family,
The little Duchy of Urbino, under the della Rovere
who had succeeded to the Montefeltri,
The Republic of Genoa,
The Republic of Lucca,
The Grand Duchy of Tuscany, under the Medici,
The Papal States,
The Spanish province of Naples,
The Spanish province of Sicily.

Over them all, Spanish provinces, independent republics, Italian duchies, and Papal States, falls the shadow cast by the royal standard of Spain. Next to our consciousness of that dreaded banner, the most vivid impression which we take away is the contrast between the vigour of the Papacy and the weakness of Italy, and we draw the necessary inference that the fortunes of the two not only have wholly parted company, but also are wholly irreconcilable.

CHAPTER XXX: THE CINQUECENTO (16th Century)

The Cinquecento, as the Italians call the sixteenth century, exhibits in the arts the same disintegration and decay that we have found in the political life of Italy. Honesty, independence, genuineness fade away, and in their stead we find cleverness and effort. The high tide of the Renaissance was in the pontificate of Julius II, but the flood lingered on at the full till 1540, and then the ebb began. This is the date which the famous German scholar and critic, Jakob Burckhardt, assigns as the limit of the Golden Age; and it is interesting to find how closely it corresponds with the political dates which marked the establishment of the new political order in Italy. In 1530 Florence was definitely handed over to the Medici; in 1535 the duchy of Milan was annexed to Spain; in 1540 the Pope sanctioned the Order of Jesus; in 1542 he established the Holy Office in Rome; in 1543 he accepted the scheme of an Index Librorum Prohibitorum; and in 1545 the Council of Trent was opened.

The change from maturity to decay was all-pervasive; yet it was slow, and a period of excellence and good taste intervened between the High Renaissance and the Baroque. This process is most clearly marked in architecture. During the High Renaissance dignity was law, the grand manner dominated, and charm determined subordinate parts. Domes were noble, loggias elegant, pilasters decorative, cornices well proportioned, ceilings splendid. After 1540 indications of decline appeared; but this fading brilliance was a kind of götterdämmerung, and, though it heralded the Baroque, displayed at times a purity of detail and a noble restraint worthy of the earlier period.

Of the architects of this intervening stage the greatest was Giacomo Barozzi, surnamed Vignola after the little town where he was born in the province of Modena. He was a man of theories, had great knowledge of classical architecture, and wrote a manual on the architectural orders which enjoyed great authority for two centuries and more. He built various buildings at Bologna, and designed a gigantic palace at Piacenza for the Farnesi, the ducal children of Alexander Farnese, Paul III, and nephews of the beautiful Giulia. The art of making gardens, of using cypress trees, greensward, pools, terraces, and clumps of ilex as joint partners with stone, brick, and stucco, in one artistic whole, had come into being in the sixteenth century; and Vignola was one of the masters of this new art. He designed the Farnese gardens on the Palatine Hill, since destroyed by time, neglect, subsequent owners, and eager archæologists. He was an artist of great ideas, and sometimes caught the grand manner. On the other hand, he also helped to bring on the Baroque. His famous church at Rome, the Gesù, despite its vast, high-arching nave, lent itself with fatal facility to a gorgeous hideousness of decoration, and set the fashion for many imitative Jesuit churches, which caught the hideous gorgeousness but missed the grandeur of their exemplar. He had an important part in building the Villa di Papa Giulio (Pope Julius III), a little outside the city walls, charming in its grace, its variety, and its succession of arcades, courts, loggias, balustrades, grotto, terrace, and garden.

The next in rank, Bartolommeo Ammanati of Florence, may be called the court architect of Duke Cosimo I. He built two bridges across the Arno, the Ponte alia Carraia and the Ponte Santa

Trinità, finished the main body of the Pitti Palace, originally designed by Brunelleschi, and completed the elaborate Boboli garden, the pleasure grounds behind the palace. He also was drawn to Rome at the behest of villa-building Popes, and had a share in elaborating the plans of the Villa of Papa Giulio. Giorgio Vasari, architect, painter, biographer, designed the Uffizi at Florence, painted many indifferent pictures, and wrote "Lives of the Painters," a garrulous, discursive, inaccurate, and delightful book. Galeazzo Alessi of Perugia built the stately, tourist-haunted palaces of Genoa, once occupied by opulent merchants, and also the gigantic church of S. Maria degli Angeli, which covers the Portiuncula of St. Francis, like a bowl turned over a forget-me-not. Jacopo Tatti Sansovino of Florence was the architect of many noble buildings in Venice. Andrea Palladio of Vicenza embodied his passionate love of classical architecture in palaces and churches in his native town and in Venice. During the revival of classic enthusiasm in the eighteenth century Palladio became a demi-god. The captivated Goethe, as soon as he arrived at Vicenza, hurried to see the Palladian palaces. "When we stand face to face with these buildings, then we first realize their great excellence; their bulk and massiveness fill the eye, while the lovely harmony of their proportions, admirable in the advance and retreat of perspective, brings peace to the spirit." In Venice, he says, "Before all things I hastened to the Carità.... Alas! scarcely a tenth part of the edifice is finished. However, even this part is worthy of that heavenly genius.... One ought to pass whole years in the contemplation of such a work."

These men and their rivals kept alive the traditions of the great period; nevertheless, in course of time stiltedness and exaggeration usurped the place of elegance and force. A servile imitation of Roman models, an absolute acceptance of classical correctness, prevailed; the classic orders, especially the Corinthian, spread themselves everywhere; in one place barren and formal simplicity obtruded itself, in another pretentious magnificence. After 1580 the transition is complete; the baroque triumphs; sham tyrannizes, wood and plaster mimic stone, columns twist themselves awry; monstrous scrolls, heavy mouldings, crazy statues, gilt deformities, and all the contortions to which stucco and other cohesive substances will submit, hang and cling everywhere, inside and out. But this is to anticipate, for the full revel of the Baroque takes place in the seventeenth century.

The same degeneration prevailed in sculpture. Michelangelo, in his statues in the Medicean chapel at Florence, "Night" and "Day," "Evening" and "Dawn" (1529-34), had achieved the utmost which thought and emotion could express in marble. They stand, pillars set up by Hercules, at the end of the noble sculpture of the Renaissance. His successors tried to imitate him, in vain; they produced bulk, or writhing or distortion. Yet some men of this period did excellent work: Benvenuto Cellini, delicate goldsmith, and sculptor of the Florentine Perseus; John of Bologna, who modelled the Flying Mercury; Taddeo Landini of Florence, who designed the charming fountain in Rome, in which several boys are boosting turtles into a basin above; Bandinelli, whose big statues are familiar in Florence, "a man strangely composed," as Burckhardt says, "of natural talent, of reminiscence of the old school, and of a false originality which carried him beyond a disregard of nicety even to grossness." After these men and a few others, sculpture followed architecture in its facile descent into the Baroque, and expressed itself in prophets, saints, and Popes, who stand in swaying and vacillating postures in nave and aisle, on roof and balustrade. These decadent sculptors strictly belong to the next century; they are but heralded by the last works of the Cinquecento.

In painting, too, the same story is repeated all over Italy. In Florence after the close of the High Renaissance twilight darkened rapidly. There are few artists of note except two fashionable portrait painters, Pontormo and Bronzino, who display the characteristics of the period. Bronzino's picture of the Descent of Christ into Hades almost justifies Ruskin's comment, a "heap of cumbrous nothingness and sickening offensiveness;" on the other hand, Pontormo's decorations in the great hall of the Medicean Villa at Poggio a Caiano are as graceful, gay, and charming as can well be imagined. After them in dreary succession come the decadent painters, who painted figures bigger and bigger in would-be Michelangelesque attitudes, as may be seen in one of the rooms of the Belle Arti in Florence. Elsewhere, also, the generation bred under the great masters faded away,—the sweet Luini of Milan, Leonardo's follower; the facile Giulio Romano, Raphael's pupil; the beauty-loving Sodoma of Siena; the romantic Dosso Dossi of Ferrara. These names show how loath the genius of painting was to leave Italy, but she obeyed fate; and, at the end of the century, we have the Caracci beginning to paint in Bologna, and Caravaggio (1569-1609) in Naples. It needs but a glance at these later pictures to see what a change had come over the spirit of beauty during the hundred years since Botticelli painted Venus fresh from the salt sea foam.

In literature, also, at the opening of the sixteenth century, we had the historian, Guicciardini; the political writer, Machiavelli; the poet, Ariosto; the cultivated Castiglione: at the end we have the pathetic figure of Torquato Tasso (1544-95), who stands drooping, like a symbol of Italy. Tasso is always inscribed in textbooks as one of the four greatest Italian poets, and it would be useless and impertinent to dispute the concordant testimony of many witnesses. Byron apostrophizes him, "O victor unsurpassed in modern song;" yet one with difficulty avoids thinking that his sad story has added to the beauty of his poetry and heightened his reputation.

Torquato Tasso was the last great genius of the Italian Renaissance, and stands there facing the oncoming decadence in gifted helplessness; he had many talents, a noble nature, a melancholy temperament, and a weak character. In boyhood his religious emotions and his intellectual faculties were both over-stimulated. His story is a medley of court favour, success, rivalry, suspicion. His home was Ferrara, but he wandered about, as a sick person seeks to ease his body by changing posture. Early forcing and some natural weakness combined to bring too great a strain upon his mind, which gave way, and the unfortunate man was put in a madhouse by his patron, the Duke of Ferrara. He was confined for seven years, but not ill treated. He died in the monastery of Sant' Onofrio on the Janiculum at Rome, where tourists stop to gaze at the poor remnant of an oak tree, under whose shade he used to sit. Carducci, the great poet, says: "Italy's great literature, the living, national, and at the same time, human literature, with which she reconciled Antiquity and the Middle Ages, and, in a Roman way, represented a renewed Europe, ended with Tasso." His sad story is a fitting epilogue to the Italian Renaissance.

This general course of ascent, culmination, and decline holds true even of Venice, except in chronology; for Venice preserved her independence from the normal Italian experience almost as resolutely in the arts as in politics. She produced no literature, piqued perhaps because Italy had taken the Tuscan dialect rather than hers for the national language; but in the arts, after decay had elsewhere set in, she bloomed in the fulness of perfection, as late roses blossom when other bushes show nothing but hips. Of her individual career a few words must be said.

In architecture and sculpture, the Lombardi, a Venetian family probably from Lombardy, flourished for nearly a hundred years (1452-1537), and left their mark on Venice, in tombs and statues, in churches and palaces. Contemporary with the last generation of Lombardi came the more gifted Alessandro Leopardi, who completed the great statue of Colleoni designed by Verrocchio, and gave a new impulse to Venetian sculpture. While the Tuscan sculptors had been studying Roman remains, the Isles of Greece had been giving Greek models to their Venetian conquerors, and Leopardi in particular profited greatly by them. In the sister art the first famous architect after the Lombardi was the Florentine, Jacopo Sansovino, who spent most of a long life in Venice, where he built the Zecca, the Loggetta, the Libreria Vecchia (the Old Library), and also the Scala d'Oro (the Golden Stairway) of the ducal palace. Sanmicheli, a military engineer, as well as a builder of palaces, came from Verona to work in Venice. Palladio (1508-80), of whom we have spoken, came from Vicenza, and bequeathed his name to the neo-classic style, known as Palladian.

In painting first came the famous Bellini family, Jacopo (1400-64?) and his two sons, Gentile and the more gifted Giovanni, painter of tenderest Madonnas; after them came Carpaccio, painter of St. Jerome and his lion, and of St. George and his dragon. Then followed in rapid succession the most gifted group of painters that ever lived together, all born within twenty years of one another, as if to prove how prodigally Nature could endow a petty province that had the luck to please her: Giorgione, from Castelfranco on the Venetian mainland, of highest fame and disputed pictures; Titian, of Cadore, noblest of portrait painters; Palma Vecchio, of Bergamo, creator of the most glorious of animals, the superb Venetian women; Sebastiano del Piombo, who painted the Fornarina of the Uffizi Gallery long attributed to Raphael, and deserved his fortune of being pupil to Giorgione and friend to Michelangelo; Lorenzo Lotto, of Bergamo, another painter of exquisite women, high-bred men, noble saints, and poetical angels; Giovanni Antonio da Pordenone, inferior only to Titian; Bonifazio from Verona, painter of patrician luxury; Paris Bordone, of Treviso, so uncertain in merit, yet at his best so rich in hue, so tender in sentiment, so admirable in his pictures of Venetian ceremonial; and at the close, the giant Tintoretto (1512-94) and Paolo Veronese (1528-88) the glorious: all, though in different degrees, splendid in colour, voluptuous ministers to the sensuous eye. This cluster of names serves to show that while elsewhere in Italy art was dwindling into mannerism and exaggeration, Venice put forth an extraordinary burst of pictorial magnificence; yet even in Venice at the end of the century none of the great men were left.

The reason for this decadence of the arts from their splendour in the early decades of the century is not easy to assign; no one can say why genius spurts up in one spot or in one individual, why the brilliant Italian race should have achieved so many masterpieces and then have become ineffectual. One can merely notice, whether as a cause or an accompanying phenomenon, that, with individual exceptions,—no man could be nobler than Michelangelo,— Italy of the High Renaissance was a great moral failure. In intellectual achievement the Italians eclipsed the world; in morality they stumbled about like blind men. This lack of morality finds its fullest expression, at least its most conspicuous expression, at the very time of the culmination of the arts. Let me illustrate.

The night that the Duke of Gandia, son of Pope Borgia, was murdered in Rome (1497), a wood-seller, living beside the Tiber, saw several men come cautiously to the river. They peered about and made a sign to some one behind. Up came a horseman, with a dead body lying across his horse's back, head and heels dangling down; the horse was turned rump to the river, and two men on foot seized the body and flung it into the water. The wood-seller was asked why he had not reported the fact. He answered that he had seen some hundred bodies thrown into the river at that spot, and had never heard any inquiries made. The duke's brother, Cæsar, was at the time believed to have done the deed, but evidence fails.

The same Cæsar Borgia, bearing the somewhat ambitious motto Aut Cæsar aut nihil, energetic, ruthless, vigorous, ingenious, and plausible, embodied the Italian conception of what a political leader should be; so much so, that Machiavelli, the greatest of Italian political writers, cites him as a model. Machiavelli was a patriot, animated by real love of his country, but he was free from our conceptions of morality, or perhaps sceptical of Italian virtue, and believed that the achievement of liberating Italy from foreign tyranny could only be accomplished by the qualities of an Iago. In the chapter in "The Prince" entitled "In what manner Princes should keep faith," he says: "How praiseworthy it is for a Prince to keep faith, to practise integrity and eschew trickery, everybody knows; nevertheless, within our own lifetime and our own experience, we know that those Princes have done great things who have made small account of good faith and have known how to turn men's heads by means of trickery, and in the end have surpassed those who planted themselves on loyalty.... Therefore a prudent lord ought not to keep faith, when keeping faith would make against him, and the reasons which made him promise are no more. If men were all good this precept would not be good; but as they are bad and would not keep faith with you, you, too, ought not to keep faith with them; and a Prince will never lack legitimate reasons to colour the breach.... I shall even make bold to say this, that to have certain moral qualities and always observe them is bad, but to seem to have them is good; as to seem to be pious, faithful, kind, religious, honest, or even to be so, provided your mind be so adjusted that, in case of need, you will know how to be the opposite. For you must know that a Prince, and especially a newly crowned Prince, cannot do all the things for which men are esteemed good, for, in order to maintain the state, they are often obliged to act contrary to humanity, contrary to charity, contrary to religion; therefore, he must have a mind prompt to veer with the wind and the fluctuations of fortune; and, as I have said, not to forsake the good, if may be, but to know how to cleave to evil, if he must."

Another illustration shall be the life of Pietro Aretino (1492-1557), born the child of an artist's model in a hospital at Arezzo, who, by wit and infinite impudence, by toadying, bullying, and blackmail, worked his way to such a position that he could say, "Without serving courts I have compelled the great world, dukes, princes, kings, to pay tribute to my genius." Once a pious lady, the Marchesa di Pesaro, remonstrated with him upon his life, and bade him mend his ways. He wrote back: "I must say that I am not less useful to the world, or less pleasing to Jesus, spending my vigils upon trifles than if I had employed them on works of piety. But why do I do this? If princes were as devout as I am needy, my pen would write nothing but misereres.... Let us see. I have a friend named Brucioli, who dedicated his translation of the Bible to the Most Christian King [of France]. Four years passed and he got no answer. On the other hand, my comedy, 'The Courtesan,' won a rich necklace from this same king; so that my Courtesan would have felt tempted to make fun of the Old Testament, if that were not a trifle unbecoming. Forgive me lady for the jests I have written, not from malice, but for a livelihood. All the world does not possess the inspiration of divine grace. Music and comedy are to us what prayer and preaching are to you. May Jesus grant you His grace to get for me from Sebastiano di Pesaro [her husband?] the rest of the money of which I have only received thirty scudi; for this I am in anticipation your debtor." Of Pietro Aretino a recent Italian critic says: "His memory is infamous; no gentleman would mention his name before a lady." Yet, perhaps, we may doubt if he was peculiarly bad; he possessed the cynical views of morality current at the time. Aretino made a fortune, received knighthood from the Pope, nearly obtained a cardinal's hat, and was painted by Titian.

The following anecdote is taken from the autobiography of the famous goldsmith and sculptor, Benvenuto Cellini (1500-71). He was travelling on a sort of canal boat on his way from Venice to Florence. "We went to lodge for the night in an inn on this side of Chioggia, on the left as we were approaching Ferrara. Our host wished to be paid, according to his custom, before we went to bed. I told him that in other places it was the custom to pay in the morning, but he said, 'I wish to be paid, according to my way, in the evening.' I replied that men who wanted their own special way would have to make a world to suit their special way, because in this world that was not the way things were done. The host answered that I need not vex my wits, for he wished to do according to his way. My companion was trembling for fear, and poked me to be quiet lest the host do worse; so we paid him, according to his way, and went to bed. We had excellent new beds, everything new, spick and span; in spite of this I did not sleep a wink, thinking all night long what I could do to revenge myself; first I thought of setting fire to the house, next of cutting the throats of the four good horses that he had in his stable; I could see that this would be easy to do, but not how it would be easy for me and my companion to escape afterwards. At last I hit on a plan. In the morning I put my companion and all the things into the canal boat. When the horses were hitched to the rope that pulled the boat, I said that they must not start the boat till I got back, as I had left a pair of slippers in my room.... When I got in the room I took my knife, which was sharp as a razor, and I cut the mattresses on the four beds to little bits, so that I knew I had done more than fifty scudi worth of damage." Throughout a delightful autobiography, which we need not accept too literally, Cellini exhibits a perfectly unmoral disposition, a mind with no sense of social law and no respect for anything except Michelangelo and art.

These four men, Cæsar Borgia, Machiavelli, Aretino, and Cellini, possessed fortitude, energy, subtlety, and courage, but they showed no appreciation of the fundamental social virtues, loyalty, trust, subordination of self to the general good; and for this reason they enable us to understand why Italy fell like a ripe apple, without resistance, into the lap of foreigners and lay helpless under Jesuit, inquisitor, petty duke, and Spanish viceroy, and why freedom to think and freedom to act faded from art and intellectual life as well as from political life.

.

CHAPTER XXXI: A SURVEY OF ITALY (1580-1581)

At the end of the sixteenth century Italy is well under way on a new stretch of history, which lasted until the nineteenth century. Except Venice, always individual, and the Papacy, freshly revivified, Italy has lost all moral force, and become wholly effeminate. In twenty-five years three hundred and twenty-six volumes of sonnets were published. Her political life has become what one may call grand-ducal; her religion formal, superstitious; her literature affected, stilted; her architecture Baroque; her painting and sculpture steeped in mannerism and exaggeration. Nevertheless, Italy is Italy, and has her own charm, her own individuality, her own coquetry. As formerly she lured Barbarian nations, so now she lures individual Barbarians, and becomes the roaming-ground of travellers. She seems less a real country than a theatre, where rococo dukes, cavaliers, and ladies curl their hair and powder their cheeks.

For two centuries this artificial existence continued. Its history is not to be found in the solemn volumes of Cesare Cantù, Carlo Botta, or other Italian historians, but in the journals of German, French, and English travellers: for during these centuries Italy was not a country in either a political or a sentimental sense; it was a place of recreation for gentlemen on the grand tour, pious folk bound Romeward, virtuosi seeking classical remains, and elderly statesmen hoping to cure the gout. The several petty states were so many artificial gardens, where the peasants wore pretty costumes, the dukes sang prize songs, the duchesses trilled tra la la in rival endeavour, and the ecclesiastics trolled out the chorus. It was the Italian opera bouffe on the most charming stage in the world. The best summary of the history of the coming century will be a series of extracts from the diary of a keen-witted French gentleman, travelling for pleasure, Michel de Montaigne, who, in the company of some friends, spent several months in Italy (1580-81). They crossed the Alps over the Brenner Pass and went by way of Trent. Montaigne's diary is sometimes written in the second and sometimes in the third person. He describes many of the principal cities.

Verona (within the territory of the Republic of Venice). "Without health certificates which they had got at Trent they could not have entered the city, although there was no rumour of any danger of pest; but it is the custom (in order to cheat us of the few pennies they cost). We went to see the cathedral, where Montaigne deemed the behaviour of the men at High Mass very peculiar; they chatted even in the choir of the church, standing up, with their hats on and their backs turned to the altar, and did not seem to pay any attention to the service except on the elevation of the Host. There were organs and violins to accompany the mass.... We went to see the castle and were shown all over by the lieutenant in charge. The [Venetian] government keeps sixty soldiers there, rather, according to what they said to Montaigne, against the people of the city than against foreigners. We also saw a congregation of monks called the Gesuati of St. Jerome [not Jesuits]. They are not priests; they neither say mass nor preach; most of them are ignorant, but they carry on a business of distilling lemon-flower water, both in Verona and elsewhere. They are dressed in white, with little white caps, and a dark brown gown over it; good-looking young men." They visited the Ghetto (Jews' quarter), and the Roman amphitheatre, which Montaigne thought the noblest building he had ever seen.

Vicenza. "It is a big city, a little smaller than Verona, all full of palaces of the nobility." The fair, which was held twice a year, was going on upon the parade-ground; booths had been built on purpose, and no shops in the city were allowed to keep open. In the town there was another establishment of the Gesuati, selling their perfumes and also medicines for every ailment. "These monks tell us that they whip themselves every day; each one has his switch at his post in the oratory, where they meet at certain hours of the day and pray, but they have no singing.... The old wine has given out, which vexed me, as it is not good for me, on account of my colic, to drink the new wines, though they are very good in their way." From Vicenza they journeyed by a broad straight road, ditched on either side and raised a little, which ran through a fertile champaign with mountains in the distance, to Padua. The inns here could not be compared with German inns except that they were cheaper by a third. "The streets narrow and ugly, not many people, few handsome houses. We went about all the next day and saw the schools of fencing, dancing, and riding, where there were more than a hundred French gentlemen together." In fact, young men went in great numbers, young Frenchmen in particular, to the schools of Padua, less to acquire a knowledge of books than to acquire the accomplishments which were then the mode. One of Montaigne's party stopped here and found good lodging for seven crowns a month, and "he might have lodged a valet for five crowns more; ordinarily, however, they do not have valets, only a general servant for the house, or else maids; every one has a nice bedroom, but fire and lights in the bedroom are extra. The accommodation was very good, and you can live there very reasonably, and that, I think, is the reason why many strangers go there to live, even those who are not students."

Venice. Here he dined with the French ambassador "very well;" among other things "that the ambassador told him this seemed odd, that he had no social relations whatever with anybody in the city, because the people were so suspicious that a [Venetian] gentleman who should speak to him twice would fall under distrust." One is inclined, however, considering the fate of Milan, to regard a certain distrust of foreigners as not unnatural. Montaigne thought that the four most remarkable things about Venice were the situation, the police, the Piazza of St. Mark's, and the crowds of foreigners. He received as a gift a little book of "Letters" from a Venetian lady, one of that celebrated class of Venetian women who were outside the matrimonial pale yet lived in ostentatious luxury, recognized by the government and by masculine society. This lady at mid-life had changed her ways and devoted herself to literature, and hearing of the famous French author, sent him her book.

Returning by way of Padua, Montaigne passed the sulphur springs, frequented in May and August by the fashionable sick, who took mud or vapour baths and drank the waters. He noted the canals; the system of irrigation in the plains, where rows of vine-laden trees intersected fields of wheat; the big, strong, gray oxen; the broad mud flats, once swamps, which the government was struggling to reclaim.

Rovigo, a little town in Venetian territory near the Adige. "There is as great abundance of meat here as in France, whatever it may be the custom to say, and though they use no lard for the roast, they do not take away the savour. The bedrooms, because there is no glass and they don't shut the windows, are not so clean as in France; the beds are better made, smoother, and well supplied with mattresses, but they have nothing but coarse coverings, and they are very sparing of white sheets; if a man travels alone, or with little style, he won't get any. It is about as dear as in France, or a little dearer."

He crossed the Po, as he had crossed the Adige, upon some kind of pontoon bridge, and went on to

Ferrara (duchy of Ferrara), where he was delayed on account of his health certificate. The ducal regulations on this point were very particular. On the door of every room in the inn was written up, "Remember the health certificate;" immediately on arrival, names of travellers were reported to the magistrates. Montaigne found most of the streets broad and straight, all paved with bricks; there were many palaces, but few people, and he missed the porticos of Padua, so convenient against the rain. He did the town, paid his respects to the duke, saw Tasso in the madhouse, and found the lemon-flower distilling Gesuates again.

At Bologna (in the Papal States), a large, fine city, bigger than Ferrara, and with many more people; he also found young Frenchmen come to learn riding and fencing. He admired the fine porticos, that covered almost every sidewalk, the handsome palaces, the buildings of the School of Sciences, the bronze statue of Neptune designed by John of Bologna, and enjoyed a company of players. "The cost of living was about the same as at Padua, very reasonable; but the city is less peaceful in the older quarters, which make debatable land between the partisans of different nations, on one side always the French, and on the other the Spaniards, who are there in great numbers."

This unpeaceful and factional condition was not confined to Bologna, but spread throughout the Papal States. Even fifty years later a perplexed visitor to Ravenna wrote: "The city is divided, as you know, into Guelfs and Ghibellines, so much so that one man won't go to another's church, and each side has its place in the public square; a tailor who works for one need not look for employment from the other, and so with all the trades; they distinguish one faction from the other by the way they wear their hair, their caps," etc. But these pale shadows of the great old parties were slight inconveniences compared with the banditti, who also decked themselves with old names, and, under pretence of fighting one another, robbed, burnt, pillaged, and murdered with perfect impartiality. The soldiers and the common people united against these rascals, but they were too strong to be utterly extirpated. In the Papal States, one Piccolomini, a member of a famous Sienese family, raided where he chose, and once led a band of two hundred men within a mile or two of the walls of Rome. Terms were made with him, for he was under the protection of the Grand Duke of Tuscany, and although he confessed to three hundred and seventy murders within twenty-five years, he was pardoned and absolved.

Leaving Bologna, Montaigne hesitated in his choice of roads on account of brigands, and chose wisely for he was not molested. He crossed the Apennines by a road, which he says is the first that could be called bad, and entered the Grand Duchy of Tuscany. One village on the way, still in papal territory, was famous for the knavery of the innkeepers, who made wonderful promises till the traveller was safely housed, and then rendered the scantest performance. At the next village, which was in Tuscany, rival hosts rode out to meet the traveller, and struggled to secure him, promising everything. One offered to serve a rabbit for dinner free, if Montaigne would lodge with him. The party prudently rode about to all the inns on a tour of inspection, examining food and wine, and making their bargain before dismounting; the host, however, managed to put extras on the bill, it being impossible to remember beforehand every item, wood, candles, linen, hay, etc.

Next day Montaigne rode out of his way to see Pratolino, the Grand Duke's famous country place, with its gardens, alleys, wonderful grottos, all decked with Nereids and Tritons, and fountains of extravagant baroque designs. From there he went on to

Florence, which appeared to him smaller than Ferrara. He went to see the ducal stables, the ducal menagerie, Michelangelo's statues, Giotto's campanile; and remarked that he had never seen a country with so few handsome women as Italy. Lodgings were inferior in comfort to those in France, and the food was far less generous and less well served than in Germany, where, also, sauces and seasonings were far superior; the windows were big and always open, for there was no glass, and if the shutters were shut they excluded light and air as well as wind; the beds were uncomfortable, the wines too sweet; moreover, Florence was esteemed the most expensive city in Italy.

Montaigne dined with the duke, Francesco I (son of Cosimo I), and his second wife, Bianca Cappello, the famous Venetian, who sat at the head of the table. She had a pleasant face, was reputed handsome, and seemed to have been able to keep her husband devoted to her for a long time. The duke mixed water freely with his wine; she scarcely at all. After a brief stay, during which he visited gardens and the environs of the city, which he admired greatly, Montaigne rode southward to

Siena. The country was cultivated everywhere and tolerably fertile, but the road was rough and stony. At Siena he notes the Duomo, the palaces, the piazza, the fountains, and, important point, that "there are good cellars and fresh;" also, that in Tuscany the city walls are let go to ruin, while the citadels are carefully fortified and no one is permitted to go near, showing that the duke feared domestic insurrection more than foreign attack. He observes "the French are kept in such affectionate remembrance here by the people of the country, that at any mention of them tears well up in their eyes, for war itself, with freedom in some form, seems to them sweeter than the peace which they enjoy under this tyranny." The French had aided Siena in its brave struggle for liberty, and a valiant remnant of French and Sienese had held out till the Peace of Cateau-Cambrésis (1559), when France abandoned them to Cosimo dei Medici.

From Siena he rode southward past Bolsena, Viterbo, and a pleasant valley surrounded by hills covered with wood, "a commodity somewhat rare in this country." Incidentally he commends the customs: in good houses dinner was served at two o'clock and supper at nine; and if there was a play, it began at six and was over by supper time. "It is a good country for a lazy fellow for they get up late."

At Rome he put up for a day at the Bear, and then took lodgings, three good bedrooms, parlour, dining-room, kitchen, and stable, for twenty crowns a month, the host providing the cook and fire for the kitchen. "Apartments are ordinarily somewhat better furnished than in Paris, especially as they have a great deal of gilt leather, with which the walls of apartments of a certain grade are hung." He might have hired another apartment for the same price, furnished in silk and cloth of gold, but he did not think this luxury suitable, and the rooms were not so convenient. Ancient Rome impressed him immensely, and the modern city, too; he was astonished by the papal court, the number of prelates, the crowd of ecclesiasts, by the streets, so full of richly dressed men, of horses and coaches.

Making a comparison between freedom in Venice and in Rome, he argued for Venice, and adduced these reasons: "Item, that in Rome houses were so insecure, that those who had considerable sums of money were advised to leave their purses at their bankers, so as not to find their chest broken open; item, that it was not very safe to go out at night; item, that, in the very first month of his visit, the General of the Cordeliers was abruptly dismissed from his post and put in prison, because in a sermon, which he preached before the Pope [Gregory XIII] and the cardinals, he had accused prelates of laziness and luxury, but without going into details, and using (with some asperity of voice) only perfectly common and current phrases on the subject; item, that his luggage had been examined on entering the city for the customs, and had been ransacked down to the smallest article of clothing, whereas in most of the other cities in Italy the officials had been satisfied with the mere offer to submit to examination; besides that, they had taken all the books they found in order to examine them, and took so long about it, that a man who had something to do might put them down as lost; add to that, that their rules were so extraordinary that the 'Book of Hours of Our Lady' fell under their suspicion, because it came from Paris and not from Rome, and they also kept books, written by some German doctors against heretics, because in combating them they made mention of their errors."

On Christmas day at St. Peter's during mass, Montaigne "was surprised to see Pope, cardinals, and other prelates, seated almost all through the mass, talking and conversing together. The ceremony seemed more magnificent than devotional." He obtained an interview with the Pope, very ceremonious; and dined with a French cardinal, where the benedicite and repetitions of grace, very long, were recited antiphonally by two chaplains. During dinner the Bible was read, and after the table was cleared, service was held; everything was exceedingly formal, but the chef does not appear to have equalled Cardinal Caraffa's chef, a culinary enthusiast, with whom Montaigne had a long talk on sauces, soups, and serving. Montaigne attended the Carnival sports on the Corso, a festival already at that time more than a hundred years old, where boys, Jews, old men, horses, asses, and buffalo ran races; fair ladies, without masks, looked on, and young cavaliers congregated where the ladies could see them; the ladies were richly clad, the gentlemen simply; and (Montaigne adds) the appearance of the dukes, counts, and marquesses was not equal to their titles.

Montaigne's "Essays" had been submitted to the Master of the Palace, who examined them with the aid of a French friar, for the Master knew no French. After a delay they were returned, and the Master left it to Montaigne's conscience to alter what might seem to be in bad taste, especially in those points to which the French friar objected; item, that Montaigne had used the word Fortune; item, that he had named poets who were heretics; item, that he had made an apology for Julian the Apostate; item, that he had suggested that when a man was saying his prayers he ought at that moment to be free from any unworthy inclination; item, that he judged any punishment in excess of death, cruelty; item, that a child should be educated to do all sorts of things, etc. Another book belonging to Montaigne, a history of the Swiss, was confiscated, because the translator was a heretic.

On Maundy Thursday he saw the Pope come forth on the balcony of St. Peter's attended by his cardinals. On one side a canon, speaking Latin; on the other, a cardinal read, in Italian, a long bull which excommunicated an everlasting list of people, including the Huguenots and all princes who withheld any portion of the territory of the Church. At this last article Cardinals Medici and Caraffa laughed heartily. At night there was a great procession of religious guilds, with twelve thousand torches, including files of Penitents, who scourged their bare backs till the blood ran. Montaigne, however, was of opinion that these Penitents were hired for this purpose. He agreed with the French ambassador, that the poor people were incomparably more devout in France than here, but that in Rome the rich, and especially the courtiers, were more devout than in France.

From Rome Montaigne made his way northward by Spoleto, where there was great alarm caused by a noted brigand. On the way he notes his food,—salt fish, beans uncooked, artichokes also uncooked, peas, green almonds, eggs, cheese, wine, and, in little places, olive oil instead of butter. "You meet monks every now and then who give holy water to travellers and expect alms in return, and a lot of children who beg and hold out their beads, promising to say a string of paternosters for the person who will give them something."

The Umbrian plain was beautiful and fertile, with grains and fruits in abundance, the whole country rich beyond description. So, too, had been the Roman Campagna, but that was not tenanted, for its owners, the Roman barons, had let it to merchant farmers, who did not maintain peasants there, but in harvest time hired husbandmen from all over Italy, to the number of forty thousand, to gather in the crops. From Foligno he turned to the right and crossed the Apennines just below Assisi, and travelled toward the Adriatic coast, making a pilgrimage to Loreto, a place like Lourdes, celebrated for its miracles, and for the "very same little house in which Jesus Christ was born in Nazareth." Here he found the people much more religious than elsewhere; even the attendants in the Church were ready to do anything, and would accept no tips. Thence he went to Ancona, Sinigaglia, Urbino, where he inspected the famous palace begun by Federigo da Montefeltro; then back to Florence, once more to admire the beautiful villas which decked the hills round about, and on to Prato and Pistoia, stagnating little towns, whose civic life had been crushed out by the Medici. So he rode on through lovely country, where long lines of little trees, trellised with vines, divided the rich fields of grain, skirting the hills covered with olive, mulberry, and chestnut, till he reached Lucca, which had saved itself from the clutch of the Medici by clinging to the skirts of Austria.

Lucca, girdled by fortifications worthy of a most martial ardour, maintained a comfortable prosperity by the manufacture of silk; but here, as elsewhere, it was becoming unfashionable to engage in trade, partly on account of decreasing returns and the general waning of energy, and partly from Spanish influences. Gentlemen retired from business, invested their money in landed estates, and were rapidly tending to become the characters which we find in Goldoni's comedies.

From Lucca Montaigne went to the Baths of Lucca and took the cure for near two months. He found the country lovely, but society a little slow; most of the men were apothecaries. After the cure he made another tour southward, then back to Lucca for more baths, from there northward, on the road to Milan, stopping at Pontremoli. At the inn in this place, the dinner began with cheese alla milanese, included a dish of olives, their pits taken out, dressed with oil and vinegar alla genovese; on a bench stood one basin in which all the guests washed their hands in the same water, alla pontremolese. From there he crossed the Apennines, where the mountaineers, horrid people, charged them most cruel prices, and went on into the duchy of Parma, where Alessandro Farnese, the great general, was the reigning duke. At Piacenza, the King of Spain, out of his abundant caution, still maintained a Spanish garrison in the castle, "badly paid as they told me." Thence they proceeded into the duchy of Milan.

At Pavia Montaigne remarks, that from Rome northward the best inn he had lodged at was the Post at Piacenza, and the worst the Falcon at Pavia: "You pay extra for wood, and there are no mattresses on the beds." Milan was the largest city in Italy, not unlike Paris, full of merchandise and craftsmen; it lacked the palaces of other cities, but in size excelled them all, and in throng of people rivalled Venice.

From Milan he rode westward, and entered the domains of the Duke of Savoy, crossing the Sesia near Vercelli, where the duke was building a fort in such haste, that he aroused the suspicion of his Spanish neighbours. Thence he went to Turin. Here the people imitated French ways, looked up to Paris, usually spoke French, or rather French words with Italian pronunciation, and altogether seemed very devoted to France. Montaigne liked Piedmont, finding the inns there better than elsewhere in Italy. The bread was bad but the wine good, there was plenty to eat, and the innkeepers were polite. He crossed the Alps over the Mt. Cenis Pass, half the time on horseback, half the time in a chaise borne by four porters, and then entered Savoy proper, passing its capital, Chambéri, crossing the Rhone to the north and then the little river Ain to the westward, and came to Montluel, the last town of Savoy, and so on to the Saône, Lyons, and French soil (November, 1581).

Such was the Italy of the long period from 1580 to 1789, the land of olives, mulberries, and chestnuts, of fertile fields crossed by vine-laden trees, of irrigated plains and treeless mountains, of innkeepers, good, bad, and indifferent, of Spanish garrisons, ducal citadels, and dare-devil banditti, of begging urchins, perfuming friars, of gentlemen too genteel to work, of prelates in coaches, of antique ruins and Renaissance glory, of blue sky and vivacious manners, in short, almost the Italy that our fathers knew before the perturbations of 1848.

CHAPTER XXXII: THE AGE OF STAGNATION, POLITICS (1580-1789)

We have now reached a period of comparative stability in which dukes, viceroys, oligarchs, and Popes sit settled in their respective dominions with a security that appears a little tame after the whir and uproar of Barbarian invasion. To be sure, the wars between Spain, France, and Austria, waged first to abate the over-greatness of the House of Hapsburg and afterwards that of the House of Bourbon, were often fought out in the north of Italy; nevertheless, the period of confusion has passed, and each principality has a consecutive political history, which runs along for two hundred years. Our best course will be to glance at the careers of the several states, one by one, until they reach the tumultuous influences of the French Revolution. Venice, the noblest as well as the most powerful, deserves to come first.

Venice

Venice still ranked as one of the great powers of Europe; she was sought as an ally, she took part in European counsels, and bore herself with resolute dignity and pride. The change that was going on went on so slowly, and her statesmen were so well trained and so far-sighted, that her reputation remained intact after the power which had created it had shrunk and dwindled. In spite of the battle of Lepanto she lost the island of Cyprus to the Turks, but secured a peace which lasted for two generations, a surprisingly long time, considering that the two states were destined to fight each other till both were exhausted. She was less successful in keeping at peace with her Christian neighbours, and became embroiled in a celebrated quarrel with the Holy See.

There was an irritating papal bull which was issued and reissued under the stimulus of the reinvigorating Counter-Reformation, entitled In Coena Domini (for the Lord's Supper), usually read on Maundy Thursday. It was probably the very bull that Montaigne heard read from the balcony of St. Peter's. This bull asserted papal claims of extreme character, not unworthy of Boniface VIII, and, in fact, revealed complete consciousness of renewed youth and vitality. Other states in Italy bowed and accepted, or pretended to accept, this declaration of papal authority; but Venice refused to publish the bull. In fact, though Venice had always professed great respect for the Holy See, she had been consistently self-willed and opposed to papal pretensions, and likewise somewhat free-thinking. Moreover, there had been festering disagreements concerning territory and politics. Venice insisted upon the right to tax Church property within the state, and to try priests charged with crime before her lay tribunals. Acting upon the latter right she arrested and tried two priests guilty of crime. This action traversed the doctrine laid down in the papal bull. The Pope put Venice under an interdict (1606). In retaliation the Signory issued a decree of banishment against all priests and monks who should obey the interdict. Various Orders quitted the city. The Pope stood firm in his position that "there could be no true piety without entire submission to the spiritual power." All Europe looked on, the Protestants backing Venice, the Catholics supporting the Pope. War was in the air; but the danger of a European mêlée was too great. The French King, Henry IV, enacted the peacemaker; and the forces in favour of compromise succeeded in reëstablishing peace.

Out of the quarrel one man issued with a noble historic reputation. Fra Paolo Sarpi (1552-

1623) was the last of the great Venetians. In boyhood he was so precocious a scholar that at eighteen he was made professor of Positive Theology, and, a little later, of Philosophy and of Mathematics. Grown up, he became a man of science, the foremost of his time excepting Francis Bacon. He discovered the valves of the veins, and also, independently of Harvey, the circulation of the blood. He made discoveries in optics. He studied heat, light, sound, colour, pneumatics, the magnetic needle. In astronomy Galileo called him, "il mio padre e maestro—my father and my master." Sir Henry Wotton, the English ambassador to Venice, said, Fra Paolo is "as expert in the history of plants as if he had never perused any book but Nature." In addition to these achievements, he wrote a very celebrated history of the Council of Trent. At the time of the breach with the Papacy, this brilliant savant was appointed Theological Counsellor to the Republic, and was abruptly flung into the confusion and passion of violent political strife. Deeply patriotic,—his last thought was for Venice, "Esto perpetua, may she live forever,"—he held a brief, as it were, for his country, and as her advocate argued her cause before all Europe with brilliant success.

At this period the Venetian Signory belonged, in spirit at least, to an international political party which was opposed to Spain and to the Papacy, and for that reason was favoured by the French, especially when Henry of Navarre was on the throne. In fact, this quarrel between Venice and the Papacy may be considered an episode in the great struggle between the party of European freedom and the tyrannical House of Hapsburg, seated on the thrones of Spain and Austria, and supported by the Papacy.

But Venice was not able to concentrate her attention upon European affairs. Later in the century war with the Turks was renewed; she was too weak to resist them single-handed, and, after a struggle which lasted for twenty-five years, she lost Crete (1669). Not many years later, having obtained allies, she renewed the war, fought with great gallantry, and actually conquered the Morea, which, on the conclusion of hostilities, was ceded to her (1699). This conquest, now best remembered from the fact that in the attack on Athens a Venetian bomb blew up the Parthenon, was the last great military exploit of the Venetians, and within twenty years the Morea was lost again.

Martial vigour ebbed slowly but surely. During the war of the Spanish Succession, when, the course of fortune having shifted, Europe combined to resist the overbearing power of Louis XIV and the House of Bourbon, Venice remained neutral. Like an old dog which has fought many good fights in its youth and prime, and now, lame and scarred, maintains a dignified abstention from canine frays, Venice lay back. In 1718, after the war with Turkey in which she lost the Morea, she took part in the treaty between Austria and Turkey. This was her last active diplomatic intervention in the affairs of Europe. She had lost Cyprus, Crete, the Morea; and now her province in Italy, bits of Illyria, and some of the Ionian Islands, alone remained from her old empire. She shut her eyes to the past, and concentrated her attention on making her beautiful city "the revel of the earth, the masque of Italy." On the eve of the mighty upheaval of the French Revolution, her old sea glory flashed up under her last great admiral, Angelo Emo (1731-92), who cleared the seas of the Algerine pirates; but it was too late, Venice had run her course, and the end was at hand.

Spanish Provinces

West of Venetian territory, the unfortunate duchy of Milan fulfilled its melancholy lot of being the prize possessed by Spain, yet coveted and fought for by France. Its history takes no special hold upon the memory. Against a constant background of French ambition (Richelieu, Mazarin, Louis XIV), the Spanish governors step forward upon the Milanese stage, levy taxes, scheme how to circumvent the French, and how to extend Spanish dominion, and then go home, a little richer but without leaving any definite impression on the page of history except as they have served to create the scenes depicted in the romantic novel "I Promessi Sposi." One has a vague idea of ceremony, bows, obeisances, ignorance, rapacity, and cruelty, but the idea is nebulous, and we need not stop.

Leaving local affairs aside, we will proceed at once to see how the titles to Milan and other Spanish provinces in Italy passed from Spain into other hands. History here acts as an attorney and coldly records the transfer from one monarch to another. Like lots of land the provinces of Italy were bartered and granted in consideration of war, dynastic love, and affection, or for the sake of the political equilibrium of Europe. The great Powers fell to blows over the succession to the crown of Spain (1700-14), to the crown of Poland (1733-35), and other matters in which Italy had no voluntary concern; and, after years of war, made treaties to reëstablish European equilibrium by an elaborate system of weights and counterweights. Where the balances hung unevenly, a province of Italy was thrown in to restore them to a level. In this way Milan, Parma, Naples, Sicily, and Sardinia were disposed of. All we need do is to remember that in place of conveyances there were treaties, and in place of offer, counter-offer, haggling, and bargaining, there were battles, sieges, devastation, and pillage.

The records of conveyances in the office of history read as follows:—

Milan was subject to only one transfer, from Spain to Austria, by the treaties of Utrecht and Rastadt (1713-14), which closed the war of the Spanish Succession. Those same treaties took Naples and the island of Sardinia from Spain and gave them to Austria, and also took Sicily from Spain and gave it to Savoy. Spain, however, was dissatisfied, and attempted to recover what she had lost; but a new European coalition forced her to renounce her claim. In the general pacification after the war, for the purpose of making a more satisfactory arrangement, Sardinia was exchanged for Sicily, giving Sardinia to Savoy and Sicily to Austria (1720). Finally, after the war of the Polish Succession by the Peace of Vienna (1738), Austria ceded Naples and Sicily to younger sons of the royal family of Spain, the Spanish Bourbons, on condition that those provinces should never be united with the crown of Spain, and received in exchange the little duchy of Parma, which had fallen to a Spanish Bourbon on the extinction of the Farnesi. But ten years later, at the close of the war of the Austrian Succession, Austria ceded Parma back again to other members of the Spanish Bourbon family.

Tuscany

Another paragraph is necessary to complete the Austrification and the Spanification of Italy. The Medici of Tuscany died out. After the first Grand Duke, Cosimo, six successors had followed, dwindling away in incapacity, luxury, and bigotry. The last died in 1737. Then, by virtue of that general reapportionment after the war of the Polish Succession, the Grand Duchy was handed over to the Duke of Lorraine, husband of Maria Theresa, of the House of Hapsburg, Empress of Austria, and became an appanage of the Austrian Empire, under the rule of the younger sons of the Imperial house. It is a relief to turn from these Austrian and Spanish provinces to the two living powers, Savoy and the Papacy.

Savoy

It would be impossible to chronicle here the history of the Savoyard dukes, who were advanced to the title of Kings of Sardinia after the acquisition of that island. Savoy lay in the way of the three fighting nations, France, Spain, and Austria. The plain of Piedmont was an admirable fighting-ground, and the combatants chose it on all possible occasions, but it would not be fair to charge the whole blame upon those three nations. The Dukes of Savoy were ambitious men, full of all sorts of schemes for increasing their dominions and their personal glory. Whenever any one of them thought he perceived an opportunity to seize some neighbouring territory, he caught at it, reckless of collision with his powerful neighbours. The general upshot was that Savoy lost its old Swiss provinces and its old French provinces, and that Piedmont became the head and front of the new Kingdom of Sardinia. Equally important to Italy was the fact that, while the people of the other Italian provinces became more and more incapable of bearing arms or of making any real martial effort, the people of Piedmont gradually became a nation of soldiers. In devastation, war, and apparent ruin, Piedmontese valour and Piedmontese character were trained and developed, and Piedmont little by little came to feel, and likewise to impress upon the other Italian States, that she, and she alone, was the refuge and hope of whatever Italian patriotism might still exist.

The Papacy

The Papacy we left at the end of the sixteenth century in the full flood of revival. The Popes were swept on by the tide. The bold and successful front opposed to the enemy was supplemented by discipline within. Heresy was traced and tracked. Inquisitors roamed about, spying what they might; they frightened the learned from publishing, printers from printing, and almost all from freedom of talk and thought. Thus traitors were rooted out. And at the same time faithful soldiers of the Church were trained and educated. Seminaries for priests of divers nations were founded in Rome; Jesuit schools were helped everywhere. Sixtus V (Felice Peretti), 1585-90, was a Pope worthy of the great period. He entertained a plan to reconquer Egypt, and make the Mediterranean and Red Seas a high-road for armies and navies that should break up the Ottoman power. He attacked the banditti of the Papal State, as his predecessors had attacked the barons, and, for a time at least, suppressed them. He was a great builder; he completed the dome of St. Peter's, set up the Egyptian obelisk in the piazza before the cathedral, substituted statues of St. Peter and St. Paul in place of Trajan and Marcus Aurelius on the tops of the two great bronze columns that adorn the Foro Trajano and the Piazza Colonna. He brought fresh water, named after him Acqua Felice, into the city from over twenty miles away, and gave Rome an aspect worthy of the capital of the Latin world. He fixed seventy for the number of cardinals; he revised the Vulgate; and pondered many great designs, for which, as he said, his strength would have been inadequate, even had he lived.

But these Popes of the Revival, who carried into effect the papal principles of the Council of Trent, vigorous, and in many respects admirable, as they were, need not detain us, for the history of the Papacy in this period scarcely belongs to Italy. It has a far wider reach, and is intimately bound up with the great Catholic, one might say the great Latin, effort to restore or extend Catholicism and Latin supremacy throughout the world. In the British Isles, in Scandinavia, in Poland, in Russia, in Germany, Austria, France, and Switzerland, the Church fought with the old Roman spirit of conquest. Everywhere the Jesuit fathers went, busy, devoted, heroic. The ardour of St. Francis Xavier, the self-abnegation of St. Francis de Sales, the passionate mysticism of St. Theresa, infected and controlled thousands of disciples. Everywhere were great manifestations of activity. In South America there were bishops and archbishops, hundreds of monasteries and innumerable priests. In Mexico there were schools of theology. In India, thousands and thousands of converts clustered around the city of Goa. In China and Japan the Jesuits built churches, and converted to Christianity disciples of Confucius and Buddha. The Church had founded an empire on which the sun never set. But our business is not with this great Latin conquest, this great Catholic revival. We must pass on to the next series of Popes, less memorable for their imitation of Scipio and Cæsar, than of Lucullus and Crassus. Here we find the names of the founders of great papal families, so familiar in Rome, not as missionaries, teachers, or martyrs, but as owners of palaces, villas, pictures and statues: Borghese (Paul V, 1605-21), the Pope who quarrelled with the Venetian Republic; Ludovisi (Gregory XV, 1621-23), in whose pontificate the Congregatio de Propaganda Fide (College for Propagating the Faith) was established; Barberini (Urban VIII, 1623-44), whose family, famous from the squib "Quod non fecerunt Barbari fecerunt Barberini," built its palaces out of Roman ruins. During the pontificate of Barberini, Galileo was brought before the Holy Office, and his opinion that the earth moved condemned as "absurd, false in philosophy, and essentially heretical."

Under his successor Panfili (Innocent X, 1644-55), Catholic Europe stopped fighting Protestant Europe, and the Thirty Years' War was closed by the Peace of Westphalia (1648). The Catholic Powers gave over the attempt to reduce the Protestant States, and acknowledged their independence. Panfili launched his bull against the treaty, but the weary world disregarded the old man's curses. After him came Chigi (Alexander VII, 1655-67), Rospigliosi (Clement IX, 1667-69), Odescalchi (Innocent XI, 1676-89), whose names mean little to us.

Long before this time the forces of revivification which had borne onward and upward the Catholic counter-charge on the Protestant ranks, had begun to fall away. The great Catholic monarchs of Europe turned their minds to personal ambitions; the Popes squandered papal revenues on their own families; the Jesuits loosened their rigid hold on their once high principles. The period of reform had passed, and the Papacy settled down into a policy of maintaining the ecclesiastical empire left to it and of enjoying its little Italian monarchy. In politics it pursued a shifting course towards Austria, Spain, and France, dictated rather by passing fears than by wisdom or lofty ambition. At the time of the close of the war of the Spanish Succession the

Papacy was hardly regarded as a European power. The proof of decline was most visible in the concessions made by the Papacy to the Catholic sovereigns, by its forced acquiescence in the repeated attacks on the Jesuits, and finally, by its bull suppressing, or rather attempting to suppress, the Order (1773).

Throughout the eighteenth century the papal part in European affairs was insignificant; and in Italy the general effects of papal rule were steadily increasing poverty, superstition, and incompetence. It is a relief to turn away, knowing that the French Revolution is blowing its refreshing blasts ahead of us.

CHAPTER XXXIII: THE AGE OF STAGNATION, THE ARTS (1580-1789)

We should do wrong to leave these centuries to stand solely on their political record. Even this dreary period has contributed not a little to the sum of Italy's attractions. After the moral vigour of republican Florence, after the freshness of the Renaissance and its later grandeur, after the elegance of the courts of Urbino, Ferrara, and Milan, it requires time to adjust ourselves to a different standard and to acquire a relish for this period of dissipated little kings and dukes. But once familiar with the altered standard of excellence, these centuries, with their arts, their habits, their idleness, become exceedingly sympathetic, and lure with peculiar dexterity the idler who seeks entertainment and the picturesque. Not that there is no serious element in them, for there is. Italy, though known to us through her lovers as a woman land, has always happily commingled feminine charm and masculine strength. Like the Apennines which stretch their grim strength from the Alps to the toe of the peninsula, virility runs throughout the length of Italian history, though at times it avoids notice. In this period it is best represented by science; and we must not omit to mention a few of the most distinguished scientific thinkers.

Giordano Bruno (1550-1600) and Campanella (1568-1639) were philosophers rather than men of science; their philosophy ran counter to the scholastic philosophy sanctioned by the Church, and they came into collision with the stern spirit of the Catholic Reaction. Campanella was persecuted and punished; Bruno was condemned as a heretic and burnt to death in the city of Rome. Greater than either was Galileo (1564-1642), whose name is one of the most illustrious in astronomy. He was born at Pisa, where he was educated in the university. He devoted himself to study, especially to mathematics, and became a professor. In 1609 he heard that a Dutchman had made an instrument which in some way by means of a lens magnified objects. Acting on this hint he constructed a telescope; and, if not strictly the inventor, he was the first to use the telescope in astronomy. The next year he made various eventful discoveries: that there are mountains in the moon, and spots on the sun; that Venus has phases; that Saturn has an appendage, which later was proved to be rings; that Jupiter has four satellites, a discovery which increased the number of heavenly bodies from the mystically sacred seven (sun, moon, Mercury, Venus, Mars, Jupiter, and Saturn) to the uninspiring eleven. These discoveries persuaded Galileo to adopt the Copernican theory, and brought him into collision with the Church. Much has been said about his cruel persecution, but he appears to have received gentle treatment and to have undergone a merely nominal imprisonment. Another philosopher, Vico (1668-1744), a Neapolitan, enjoys a very high reputation in Italy as a thinker. He wrote a philosophy of history, in which he investigated the laws that govern human progress, showed that philosophical theories must treat mankind collectively, and anticipated Comte's theory of the three stages of social development.

Science is not the characteristic trait of this period; for that is to be found in the arts or in the pleasant enervating lassitude of life. In the grand-ducal atmosphere there is a sense of having browsed on lotus-flowers. As we glance back on the great centuries, their efforts look splendid, their high purposes noble, their infinite curiosity commendable, but we are content to sit in a ducal garden, to listen to the Tritons spout into the fountains, to sip chocolate, to meditate sonnets to a partner for the minuet, to gossip about "His Highness and Contessa B——, who, so that young milord, Horry Walpole, says, was once a ballerina," and to confess our sins to fat, amiable priests. We enjoy the badinage of the abbés, the ingenious vacuity of the littérateurs, the cheerful buzz of the café, the daily saunter on the fashionable promenade, the drive in the park, and all the details of theatrical make-believe existence.

As one becomes used to this lotos-laden atmosphere, one gets lenient impressions of the arts, of their peculiar and characteristic agreeableness, and rapidly loses one's previous too scornfully classical attitude. In an earlier chapter we indulged in some high-flown denunciation of the Baroque in architecture. That was because we were fresh from the Renaissance. Now that we have eaten of the lotos, we refrain from comparison and enjoy the arts in their new phases, in and for themselves. There is hardly an Italian city that would not be poorer for the absence of the Baroque. Rome, for instance, owes most of its charm to these decadent generations, to the Villa Medici, the Villa Borghese, the Spanish Steps, the Trevi Fountain, the Piazza Navona.

A Neapolitan, Bernini (1598-1680), was the master spirit of the best Baroque, both in architecture and in sculpture. His greatest achievement is the splendid colonnade which reaches out like two arms from St. Peter's Church and clasps the sunny piazza in its embrace (1667). Bernini's statues, his fountains, his decorations and ornaments, make a good history of the time. They undoubtedly reveal decadence, yet they are respectfully imitative of the great achievements of the Renaissance, whereas the works of his numerous disciples are surcharged with contortion, obvious effort, and strain for effect. There is a maximum of visible exertion with a minimum of real accomplishment. Details are multiplied, and ornaments bear little or no relation to the organic structure of the buildings which they adorn; yet that practice is an Italian trait, and even in excess has a picturesque merit. The baser work of this style, exhibited in the vainglorious churches of the Jesuits, is sometimes called the Jesuit style. After this period of stormy ornament came a calm in the eighteenth century, façades became rectilinear, and there was a general subsidence of obvious effort.

In painting the school of Bologna, led by Lodovico Caracci (1555-1619) and his nephews, Agostino and the more noted and gifted Annibale, set the fashion. They endeavoured to combine faithfulness to nature with all the merits of all their predecessors, and are therefore called the eclectic school. They remained the cynosure of touring eyes until the middle of the nineteenth century. Sir Joshua Reynolds admired and praised them. Some of their disciples were for a long time almost as famous as Raphael. Domenichino's Last Communion of St. Jerome held a place of honour in the Vatican Gallery equal to Raphael's Transfiguration. Guido Reni's Aurora, painted on the ceiling of the casino in the Rospigliosi palace in Rome, had a tremendous vogue, and even now tourists, escaped from the critics, admire it privily. Guercino, Sassoferrato, and also the lachrymose Carlo Dolci are other celebrated members of the school. Another school, almost equally famous, was devoted to Naturalism,—imitation of starving old beggars and a general depiction of want, misery, and squalor. Of these painters the principal were Caravaggio (1569-1609), a Neapolitan, and his pupil Ribera, known as Lo Spagnoletto, because he was born in Spain. A later group, the Venetians of the eighteenth century, consisted of Canaletto, Bellotto,

Guardi, and others who painted again and again the idle canals and pleasure-loving palaces of Venice. The greatest of this group was Tiepolo (1693-1770), who attained in a measure the grand manner of the great masters of the sixteenth century.

In literature, though that also had flashes of seriousness, as in Filicaia's celebrated sonnet to Italy adapted by Lord Byron,—

Italia! O Italia! thou who hast The fatal gift of beauty—

the spirit of the Baroque, in its lightest and pleasantest manner, expressed itself to the full by means of the Academy of Arcadia. The unreality of the whole Italian world was concentrated in this Academy, which soon had branches, imitations, colonies all over the peninsula. It was founded in Rome (1692) by Gravina, a jurist, Crescimbeni, a priest, and other dilettanti, for the ennoblement of literature, the purification of taste, and other meritorious purposes. The members called themselves Arcadian shepherds and shepherdesses, took pastoral names, composed sonnets by the bushel, wrote one another's biographies, and were altogether delightfully silly. Goldoni, the playwright, gives a glimpse of these littérateurs in the eighteenth century as he observed them in Pisa.

One day he passed a garden gate and saw within the garden a crowd of ladies and gentlemen grouped by an arbour. He was told, "The assembly which you see is a colony of the Arcadia of Rome, called the Colony of Alpheus, named after a very celebrated river in Greece, which flowed through the ancient Pisa in Elis." Goldoni went up to the circle and listened to a number of gentlemen who recited poems, canzoni, ballads, sonnets, etc. He observed that the company looked at him as if desirous to know who he was. Eager to satisfy their curiosity, he asked the president if a stranger might be permitted to express in poetry the satisfaction which he experienced in being present on so interesting an occasion. Goldoni had a sonnet in his head, composed by him in his youth for some similar festival; he hastily changed a few words to adapt it to the present occasion, and recited the fourteen lines with the tone and inflection of voice which set off sentiment and rhyme to the best advantage. The sonnet had all the appearance of being extemporaneous, and was very much applauded. Whether the meeting had come to its appointed end or not he did not know, but everybody got up and crowded about him. Thereupon he was introduced to a whole troop of Arcadian shepherds, who welcomed him most heartily. At another meeting the president, whose proper title was Guardian of the Shepherds, drew a large packet from his pocket, and presented Goldoni with two documents, a certificate of his membership in the Arcadia of Rome under the name of Polisseno (Polixenes), and a legal deed which bestowed upon him the Fegean Fields in Greece; whereupon the whole assembly saluted him under the name of Polixenes Fegeus, and embraced him as a fellow shepherd. Goldoni says that, in spite of the formality of the conveyance, the Turks never acknowledged his title.

Mention of the Arcadia and of Goldoni leads to another art, most characteristic of these two centuries, the player's art. The drama had never been a success in Italy; Machiavelli and Ariosto wrote comedies, but they were no better from a dramatic than from an ethical point of view. After the acknowledged failure of serious comedy, another species took the field, the "Commedia dell'Arte," and definitely established itself at about the time of the beginning of the

Baroque. In this species of comedy the dramatis personæ were masked and always impersonated certain definite characters, and the dialogue was improvised. These masks were Pantalone, our Pantaloon, a Venetian merchant, who always wore a black robe and scarlet stockings, and spoke the Venetian dialect; Il Dottore, the doctor, a pompous ass from Bologna; Arlecchino, Harlequin, a silly and credulous servant in tight hose and motley jerkin, and Brighella, a quick-witted and knavish servant, both speaking the patois of Bergamo; Colombina, the soubrette, a pretty maid-servant from Tuscany; Capitano Spavento, Captain Terrible, a fire-eater from Naples, etc. This comedy, necessarily kept within narrow limits by these characters, was strictly improvisation, except that the playwright provided a scenario, a skeleton plot. It had great success, and troops of Italian comedians went all over Europe; but by the eighteenth century it had run its course and become mere vulgar horseplay, and Goldoni (1707-93), the only brilliant comic playwright that Italy has produced, gave it a death-blow.

Goldoni was a Venetian, and a perfect embodiment of the happy, careless, amiable, entertaining society of the time. He led a roaming life, going to Tuscany to learn good Italian, and finally ending his career with twenty years in Paris. Some of his plays are in the Venetian dialect; two were written in French. There are more than a hundred, counting tragedies, interludes, and all. Their virtue is their lightness. They are made of foam, a delicious dramatic soufflé, and in the hands of accomplished Italian actors, like Eleonora Duse or Ermete Novelli, retain their charm to this day. They are essential for the history of the period, with their counts, barons, marquesses, their ladies, their waiting-maids, their innkeepers, camerieri, cobblers, adventurers, and all their gay mockery of the idle habits of the time.

It will throw a little more light upon the customs of that day to mention cicisbeismo, an unwritten rule of an artificial and idle society, which prescribed that a lady should have a cavaliere servente, a gentleman dangling in attendance upon her. Every lady had a husband, as maidens were not allowed in society, and widows had to choose between a convent and a second marriage; but the husband could not wait upon her, for his own duty as cavaliere servente required him to be in attendance upon somebody else's wife. The duties of the cavaliere servente were to devote himself solely to his lady, to write billets-doux, compose sonnets to her lapdog, to hand her chocolate at conversazioni, to give her his arm on all occasions, to ride beside her coach when she was out driving, and so on. In fact, he was required to do all those little offices, petits soins, which a young gentleman is accustomed to render to the lady whom he is engaged to marry. It was a state of active flirtation, not only sanctioned but required by society. It is said that in some cases the cavaliere servente was agreed upon before marriage, and his name inserted in the marriage contract.

Besides Goldoni's comic drama and the "Commedia dell'Arte" this Baroque Italy gave the world another and far more important gift, the Opera. Italian genius flared up once more and led the world in music. As far back as the days of the Council of Trent the reforming spirit of the Church found its noblest expression in Palestrina's (1524?-94) masses, but after his death, after the Catholic Revival had lost its deeply serious feeling, music took another step. Florence, the old home of genius, was the spot. A group of music lovers, who were full of classic theories about art, wished to revive antique Greek drama, with its combination of poetry, music, and dance. They decided that the words were the chief element, that the music must be subservient to the full emotional expression of the poetry, must intensify the dramatic significance of the story. To give effect to their opinion they devised a method of setting music to declamation, the earliest form of recitative. They meant to revive the Greek drama, but they produced the opera. After a few years of work over the new ideas, in 1600, at the Pitti Palace, an opera was publicly performed in honor of the espousals of Maria dei Medici and Henry IV of France. This was the first public performance of a secular opera. Soon afterwards Monteverdi (1567-1643), a revolutionary genius in the history of music, produced his operas at Mantua. In 1637 the first public opera house was opened in Venice; others quickly followed; the opera became a favourite diversion, and Italian singers carried it to France, Germany, Austria, and England. In the same year as the performance in the Pitti Palace, a dramatic oratorio, "The Soul and the Body," was publicly performed in Rome. The oratorio was greatly developed by Carissimi (1604-74) of the Roman school, and with him and his successors acquired much stateliness and beauty. Its influence on the opera, however, was not good, at least if we adopt the opinion of those Florentine Hellenes and of Wagner, for it developed music as an independent element, and did not subordinate it to dramatic action.

With the exception of this misdevelopment of the opera, all music evolved brilliantly and well in Italy, and especially in Naples, which eclipsed all other cities, and showed that she, too, had her individual genius. Alessandro Scarlatti (1659-1725) wrote a great number of operas and oratorios, and composed a vast quantity of ecclesiastical music. He was followed by his son Domenico Scarlatti, by Durante, Leo, and Jommelli, by Pergolesi, Piccinni, Cimarosa, and Paisiello, who followed one another, like a flight of singing birds, through the eighteenth century. The Italian opera, even then, had the characteristics of subordinating dramatic propriety and all semblance of reality to arias, trills, and vocal exaggeration, but it was not till the beginning of the nineteenth century—with Rossini, Bellini, Donizetti—that the Italian opera (if I may venture to adapt a famous phrase) became melted Baroque. There were other schools of music at Rome, Bologna, and Venice. It was in Venice that the four famous asylums for girls, conservatori, were turned into music schools, and gave their name to training schools for musicians all over the world.

Besides the opera one must note, in mentioning Italian musical genius, the violin-makers, the Amati of Cremona, the greater Stradivarius (1644-1737), and other famous makers of Cremona, Brescia, and Venice; also the organ-builders, the Antignati of Brescia; the great Italian singers, then as now favourites of the world; as well as the greatest of libretto-writers, Metastasio.

Metastasio (1698-1782) had a career that can only be compared to that of a successful prima donna. As a boy he was adopted by the Arcadian lawyer, Gravina, and brought early to drink of the Pierian spring. After Gravina's death he spent his money, got into the company of singers and musicians at Naples, and composed the words of an opera "Dido," while still a youth of five-and-twenty. "Dido" had immense success, and from this time on Metastasio poured out play after play in words that went halfway and more to meet the accompanying music. His renown was triumphant throughout Europe; he became the pet of lords, ladies, kings, and Popes. He flitted from court to court, and sipped the honey of facile success; he serves as the embodiment of the Italian opera, or rather as a poetical spirit, a kind of baroque nightingale, to chant the charm, the sentiment, the sweetness, the unreality, of these two make-believe centuries.

As we take leave of the Seventeenth and Eighteenth Centuries (a somewhat ignoble pair), their architecture, painting, literature, and music, we must, as in other matters, remember the good and forget the bad. We must keep in mind the Spanish Steps, which offer at their base ample room for all the flowers of all the flower-sellers of Rome, then rise in easy flight, pause, rest, and mount again, tier upon tier, till the top step stretches out into a terrace, where the pedestrian, glad to pause, turns and looks back over Rome towards the majestic dome of St. Peter's. We must remember the Trevi Fountain where gods and nymphs and waters splash and frolic together, or Guido's Aurora, where Apollo looses the rein to his heavenly horses as they gallop after Lucifer, while the straight-backed hours dance divinely alongside. We must recall the sweet sentiment in Metastasio, the light nothingness of Goldoni, the merriment of Harlequin and Columbine, the violins of Stradivarius, the singing of Farinello and Pacchierotti, the melodies of Pergolesi, and the general pleasantness of an idle, amiable society. Then we want to join the eighteenth-century travellers,—Addison, Walpole, President de Brosses, or Goethe,—and we look back with vain regret to that happy lotos-eating time, and wish it would return again.

CHAPTER XXXIV: THE NAPOLEONIC ERA (1789-1820)

Now come those great events, most important to Italy, the French Revolution and the invasion by Napoleon. The storm burst upon a scene of quiet. Italy was still like a comedy of Goldoni, dukes enjoying taxes and mistresses, priests accepting oblations and snuff, nobles sipping chocolate and pocketing rent, while the poor peasants, kept behind the scenes, sweated and toiled for a bare subsistence.

Before the Revolution came the premonitory breezes of philosophical philanthropy wafted across the Alps from the Encyclopedists. As they affected the various rulers differently, it is necessary to descend to some particulars. In Piedmont no philosophical philanthropy warmed the king; he wrapped his cloak tighter about him, and deemed the old ways good enough. He maintained his court in imitation of Versailles, and drilled his soldiers in imitation of Frederick the Great. Nobles alone were employed in the higher ranks of the civil service, nobles alone were made officers in the army; in return, they were treated like schoolboys, not allowed to leave a prescribed path without permission. The clergy had the privileges of the old régime; their tribunals had sole jurisdiction over priests, and tried to maintain jurisdiction over the laity for all offences that had a smack of sin. King, nobility, and clergy clung to the autocracy, and were resolved to maintain it in full vigour. A rash admirer of Montesquieu wrote a treatise upon "Constitutional Monarchy," and was put in prison.

In Lombardy the House of Austria really plunged into reform; it reorganized the administration, reapportioned taxes, curtailed clerical privileges, abolished the Inquisition, improved roads, favoured agriculture, stimulated trade, and encouraged manufacture. New ideas were broached. Beccaria published his famous book "On Crimes and Punishments," which began the attack on the atrocious, old penal cruelties. French philosophy was discussed. The physicist Volta, famous for his electrical discoveries, occupied a chair in the university at Pavia. Austrian garrisons indeed were on duty, but Lombardy prospered as it had not done since the days of the Sforzas.

In Venice the new ideas did not affect the government. The old system continued. The Great Council of Patricians sat in conservative indolence; the ornamental Doge shuffled about, the Senate talked, and the Council of Ten maintained its petty despotism. Venice was moribund. Her voice was no more heard in European affairs. Her army had dwindled to a few undisciplined and inefficient regiments; her arsenal was little employed. Gayety, luxury, vice, reigned triumphant; all the young blades of Europe went thither to carouse.

In Parma the flood of philanthropic reform had flowed strong; the minister of state, a Frenchman, full of Parisian ideas, had introduced many beneficial changes, but a new duke, dissipated and devout, slipped back into the old ways; and its little neighbour, Modena, concentrated its attention on avoidance of all possible offence to its neighbours.

In Tuscany, an appanage of Austria, reform bounded along. The Grand Duke, Leopold I, proposed to destroy every remnant of the Middle Ages; he attacked the power of the ubiquitous priests, granted free trade in grain, and equalized taxes,—without discrimination even in favour of his own estates. He improved the universities of Pisa and Siena, drained the marshes of the Maremma, and led the way in abolishing torture and capital punishment; he rendered a public account of the state's revenues; and, in short, put in practice the advanced philanthropic ideas on government.

In the Papal States, on the other hand, mediævalism lay heavy. There was no commerce, no manufacture, little agriculture. Priests were everywhere, greedy relations of the Pope almost everywhere. No laymen were given office. Ancona, a seaport, and Bologna, with its university, were the only exceptions to general wretchedness. The finances were in extreme confusion; the offerings of the faithful, the sale of offices, the multiplication of taxes, did little more than pay interest on the bonded debts. Rome was a little, unimportant, ecclesiastical city.

In Naples, however, even the Bourbons felt the fresh breath of reformation. A reforming minister expelled the Jesuits and tried to reduce the number of superfluous priests, monks, and nuns, and to root out the old feudal privileges. In the city itself a goodly company of men gathered together, cultivated ideas, and followed the lead of the French philosophers. Poor Sicily, overridden by barons and priests, lagged behind, a prey to the feudal system, and so unsusceptible to new ideas that the reforming prime minister could not budge the dead weight of custom. The people preferred to help one another in their own way, and resorted to that mysterious society, the Mafia.

Thus was Italy, half philanthropically inclined, half despotically, with few outward indications of the great awakening of the nineteenth century. One such indication might have been found in the life and character of a gentleman of Turin. Vittorio Alfieri (1749-1803) was a kind of antique Roman, a new Brutus, of passionate and lofty nature. He embodied his ideas of liberty in classic tragedies, which stirred Italian manhood in those days, but now are extremely tedious to read. He boldly gave vent to his hatred of foreign oppression, preached freedom, and appealed to the "future Italian people." His autobiography, somewhat condensed and expurgated, might be put into Plutarch. He stands in history, not as a great tragedian, but as the first example of the rebirth of that antique virility which was to display itself so brilliantly in the nineteenth century.

Down into this little world of periwigs and lavender came the French Revolution. All who had applauded Alfieri's tragedies were delighted, except Alfieri himself, who hated the French. But the Italian princes took fright at the democratic volcano, and talked of a general union against France. Piedmont alone was vigorous enough to take action; she made a league with Austria (1792). Nothing important happened until young Napoleon took command of the French army of invasion (1796), and began to tear "the heart out of Glory." It would be useless to relate in detail his wonderful career in Italy. He arranged the peninsula as a housekeeper shifts the furniture in an unsatisfactory room. He took Nice and Savoy from Piedmont, Lombardy from Austria, formed the little states south of the Po into a republic, took the temporal power from the Pope, and set up a Roman Republic. He turned the Kingdom of Naples into a republic and then back again into a kingdom, first for his brother Joseph, and then for his general, Murat (1808). He converted Genoa into the Republic of Liguria. Venice, like old Priam before bloody Pyrrhus, fell at the whiff and wind of the victor's sword; the Great Council resigned without a struggle, and the Republic of St. Mark after an existence of a thousand years came to its end. It was then handed over to Austria, but after Austerlitz taken back again. In 1805, having become Emperor, Napoleon turned the northern part of the peninsula into the Kingdom of Italy, and put the iron crown of Lombardy on his own head, saying, "God has given it to me, woe to him that touches it." In 1806 he put an end to the Holy Roman Empire, and forced the Emperor, Francis II, to resign the Imperial crown.

The old laws of political gravitation ceased to act, and Italy was moulded and broken and moulded anew, as if creation had begun again. The revolutionary ideas on which Napoleon's power at first rested had spread everywhere; liberty, equality, democracy were a part of every man's stock of familiar thoughts, and the conception of an Italian kingdom, vaguely associated with the poetic dreams of Dante, Petrarch, Machiavelli, had become a political fact. Italy was changed forever, the old Goldoni comedy was gone; Napoleon had given the coup de grâce to the old régime.

There was another side to the Napoleonic domination. A multitude of men had been forcibly enlisted in Napoleon's armies; twenty-six thousand, it is said, perished in the terrible retreat from Moscow. The French were arrogant and they were foreigners. Changes had been made too quickly and with too reckless a disregard for Italian wishes. Nobles and clergy had been despoiled of privileges, peasants had been confused and bewildered, the pious had been scandalized by Napoleon's treatment of the Pope; all these longed for the restoration of the old political divisions and of the old easy ways.

After Napoleon's overthrow the Napoleonic states in Italy fell almost immediately. The viceroy of the Italian kingdom, Napoleon's stepson Eugène Beauharnais, slunk away; and in the south, after some vicissitudes, Murat was caught and shot (1815). Kings, dukes, and Pope came tripping back to their thrones. The Congress of Vienna decided that the doctrines of the French Revolution were quite wrong, that law, order, and the principle of legitimacy were bound up together, that states belonged to their royal families in tail male, and reparcelled Italy among its petty sovereigns, acting quite as despotically as Napoleon had done. It gave Venice to Austria, Genoa to Piedmont, and Parma to Marie Louise, the Austrian wife of Napoleon, for her life, as she had to be decently provided for. The Dukes of Parma received Lucca until her death, when they were to return to Parma, and then Lucca was to be annexed to Tuscany. Metternich, Hardenberg, Castlereagh, Talleyrand, and their associates complimented one another on the happy completion of their task, and the Congress broke up.

In Piedmont the king, loyally welcomed home, put back everything to the position in which it was before the disturbances; the old dispossessed nobles were restored to their places in the civil and military service, and the carrière ouverte aux talents was closed. In Lombardy and Venice Austrian officials held a tight rein, and a watchful secret service (sbirri) prowled about ready to pounce on plotting youth like owls upon field mice. In Parma and Modena the eye of the Austrian government was always peering and peeping. In Tuscany Austrian influence also was dominant; but the Grand Duke was a gentle, kindly, paternal person, and his subjects were placidly content, for the old Tuscan fire had died out, and no Tuscan was so crazy as to dream of revolution or of a united Italy. In the Papal States the reaction was complete; the Inquisition was restored, the Jesuits recalled, the civil service limited to priests. But in Naples the reaction was worst. The despicable Ferdinand, who dropped his number IV of Naples to become Ferdinand I of the Two Sicilies, restored the old régime, and swept away the autonomy of Sicily, which had had a separate parliament for hundreds of years, and since 1812 a constitution also. Ferdinand humbly followed every hint from Austria. The will of Austria was supreme from Venice to Naples, and behind Austria was the conservative judgment of the ruling classes of all Europe, still frightened by the Revolution. European nobles and landowners agreed that the riotous desires of the middle class and proletariat for political privileges must be crushed down.

CHAPTER XXXV: THE REAWAKENING (1820-1821)

Outwardly despotism had been triumphantly reëstablished, and Popes, princes, and privileged persons in general made a gallant attempt to pretend that the French Revolution and the Napoleonic upheaval had never taken place. Nevertheless, the quiet on the surface did not extend underneath. Inwardly the new ideas and aspirations were fermenting from Piedmont to Calabria. The Carbonari (Charcoal-burners), a secret society organized against despotism, plotted for freedom and for constitutions. Their members were thickest in the Kingdom of Naples, but spread throughout Italy. The spark necessary to set ablaze this hidden discontent came from Spain. There a successful rebellion obtained a constitution. The thrill stirred Naples. A company of soldiers under two young lieutenants rebelled (1820), many joined them, a general put himself at their head. The army would not fight them. The insurgents demanded a constitution, with a parliament, a free press, trials according to law, etc. The dastardly king was frightened into promises, but as the insurgents were not content with promises, he granted a constitution, and solemnly swore to maintain it. These revolutionary tumults, however, had alarmed the comfortable, conservative ruling classes and their leaders, the Emperors of Austria, Prussia, and Russia. An Imperial conference was held at Laybach (1821), and Ferdinand attended. The new constitution, indeed, forbade him to leave the kingdom without permission from parliament, but he had obtained leave by promising to argue in favour of the new régime. Whatever his arguments were the Holy Alliance disregarded them, and charged Austria with the duty of restoring despotism in Naples. Austria obeyed. An overpowering army easily scattered the Neapolitan constitutionalists and put Ferdinand back. The constitution, parliament, free press, and all the other obnoxious revolutionary institutions were brushed away, and Ferdinand, having hung up in church a lamp of gold and silver as an offset to his perjury, inflicted punishment on the late rebels as fast as he could.

Meanwhile the North had felt the thrill. In Lombardy the hawk-eyed government pounced down on possible conspirators. Silvio Pellico, the pathetic author of "Le Mie Prigioni" (My Prisons), and his friend Maroncelli, were arrested and put into prison (1820), there to stay for ten years. A little later Confalonieri, head of the Milanese nobility, and a group of gentlemen were seized and sent to prison. They were set free only in 1836, on the accession of a new Emperor. Some of them, Castillia, Foresti, and Albinola, then sought refuge in the United States. I quote from the unpublished diary of an American to show what kind of men these conspirators were: "Castillia is an Italian, of an honourable Milanese family. At the age of twenty-three he, with other noble and brave Italians, lovers of their country, was thrown into the dungeons of Spielberg (Moravia) by Austrian despots, and there chained and confined, sometimes in total solitude, enduring the sharpest privations and basest ignominies for seventeen years. Then on the accession of a new Emperor they were released and exiled to America—they were men of superior intelligence and education, honourable gentlemen, true-hearted, loving men—Castillia possessed all the virtues that one can name and in their most attractive forms."

What these gentlemen suffered for love of their country may be read in "Le Mie Prigioni."

Pellico himself was a Christian saint. After years of solitary confinement he and Maroncelli were put together. Maroncelli had a tumour on his leg, which grew so painful that whenever it was necessary to move Pellico helped him. "Sometimes to make the slightest shift from one position to another cost a quarter of an hour of agony." The wound was frightful and disgusting. I quote from Pellico: "In that deplorable condition Maroncelli composed poetry, he sang and talked, and did everything to deceive me and hide from me a part of his pain. He could not digest, or sleep; he grew alarmingly thin, and often went out of his head; and yet, in a few minutes gathered himself together and cheered me up. What he suffered for nine months is indescribable. Amputation was necessary; but first the surgeon had to get permission from Vienna. Maroncelli uttered no cry at the operation, and when he saw the leg carried off said to the surgeon, 'You have liberated me from an enemy, and I have no way to thank you.' By the window stood a tumbler with a rose in it. 'Please give me that rose,' he said to me. I handed it to him, and he gave it to the old surgeon, saying, 'I have nothing else to give you in testimony of my gratitude.' The surgeon took the rose and burst into tears." Such was the character of the men who plotted for the freedom of Italy.

The Papal States likewise had been quivering. Lord Byron was in Ravenna at the time. He enrolled in the Carbonari, and sent a thousand louis to the Neapolitan Constitutional Government with an offer to serve wherever and in whatever capacity they should desire. His letters and diary help us to understand the situation.

BYRON TO MURRAY, HIS PUBLISHER

November 23, 1820.

Of the state of things here it would be difficult and not very prudent to speak at large, the Huns [Austrians] opening all letters. I wonder if they can read them when they have opened them; if so they may see in my most legible hand that I think them damned scoundrels and barbarians, and their Emperor a fool, and themselves more fools than he; all which they may send to Vienna for anything I care. They have got themselves masters of the papal police and are bullying away, but some day or other they will pay for all; it may not be very soon because these unhappy Italians have no consistency among themselves; but I suppose that Providence will get tired of them at last.

SAME TO SAME

December 9.

I open my letter to tell you a fact which will show the state of this country better than I can. The commandant of the troops is now lying dead in my house. He was shot about two hundred paces from my door.... As nobody could or would do anything but howl and pray, and as no one would stir a finger to move him for fear of consequences, I had the commandant carried upstairs to my own quarters.... Poor fellow, he was a brave officer but much disliked by the people.

EXTRACTS FROM BYRON'S DIARY

January 6, 1821.

To-night at the theatre, there being a prince on his throne in the last scene of the comedy, the audience laughed and asked him for a constitution. This shows the state of the public mind here as well as the assassinations. It won't do. There must be a universal republic, and there ought to be.

January 7.

The Count Pietro Gamba took me aside to say that the Patriots had had notice from Forlì [twenty miles away] that to-night the government and its party mean to strike a stroke, that the Cardinal here has had orders to make several arrests immediately, and that in consequence the Liberals are arriving and have posted patrols in the streets, to sound the alarm and give notice to fight. He asked me "what should be done." I answered, "Fight for it, rather than be taken in detail;" and offered if any of them are in immediate apprehension of arrest to receive them in my house (which is defensible), and to defend them with my servants and themselves (we have arms and ammunition) as long as we can, or to try to get them away under cloud of night. On going home I offered him the pistols which I had about me.

January 8.

Rose and found Count Pietro Gamba in my apartments. Sent away the servant. He told me that according to the best information, the government had not issued orders for the arrests apprehended; and that as yet they are still only in apprehension. He asked me for some arms of a better sort, which I gave him. Settled that in case of a row the Liberals were to assemble here (with me) and that he had given the word to the others for that purpose. Concerted operations. I advised them to attack in detail and in different parties, in different places, though at the same time, so as to divide the attention of the troops, who though few yet being disciplined would beat any body of people (not trained) in a regular fight, unless dispersed in small parties and distracted with different assaults. Offered to let them assemble here if they chose. It is a strongish post—narrow street, commanded from within—and tenable walls....

I wonder what figure these Italians will make in a regular row. I sometimes think that like the Irishman's crooked gun they will do only for shooting round a corner; at least this sort of shooting has been the late tenour of their exploits. And yet there are materials in this people and a noble energy if well directed. But who is to direct them? No matter. Out of such times heroes spring. Difficulties are the hotbed of high spirits and Freedom the mother of the few virtues incident to human nature.

January 9.

They say the King of Naples has declared, by couriers from Florence, to the Powers (as they call now those wretches with crowns) that his constitution was compulsive, and that the Austrian barbarians are placed again on war pay and will march. Let them,—"they come like sacrifices in their trim,"—the hounds of hell! Let it be a hope to see their bones piled like those of the human dogs at Morat, in Switzerland.

January 29.

Met a company of the sect (a kind of Liberal Club) called the Americani in the forest, and singing with all their might in Romagnuol "Sem tutti soldat' per la libertà"—(We are all soldiers for liberty). They cheered me as I passed; I returned their salute and rode on. This may show the spirit of Italy at present.

They say that the Piedmontese have at length risen—ça ira!

The news from Piedmont was true. Some officers in the army proposed to demand a constitution from the king and then force him into war with Austria. They believed that Prince Carlo Alberto, who stood next but one in succession to the throne, though only a distant cousin of the sonless king, was in sympathy with them and would act with them. How far they were justified in this belief is uncertain. The leading conspirators had an interview with him, and thought they received satisfactory assurances. In subsequent explanations he denied any such assurances. Thus encouraged, the garrisons of Alexandria and Turin hoisted the tricolour of the Carbonari, and made their demands. The old king, Vittorio Emanuele, not knowing what to do, resigned in favour of his younger brother, Carlo Felice, who was then absent, and appointed Carlo Alberto regent during the new king's absence. Carlo Alberto, always infirm of purpose, with doubt and hesitation took the opportunity and proclaimed a constitution (March, 1821). But the new king, apprised of this wild act, at once annulled it, and bade Carlo Alberto leave the country. Poor Carlo Alberto was in a sad dilemma: should he obey his king and abandon his liberal friends, or cleave to them and be disloyal to the king? He obeyed and went to Tuscany. An Austrian army aided the king to suppress the revolt. The liberals escaped as best they could. Some fled to Spain by way of Genoa, where they were seen by Giuseppe Mazzini, a lad of sixteen, who thereupon resolved "that one could, and therefore one must, struggle for the liberty of Italy."

Thus the revolutionary storms swept by; the sbirri resumed their old methods of prying and spying, and dukes and kings deemed themselves secure of their own again.

CHAPTER XXXVI: PERTURBED INACTIVITY (1821-1847)

After 1821 followed ten years of outward repose. Times were hard for lovers of independence, but hope and purpose had been let loose, and in dark corners, cloaking themselves as best they could, the friends of freedom groped their way. Openly little was done except by exiles, but indirect aid came from literature, which followed the romantic movement, and loudly asserted the revolutionary ideas. There was Ugo Foscolo, the poet, half Venetian, half Greek, who after the return of the Austrians refused to take the oath of allegiance and fled to England, giving, as was said, "to New Italy a new institution, Exile;" Giovanni Berchet, of Milan, poet and man of letters; Gabriele Rossetti, of the Abruzzi, father of Dante Rossetti, a poet himself; and many others. By far the most distinguished was Alessandro Manzoni, a quiet, dignified Milanese gentleman, who wrote patriotic plays, and the famous romance, "I Promessi Sposi" (The Plighted Lovers). He cheered and comforted his compatriots with the thought that in him they possessed a man of letters whom Europe recognized as the peer of Scott, Byron, and Goethe. Scott praised "I Promessi Sposi" most generously, and Goethe said, "It satisfies us like perfectly ripe fruit."

Greater than Manzoni, though at the time less widely known, was the sad poet, Giacomo Leopardi, indisputably the greatest Italian poet since Tasso, and in the judgment of some men to-day, owing perhaps to greater sympathy with his sentiments, superior to Tasso. Leopardi raised Italian self-respect, as Manzoni did, by proof that the genius of the race still lived. He wrote the most patriotic odes since Petrarch. Of these the poem "To Italy" is perhaps most famous. It begins:—

O my country, I see the walls, the arches, The columns, the statues, the defenceless towers Of our forefathers, But the glory I do not see.

Leopardi's wretchedness, in great measure purely personal, was matched by that of his country. Austrian soldiers, ducal sbirri, and Jesuits did their best to destroy all vigour, life, and freedom. The press was stifled; no allusion to freedom was allowed. In a chorus of Bellini's opera "I Puritani" the word liberty was stricken out by the censor and loyalty substituted; and a singer who forgot the change was sent to prison for three days. Things were best in Tuscany and worst in Naples, where Francis I, a rake, bigot, and coward, practised the utmost cruelty. After an insurrection in a village, twenty-six heads were cut off at his command, and exhibited in cages; and once, when a grandmother besought mercy for her two grandsons who were condemned to death, he bade her choose one. She chose one; the other was shot, and she went mad.

The ten long years of inaction at last passed away, and another wave of exasperated independence and patriotism swept over the peninsula. The French Revolution of 1830 was the proximate cause. This time, while Piedmont and Naples remained quiet, for most of their leaders were in exile or in prison, Parma, Modena, and the Romagna burst into insurrection; but the Austrian soldiers marched in, suppressed the revolt, and reseated duke, duchess, and Pope. The attention of the world, however, had been called to priestly government in the Romagna, and the five great Powers,—England, France, Austria, Prussia, and Russia,—not wishing a hotbed of justifiable revolt on the same Continent with comfortable and privileged ruling classes, wrote a collective note to the Pope in which they insisted on certain reforms as indispensable. The papal Curia made promises, but did nothing, and all Italy relapsed outwardly into the condition in which she had been during the ten years of inaction.

Nevertheless, the forces underneath, plotting and conspiring for freedom, were stronger than before, and here and there indications of this growing sentiment cropped out. In 1831, after the ill-fated, melancholy, distrusting, and distrusted Carlo Alberto had succeeded to the Kingdom of Sardinia, an anonymous letter addressed to him was spread broadcast over Italy. This letter bade him choose between two courses,—either to lead the national movement, or to be basely servile to Austria. "Bend your back under the German (Austrian) whip and be a tyrant—But, if as you read these words your mind runs back to that time when you dared look higher than the lordship of a German fief, and if you hear within a voice that cries 'You were born for something great,' oh, obey that voice; it is the voice of genius, of opportunity, that offers you its hand to mount from century to century as far as immortality; it is the voice of all Italy, who awaits but one word, one single word, to make herself all your own. Give her that word. Put yourself at the head of the nation, and on your banner write Union, Freedom, Independence. Sire, according to your answer, be sure that posterity will pronounce you either the first of Italian Men, or the last of Italian Tyrants. Choose."

Carlo Alberto, melancholy as Hamlet, for the burden put upon him was greater than his strength, continued inactive, distrusted, and distrusting. His only answer was to give sharper orders against conspirators. The writer of the letter was a young Genoese of grave countenance, with a sweet mouth and sad, handsome eyes, Giuseppe Mazzini, aged twenty-six, who had already abandoned law for literature, and literature for his country. Suspected of being a Carbonaro, he had been arrested and put in prison. His father, having asked the reason, was told that "his son was a young man of talents, very fond of solitary walks at night, and habitually silent as to the subject of his meditations, and that the Sardinian government was not fond of young men of talents the subject of whose meditations it did not know." In prison Mazzini became convinced that the true aim of patriots was the unity of all Italy, and that the means should be the people, not the princes. After a few months of imprisonment he was banished. It was then that he wrote the letter.

In exile he began the task of rousing the Italian people throughout the peninsula to the need of common effort for a common end. He organized a secret society, and named it Young Italy. Its purpose was to make Italy free, united, and republican. The first article of its constitution read: "This society is instituted for the destruction, now become indispensable, of all the governments of the peninsula, and for the union of all Italy in a single state under republican government." The new society spread rapidly, and was, perhaps, the greatest individual cause of final success.

Mazzini was a master conspirator, a very St. Paul of the Risorgimento. His whole life was a passionate renunciation of all the pleasures and comforts for which most men live, and a passionate dedication of himself to his ideals. He is a striking illustration of the saying, The man whose heart is lifted up within him shall not find the path smooth before him, but the just shall live by his faith. His ideals soared higher and higher; not content with hope for Italy, he made plans for helping all Europe. He became an object of suspicion all over the Continent, and was driven from country to country, till he finally went to England, but he never ceased to preach and teach, to urge and encourage, to plot and counterplot. He believed in sacrifice, both of himself and of others, and instigated desperate uprisings. One of these, a wild invasion of Piedmont which came to nothing, is memorable because among the list of those who were subsequently proscribed for participation in it was a young seaman, a native of Nice, then a part of Savoy, Giuseppe Garibaldi. Mazzini himself stayed in England, where the cruelest accusations were made against him. He endured slander, malice, poverty, outward failure, still steadfast at his task. He says, "I have not for an instant thought that unhappiness may influence our actions." He knew Carlyle, who bore witness in his favour: "I have had the honour to know Mr. Mazzini for a series of years, and whatever I may think of his practical insight and skill in worldly affairs, I can with great freedom testify that he, if I have ever seen one such, is a man of genius and virtue, one of those rare men, numerable unfortunately but as units in this world, who are worthy to be called martyr souls; who, in silence, piously in their daily life understand and practise what is meant by that."

While Young Italy and the Carbonari worked in secret, literature continued to carry on the task of arousing enthusiasm for national achievements and national ideals. The patient piety of Silvio Pellico's "Le Mie Prigioni" was a most effective denunciation of Austrian tyranny; the plays of Giovan Battista Niccolini, of Florence, on subjects famous for Italian patriotism, were stirring appeals against despotism, civil and ecclesiastical; the romantic novels of Massimo d'Azeglio, of Piedmont, the patriot painter and statesman, reminded youth of the great days of old; other novels, passionate and patriotic, by Tommaso Grossi, of Belluno, and by Francesco Domenico Guerrazzi, of Leghorn, did likewise. These romances so pitifully uninteresting to-day did much; but a book of a different character had in its way a still more brilliant career. Vincenzo Gioberti, of Turin, began life by taking orders; he became patriotic, was suspected, imprisoned, exiled; in exile he studied, taught, and thought. In 1843 he published in Brussels "Il primato morale e civile degli Italiani" (The Moral and Civil Primacy of the Italians), a book that rehearsed the old glory of Italy and pointed out new ways by which that ancient glory might be renewed. Gioberti advocated a confederation of the Italian States (excluding the Austrian provinces) with the Pope at its head. The book had tremendous success; its ideas were accepted and became a party creed; and Gioberti is entitled to rank as one of the factors in the Risorgimento. Oddly enough, as it seems to us now, his plan was on the verge of execution.

At this time Gregory XVI was Pope, a reactionary man, devoted to ecclesiastical history, and, according to his detractors, to Orvietan wine. He showed the extreme of papal incapacity for civil administration; in the papal cities was squalor, in the country brigandage, in both dense ignorance. But on Gregory's death Cardinal Mastai-Ferretti, an amiable, smiling, charming, handsome, liberal-minded cardinal, who had applauded Gioberti, became Pius IX (July, 1846). Within a month or two Pius granted amnesty to political prisoners, appointed a commission to study the necessary reforms in his states; permitted, tacitly at least, liberty of the press; announced a Council of State to consist of lay members; and authorized the organization of a civic guard. He was hailed with enthusiasm throughout the peninsula. Here was Gioberti's ideal Pope. Here was the man to lead the Italian Guelfs and drive the Barbarians from Italy.

That the ecclesiastical head of organized conservatism, the great bulwark of authority, the maintainer of ancient things, should be hailed as a saviour by men desiring independence, freedom, and war, needs a word of further explanation. In this period of decadence and servitude, while Austrian officers played the peacock on every piazza from Milan to Naples, Italians could remember that an Italian Pope was head of the greatest corporate body in the world, that tribute was paid into his treasury from every country in Europe, that kings treated him with deference, and that from East and West hundreds of servant bishops came to the foot of his throne. These thoughts, coupled with inapplicable memories and desperate hopes, led men to regard Pius IX as the predestined leader of the liberal movement; and shouts of "Hurrah for Italy, the Pope, and the Constitution!" were heard throughout the peninsula.

Hope, too, arose in Piedmont. King Carlo Alberto received Massimo d'Azeglio in audience (1845), and bade his astonished subject tell his friends that when the occasion should present itself, his own life, his sons' lives, his treasure, and his army would all be spent for the Italian cause. A year later the king withstood Austria in a dispute over customs; and a little later still, at an agrarian congress a member rose and read a letter from the king which ended, "If ever God shall give us grace to be able to undertake a war of independence, no one but me shall command the army. Oh, what a glorious day will that be when we shall be able to utter the cry of national independence!"

Thus encouraged by king and Pope, patriots, from Piedmont to Sicily, waited in tremulous expectation for the coming of great events.

CHAPTER XXXVII: TUMULTUOUS YEARS (1848-1849)

The period of waiting for coming events was short. The whole Continent of Europe was straining like a greyhound in its leash; Italy, from end to end, was on tiptoe with excitement; and the year 1848 came rushing in with swashbuckler fury.

In Italy the revolutionary movement began in Palermo. The people attacked the Bourbon soldiers and drove them out. Their example was followed throughout the island. Across the channel Naples arose and demanded a constitution. The frightened king granted it (January 29). In Piedmont at an assemblage of journalists, the director of a newspaper, "The Risorgimento," declared that the time appropriate to petitions for the banishment of the Jesuits and for the institution of a national guard had passed, and that a constitution should be demanded. The speaker was a stoutish man of thirty-eight, with a square face under a high forehead. He wore spectacles, and under his chin a fringe of beard ran round from ear to ear like a ravelled bonnet string; he looked like a distinguished and amiable professor, except that there was a pinch to his nostrils and a compression to his lips which suggested an arrogant lineage and inherited notions of "Let those take that have the power, and let them keep that can." In fact, Count Camillo Cavour belonged to the old Piedmontese aristocracy. As a lad he served in the engineer corps of the army, then travelled in England (which he admired greatly) and in France, studying all kinds of social matters, from machinery to constitutions. On his estates he was a practical farmer, and he took keen interest in public life. It was at this time that he first became a man of note.

The city of Turin took up Cavour's cry, and the king acceded. The Grand Duke of Tuscany granted a constitution. The Pope was slow to bestir himself, but the news of revolutionary success in Paris quickened his gait, and he too granted a constitution. In the Austrian provinces, Lombardy and Venetia, there were tumults, arrests, cavalry charges, and martial law; then came news of the revolt in Vienna itself and word that the scared Emperor promised a constitution. Venice accepted the promise; but Milan, where a citizen had been killed by the soldiers, broke into rebellion. Carts, carriages, tables, chairs, pianos, bedsteads, were heaped up to defend the streets; sixteen hundred and fifty barricades were erected; men snatched knives, hammers, arquebuses, axes; all took part,—boys, lads, old men, priests. These were the famous Five Days of Milan. Every street, every house was a battleground, and Field Marshal Radetzky, with fourteen thousand men, was driven from the city. Revolt spread through Lombardy. When the news reached Venice the citizens rose, forced the Austrian governors to surrender, and proclaimed anew the Republic of Venice. Daniele Manin was made president.

This glorious news, Venice republican, Milan victorious over Radetzky, flew to Turin. Every liberal went mad with excitement. The centuries of national humiliation seemed past. Now had come the hour for which Piedmont had trained and disciplined itself, for which it had hoped and longed; now should Piedmont uplift Italy and fight its country's battle. Cavour cried that there was but one possible course,—immediate war with Austria. A great crowd in tremulous anxiety thronged before the royal palace. At midnight on March 23, Carlo Alberto stepped out on his balcony and waved a tricolour scarf. Next day a royal proclamation stated that the Piedmontese army would march to the aid of Lombardy and Venice. A shout of joy went up throughout Italy. Modena and Parma cast out their dukes and sent recruits to help. The Grand Duke of Tuscany, the Pope, even the King of Naples, compelled by necessity, each sent an army. The war was a national crusade.

At first the campaign went well. The Italian allies numbered more than ninety thousand men; and Carlo Alberto, leading the main body, forced the Austrians under Radetzky within the quadrilateral made by the strong fortresses, Verona, Peschiera, Mantua, and Legnano. But the King of Sardinia was no general; he lacked energy, decision, character. While he dawdled, not knowing what to do, Radetzky received reinforcements. This hesitation and delay cooled the first glorious burst of union and freedom. Pius IX felt doubts; what right had the Vicar of Christ to take part in war? Were not Austrians and Italians alike in the sight of God? What had the Universal Church to do with national divisions? And might not Austria become heretic and secede from the papal rule? He said he would not fight. So great, however, were the tumults in Rome that he was forced to face about once again, but his tergiversation gave a fatal blow to the cause. In Naples the watchful Ferdinand, eager for a pretext, took advantage of some street riots to dissolve parliament, and bade his army come home. One general with a few hundred men disobeyed, but the rest turned back.

In the north the old jealousies between the Italian States wedged themselves in and broke the new-made union. Venice, instead of uniting with Piedmont in a joint political confederation, insisted upon remaining an independent republic, and Milan hesitated out of jealousy of Turin. Of these discords and hesitations the octogenarian Radetzky took advantage. Within thirty days the Tuscan army had been destroyed, the papal army made prisoners, and Piedmont was left alone to maintain the Italian cause in the field. In a three days' battle at Custoza (July 23-25) the issue was decided. The beaten Piedmontese were forced to surrender Milan, and to retreat across the river Ticino into their own land, and Austria returned triumphant into full possession of her provinces, except the city of Venice. The little Dukes of Parma and Modena returned also.

Elsewhere the current of events ran equally fast. In Sicily Ferdinand bombarded the revolted city of Messina (hence his nickname Bomba), and forced it to surrender; and in Naples he made a mock of the constitution. Rome was in horrid confusion. Pius IX appointed Pellegrino Rossi prime minister, in hope that his energy and vigour might restore peace and quiet; but Rossi was murdered on the steps of the Cancelleria. Rioters wandered at will about the city. Shots were fired near the papal palace on the Quirinal. The Pope, terribly frightened, fled from the city, and took refuge across the Neapolitan border at Gaeta. He was besought to return, but would not. The revolutionary leaders convoked an assembly of Roman citizens to decide what form of government to adopt, and, though the Pope hurled excommunications at all who should take part, the radicals met (February 5, 1849), declared the Temporal Power at an end, and established the Roman Republic. In Tuscany the republican fire likewise blazed up; the Grand Duke ran after the Pope to Gaeta, and a provisional government was appointed with a triumvirate at its head.

In the north, Piedmont and Austria renewed the war. On March 23, at Novara, a little town on the Piedmontese side of the Ticino, the deciding battle was fought. The Austrians were completely victorious. King Carlo Alberto asked for a truce. Radetzky's terms were so severe that the king, feeling himself the chief cause of this severity, resolved to be of no further detriment to his country. He abdicated in favour of his son, Vittorio Emanuele II, and went into exile, where he soon died. The young king made peace on harsh terms.

All rational hope for the Italian cause was at an end, but the dismembered parts struggled on. The men of Brescia defended themselves gloriously for days, barricading every alley and making a fort of every house, but they were overpowered; the Austrian general Haynau inflicted atrocities that made his name a byword throughout Europe. His own report says, "I ordered that no prisoner should be taken, but that every person seized with arms in his hands should be immediately put to death, and that the houses from which shots came should be burned." In Sicily the revolutionists resisted in vain, and the king's authority was reëstablished throughout the island. In Naples all liberals were shamefully and most cruelly persecuted. In Tuscany the mild-mannered Tuscans, dismayed at their own radical government, invited the Grand Duke to return; so he came, bringing Austrian soldiers with him.

In Rome still more notable events happened. Mazzini, as member of the revolutionary triumvirate, was at the head of the government. His task was hard, for the Pope had asked the Catholic Powers to restore him, and Spain, Naples, Austria, and France, hastened to obey. France interfered because Louis Napoleon, president of the new republic, wished the support of the French clerical party; nevertheless, he had to proceed cautiously in order not to vex the liberals, and pursued a wavering course. He said he would send an army to defend real liberty, and would let the Romans decide for themselves what they wanted. The French soldiers advanced to the walls of Rome (April 29, 1849); the Roman republicans were naturally suspicious and treated them as enemies. Skirmishes were fought, and the French constrained to retire. Meanwhile, an Austrian army came from the north, the Neapolitans from the south, and the Spaniards landed at the mouth of the Tiber. The French intimated to the Austrians that this was their affair; the Romans, reinforced by Garibaldi and his Legion, drove back the Neapolitans; and the Spaniards retired quietly, thus leaving France to deal with the situation as she deemed best. French reinforcements arrived, and fighting was begun again.

The Italians defended themselves for three weeks; their soldiers, though brave, were raw, many of them mere volunteers, and ineffectual against regular troops. As Mazzini was the hero in council, so Garibaldi was the hero on the field of battle. The last of knight-errants, he was the very incarnation of Romance and Revolution. Bred to the sea, this Savoyard from Nice always retained the jaunty, gallant bearing of a mariner. His countenance (childlike and lionlike),—with its broad, tranquil brow, benign eye, and resolute mouth,—in youth all sparkling, gradually changed with care and disillusion, but he still kept the seaman's mien and the seaman's lightsome eye. He was the beau ideal of a romantic hero. After his unsuccessful raid into Piedmont he had gone to South America, where he lived a wild life of guerilla warfare, fighting like a Paladin on behalf of republican revolutionaries who were struggling for their freedom. All the time he was training a band of Italian adventurers, his Legion, so that they should be ready when their country had need of them. These men rushed to the defence of Rome. Their entry into the city was most picturesque. The gaunt soldiers, wearing red shirts and pointed hats topped with plumes, their legs bare, their beards full-grown, their faces tanned to copper colour, with their long black hair dangling unkempt, looked like so many Fra Diavolos. At their head Garibaldi, in his red shirt, with loose kerchief knotted round his throat, the regular beauty of his noble, leonine face set off by his waving hair, mounted on a milk-white horse, rode like a demi-god.

Besides this Legion, troops of volunteers came from all over Italy. The character of these patriots may be learned from Mazzini's account of the young Genoese poet Goffredo Mameli, who was killed there. "For me, for us exiles of twenty years who have grown old in illusions, he was like a melody of youth, a presentiment of times that we shall not see, in which the instinct of goodness and sacrifice will dwell unconscious in the human soul, and will not be, as virtue is in us, the fruit of long and hard struggles. Of a disposition lovingly yielding, he was only happy when he could abandon himself to those he loved, as a child in his mother's caress; and yet Mameli was unshakably firm in what touched the faith he had embraced. He was handsome, but careless of his appearance, and sensitive as a woman to the charm of flowers and sweet scents. Such was he when I knew him first at Milan in 1848, and we loved each other at once. It was impossible to see him and not love him. Only twenty-two, he joined the extremes rarely found united, a childlike gentleness and the energy of a lion, to be revealed, and which was revealed, in supreme emergencies."

The defence of Rome was vain. Mazzini escaped by means of an English passport, and Garibaldi led a handful of men eastward hoping to reach Venice. The French soldiers marched into the city, and reestablished the Temporal Power of the Pope. Venice alone remained. Daniele Manin, the valiant dictator, maintained a stout defence for four months, but cholera and hunger came to the enemy's aid. On August 24 the city capitulated, and on the 30th Marshal Radetzky heard the Te Deum of Austrian gratitude played in St. Mark's. In all Italy, except Piedmont, the reaction had triumphed; Piedmont alone was left to become the centre of whatever hopes of independence and unity still existed.

CHAPTER XXXVIII: THE UNITY OF ITALY (1849-1871)

After the uprisings of 1848-49, the old tyrannical system prevailed for eight years and seemed heavier than ever. Liberalism meant suspicion, disfavour, danger. The liberals were not very numerous and did not agree among themselves. Some looked for hope to Piedmont, some to England, some to France. Some were for a republic, some for a confederation, some for unity; some wished insurrection, others lawful agitation.

In Naples the king busied himself with putting the liberals in dungeons. According to the general belief the number of prisoners for political offences in the Two Sicilies was between fifteen and thirty thousand. Among them was Baron Carlo Poerio, "a refined and accomplished gentleman, a respected and blameless character," at one time one of the ministers of the Crown. It happened that Mr. Gladstone, travelling for the benefit of a daughter's health, passed several months in Naples at this time (1850-51). He attended trials of the liberal prisoners, listened to a "long tissue of palpable lies told by witnesses suborned by the government," and visited the horrible and filthy prisons. After his return to England he published his "Letters to the Earl of Aberdeen." He set forth before the English people "the horrors—amidst which the government of that country (Naples) is now carried on." He said that "the present practices of the Government of Naples in reference to real or supposed political offenders are an outrage upon religion, upon civilization, upon humanity, and upon decency." He described the "incessant, systematic, deliberate violation of the law by the Power appointed to watch over and maintain it." "It is the wholesale persecution of virtue,—it is the awful profanation of public religion,—it is the perfect prostitution of the judicial office,—this is 'The negation of God erected into a system of government.'" He recounted Poerio's trial at length, and told how Poerio and fifteen others were confined in a room about thirteen feet long and eight feet high, in which they slept, always chained two by two. These chains were never taken off, day or night. He ended by saying, "It is time that either the veil should be lifted from scenes fitter for hell than earth, or some considerable mitigation should be voluntarily adopted. I have undertaken this wearisome and painful task, in the hope of doing something to diminish a mass of human suffering as huge, I believe, as acute, to say the least, as any that the eye of Heaven beholds."

These letters were sent by Lord Palmerston to every government in Europe, and helped to awaken general European sympathy for the oppressed liberals of Italy.

In the Papal States Pius IX put himself wholly in the hands of the reactionaries and the Jesuits. His government was practically imbecile. Brigands came and went at will. In Forlimpopoli, for instance, a city of the Romagna, a famous highwayman and his band appeared on the stage of a theatre, and made the spectators empty their pockets of their money and of their front-door keys. In Modena, Parma, and Tuscany the governments did whatever they deemed would be pleasing to Austria; and in Lombardy and Venice the Austrians repressed the slightest signs of patriotism.

In Piedmont alone was there light ahead. The young king was the embodiment of the best qualities of his race. The statues of him, carved in the first fury of patriotism, which disfigure many a piazza, reveal only his corpulence, his monstrous mustachios, and the forceful ugliness of his shrewd face. Victor Emmanuel was a soldier born, of careless manners, imperious and brusque, yet with a charm of obvious honesty that won men's hearts and gained for him the title of il re galantuomo. He reminds one of Henry of Navarre, in his dash, his impetuous energy, his shrewdness, his deserved popularity, and his eternally youthful readiness to fall in love. After the defeat at Novara (1849) pressure was put upon him to return to the autocratic system, and, it is said, Austria offered him easier terms if he would. He had been brought up with the old ideas of the royal position, but he was statesman enough to perceive that if Piedmont and the House of Savoy were to lead in the movement of Italian independence, they must win the confidence of the liberals; and he had sworn to maintain the constitution. He was always a man of his word, whatever policy might advise, and answered that he should be loyal to the constitution.

Piedmont's history for the next few years is a record of liberal legislation, as it was then understood. This legislation was especially directed against antiquated ecclesiastical privileges, with the purpose of realizing Cavour's principle, "A free Church in a free State." A little later Cavour was called to the head of the government, and for ten years, with certain brief exceptions, he remained the chief figure on the Italian stage. There are diverse judgments on the very diverse merits of the master-builders of the Italian kingdom; some admire most Mazzini, the indefatigable conspirator, the dreamy idealist, the nobly fanatical republican; others, Garibaldi, the man after Petrarch's heart, the rival of Roland or the Cid; others, Victor Emmanuel, the honourable, bold, shrewd, resolute king; but all agree that Cavour's brilliant diplomacy entitles him to rank as one of the world's great statesmen, and that his work was indispensable to the establishment of the Italian kingdom.

This period prior to the war with Austria is Cavour's. He set the finances of Piedmont on a better basis; he began a series of measures for the development of her resources; he secured various internal reforms, but his brilliant achievement was in his foreign policy. He knew that the Austrians could not be dispossessed without a war, that Piedmont was not strong enough of herself, and that in order to gain allies she must get a hearing before Europe. The Crimean War gave Cavour an opportunity. England and France would have preferred Austria as an ally, and there was much cautious proceeding; but Austria hesitated, and Piedmont offered herself. Many Italians deemed the plan of taking part in a war with which Piedmont had no visible concern a piece of folly; but Cavour carried his point. The Piedmontese army went, behaved with credit, and effaced the unfavourable impression left by the disastrous campaigns of 1848-49. The fruits of the Crimean expedition were gathered at the Congress of Paris (1856), where Cavour, supported by England and France, was able to call the attention of the Congress to the condition of Italy. He pointed to the tyranny of Austria in Lombardy and Venetia, to the abominable condition of the Papal States, to the horrible misgovernment in the Two Sicilies; and he pointed to Piedmont as the bulwark against Austrian preponderance on the one hand, and against the revolutionary spirit on the other. Nothing definite was done, but the Italian question had been broached, and Cavour's participation in the Congress was recognized as a great achievement.

Piedmont's leadership was helped by rash revolts elsewhere, easily put down and cruelly punished; and it became plainer and plainer that through the steady, orderly monarchy of

Sardinia deliverance was to come, if at all, and not through the visionary schemes of Mazzini. The dark, mysterious plans of Napoleon III now loomed on the horizon. Relations between him and Cavour became closer. Cavour, no doubt, would have liked to gain his ends without French aid, but that could not be done. The only other possible ally, England, would not interfere. In the summer of 1858 an understanding was reached between him and Napoleon that in case of Austrian aggression France would aid Piedmont. On January 1, 1859, Napoleon hinted to the world what had happened; on January 10, Victor Emmanuel at the opening of the Piedmontese parliament said that the political situation was not free from perils ahead, "for while we respect treaties, we cannot disregard the cry of pain which comes to us from so many parts of Italy." Count Cavour asked for a loan of 50,000,000 lire. Affairs moved fast. Relations between Piedmont and Austria were strained taut; but it was essential that Austria should be the aggressor. Russia and England, in order to prevent war, suggested a European Congress to consider matters. Napoleon consented; and Cavour, who knew that freedom for Italy could only be obtained by war, feared that his chance had gone. There was talk of disarmament, but no agreement had been reached, when Austria, impatient and arrogant, sent an ultimatum to Piedmont that she must disarm prior to the Congress. Victor Emmanuel refused and war was declared.

The French Emperor crossed the Alps, and in June the allies won the battles of Magenta and Solferino. The Italians believed that Austria would now be driven from every foot of Italian soil: when, suddenly, without consulting Piedmont, Napoleon, for reasons of French policy, made peace with Austria. The Emperor of Austria ceded Lombardy to Napoleon, and Napoleon transferred it to Piedmont; and, as a sop to the spirit of Italian unity, both Emperors agreed to favour the scheme of a confederation of the Italian States with the Pope at its head, but the latter plan was left in the air. This was the end of the high hopes of Italian freedom and unity. Italy had received a slap in the face. Cavour was furious; he had a stormy interview with his king, and passionately urged him not to consent, but the king had the good sense to see that he must. Cavour immediately resigned.

Meanwhile the war had caused the recall of the Austrian troops south of the Po, and the patriots had risen in joy. The Grand Duke of Tuscany, the Duke of Modena, the Duchess Regent of Parma, the papal legates of the Romagna, ran away, and provisional governments were established; but a permanent political disposition was attended with difficulties. The states themselves wished to join Piedmont, but the wish was not unanimous, for many people wanted to preserve local autonomy and their old historic boundaries. Napoleon favoured his vague confederacy, and a European Congress supported his view. Indecision reigned, but the cause of national union triumphed through the vigour of Count Bettino Ricasoli, a man of iron character, head of the provisional government in Tuscany. "We must," he wrote, "no longer speak of Piedmont, nor of Florence, nor of Tuscany; we must speak neither of fusion nor annexation, but of the union of the Italian people under the constitutional government of Victor Emmanuel." Certainly the fugitive dukes could only return by force, and though Continental Europe approved their return, there was nobody to supply the force. The little states voted to join Piedmont.

Piedmont, however, hesitated, in fear of European contradiction. Nobody but Cavour could manage the matter, and he was recalled to office (1860). Cavour appealed to the doctrine of the popular will to be expressed by a plebiscite. France, however, would only consent upon cession of Savoy and Nice, a measure already talked of as the price of the French alliance; and in spite of the reluctance of the king to surrender Savoy, the cradle of his race, the price had to be paid. The cession was made, and Parma, Modena, Tuscany, and the Romagna were united with the Kingdom of Sardinia under the name of the Kingdom of Italy (April 15, 1860).

In the mean time Ferdinand II, King of the Two Sicilies, had died, hated and despised by everybody, and his son Francis II, a weak, ignorant, bigoted lad, had mounted the throne. He refused a suggestion of Victor Emmanuel to join in the war against Austria, threw himself into the arms of the reactionary party, and made an alliance with the Pope. The discontented liberals took courage at the news from the north. In April, 1860, the revolt began in Palermo, and, though suppressed there, spread. Two young patriots, Francesco Crispi and Rosalino Pilo, went about stirring the people to action. Garibaldi was begged to put himself at the head of the proposed revolution. On the night of May 6, two ships, the Lombardy and the Piedmont, secretly left Genoa, and took Garibaldi and a thousand volunteers aboard. This band, known as i Mille, is nearly as famous and as legendary as King Arthur and his Round Table. On May 11, the ships landed at Marsala. Two Neapolitan cruisers came up, but two English men-of-war happened to be there also; and the English captains, under guise of friendly notification to the Neapolitans, took some action which delayed the latter long enough to let the last Garibaldians disembark. Once on shore, Garibaldi's volunteers ran to secure the telegraph office. They arrived just after the operator had telegraphed that two Piedmontese ships, filled with troops, had come into the harbour; a Garibaldian was able to add to the message, "I have made a mistake; they are two merchantmen." The answer came back, "Idiot." The volunteers marched inland. A provisional government was organized; Garibaldi was made dictator, and Crispi secretary of state. The cry was "Italy and Victor Emmanuel!" Garibaldi was joined by insurgent Sicilians, and, with numbers considerably increased, fought and defeated the Bourbon army. The story reads like the exploits of Hector before the Greek trenches. Victory followed victory. Palermo fell, Milazzo and Messina; then he crossed the straits and invaded Calabria (August). This marvellous triumph, for there had been thirty thousand regular troops to oppose Garibaldi, frightened King Francis; he proclaimed a constitution, appealed to Napoleon, and even to Victor Emmanuel, for help. It was too late. Garibaldi swept on victorious, and the king fled from Naples (September 6); the next day Garibaldi marched in and assumed dictatorship of the kingdom.

England approved, but Continental Europe looked askance at this irregular proceeding, and Victor Emmanuel and Cavour began to feel uneasy, apprehensive lest the Great Powers should intervene in Italian affairs. It was a difficult situation. Garibaldi was moving on northward, and proclaimed his intention of going to Rome, regardless of the French army stationed there, and then to Venice, regardless of the European treaties that gave Venice to Austria. Besides, the Pope had collected an army (largely of foreign recruits) to suppress the liberal movements in Umbria and the Marches, and to give aid to the Neapolitan king. Here were further opportunities for foreign intervention. Evidently Cavour must act promptly if he wished Piedmont to continue to control the national movement. He requested the Pope to dismiss his new army. The Pope refused. The Piedmontese army crossed the pontifical border, scattered the papal army, and took possession of all the papal territory, except the city of Rome and the country immediately about it, and then marched on across the Neapolitan boundary. Here the Bourbon army was holding Garibaldi at bay. The arrival of the Piedmontese determined the issue. A less noble man might have shown resentment at having another come at the eleventh hour and seize the fruits of victory, but Garibaldi hailed Victor Emmanuel as King of Italy, refused the proffered honours and rewards, and went home, a poor man, to the little island of Caprera. The Two Sicilies and the liberated parts of the Papal States voted to join the Kingdom of Italy. In February, 1861, the first Italian parliament was held, and Victor Emmanuel formally received the title King of Italy. Excepting Rome and Venice, Italy was free and independent.

Rome was the more pressing question of the two. A history of twenty-five hundred years, a profound sentiment, a patriotic, poetic, romantic love, had inevitably determined that Rome must be the capital of United Italy. On the other hand, opposed to the Italian national sentiment was the historic Catholic sentiment, diffused throughout Europe and strongest in France. The Pope naturally deemed his Italian birth inferior in obligation to his Catholic position. Moreover, the Temporal Power of the Popes had endured for more than a thousand years, and since the time of Julius II the pontifical title had been as good as the title to public or private property anywhere. Catholics honestly believed that this political kingdom was necessary to the independence of the Church. How could the world, they said, believe in papal impartiality if the Papacy were under the thumb of the Italian government? The difference in point of view inevitably brought the ardent Papist and the patriotic Nationalist to mutual injustice. The Italians looked on Pius IX as their worst enemy; the Roman Curia deemed the Italians robbers. French sympathy with the Papists, and especially the presence of a French army in Rome, made the question exceedingly difficult. A special circumstance aggravated the difficulty. The King of Naples, having taken refuge in Rome, armed and subsidized gangs of brigands, who raided the Neapolitan provinces and committed unspeakable outrages. These rascals, when pursued by the Piedmontese army, crossed the pontifical border and were safe. This condition was intolerable.

At this juncture the great statesman who had steadfastly pursued his policy,—a free Church in a free State,—and never lost hope of a peaceful solution of the Roman difficulty, died (June 6, 1861). The priest who shrived him was summoned to Rome, deprived of his parish, suspended from his office, and sent to finish his days in a remote monastery; so strongly did the Roman Court feel that Cavour and his abettors were wicked men.

Cavour's successors, Ricasoli and Rattazzi, with feebler gait, followed his policy as best they could; but uncertainty and hesitation prevailed. The two great questions, Rome and Venice, pressed for solution. The radicals clamored to have the Italian army march on Rome. Garibaldi's impatience would not brook further inaction. He left his island home at Caprera, and betook himself to Sicily, crying, "Rome or Death!" With a little army of hot-tempered radicals he crossed into Calabria. The Italian government had no choice. Regular troops met Garibaldi at

Aspromonte, near Reggio, and bade him withdraw; he refused; shots were fired. Which side fired first is uncertain. Garibaldi was wounded and made prisoner (August 29, 1862). This indignity to the national hero roused much hard feeling, but reasonable men perceived that the solution of the Roman question had to be found in some other way than by a filibustering expedition against a city held by the troops of a power with whom the nation was at peace.

The liberation of Venice came first. Prussia occupied a position in Germany somewhat similar to that of Piedmont in Italy. Both had somewhat similar problems. Both felt antagonism to Austria, and also a suspicion of France. In April, 1866, the two states made an alliance against Austria, who, fearing the combination, tried to break it by offering to cede Venetia to Italy if she would abandon the Prussian alliance. Victor Emmanuel refused, and war began in June. The Italians were beaten both on land and sea, to their great mortification and chagrin. The crushing Prussian victory at Sadowa, however, forced Austria to accept the victor's terms, including the cession of Venice. On November 7 Victor Emmanuel entered the city. Rome alone was left.

Garibaldi made another desperate attempt, but was defeated by the French at Mentana (1867). Not by Italian victories, but in consequence of Prussian victories, the conquest of Rome was finally effected. The French were obliged to withdraw their garrison during the Franco-Prussian War, and then the Italian government, which, to the shame of ardent patriots, had so long forborne out of obedience to the will of the French, gave notice to the world that it would annex Rome. After a useless call upon the Pope for peaceful surrender, Victor Emmanuel directed his army to march on the city. Real resistance was out of the question, but Pius IX had decided to yield only to force. On the 20th of September, 1870, a breach was made in the wall near Porta Pia, a few shots were fired, a few score soldiers killed and wounded, and the Italian army marched in and took possession of the city. A plebiscite was held, and by a vote of 133,681 to 1507 the city voted to become a part of Italy. In June, 1871, the seat of government was formally removed from Florence, and Rome once again, after fifteen hundred years, became the capital of the Kingdom of Italy.

CHAPTER XXXIX: CONCLUSION (1872-1900)

The union of Italy was so triumphant, the efforts which accomplished it so heroic, and the whole tone of Italian history throughout the Risorgimento so romantic and noble, that the period since of necessity looks flat and dull. The Italians themselves had imagined that the union of Italy would be followed by some career, political, moral, or intellectual, that would be comparable to the career of ancient Rome. A reaction was inevitable. No nation could continue at so enthusiastic a pitch. Moreover, the difficulties before it were great.

Chief of these difficulties was the persistent hostility of the Papacy. Pius IX, a kind, lovable, timid man, wholly inadequate to cope with a revolutionary situation, had passed from his early sympathy with the liberal movement to the opposite extreme, and hated it with the hatred of fear. His hatred of liberal ideas may be seen in his conduct with regard to ecclesiastical matters. He insisted upon the extremest conservative dogma, as if it were a shield to protect the Papacy, the papal city, the Papal States, and the whole Catholic world, from all assaults of Satan and his liberal crew. First he proclaimed the dogma of the Immaculate Conception of the Virgin Mary, next he published the "Syllabus," which is a condemnation of all those doctrines commonly embodied in Bills of Rights. Finally, he convoked the Vatican Council (1869-70), and procured a decree that the Pope is infallible in matters of faith and morals. This decree gave the death-blow to whatever remains of republicanism there were in the Church, and established the Pope as absolute monarch. An Ecumenical Council, representing the Church, had previously been the infallible head of the Church; now the Pope was substituted for the Council.

In this way the Church more and more assumed an attitude of irreconcilable hostility to the ideas that prevailed among the educated classes in Italy. After the occupation of Rome by the Italian government, Pius shut himself up in the Vatican palace and proclaimed himself a prisoner. He first advised and then commanded Catholics to stay away from the polls at national elections, and directed his foreign policy to the end of reëstablishing his Temporal Power. This policy, judged by the popular belief in the divine right of nationality and of majorities, is of course wrong; judged by one who regards the interests of the Church as paramount, it may be defended as an attempt to adhere to the old ways under which the Catholic Church had played its extraordinary part in European history. After the occupation of Rome the Italian government passed the Law of Guarantees (May 10, 1871), which guaranteed to the Pope an annual subsidy of somewhat more than 3,000,000 lire a year, and also the personal and diplomatic rights of a sovereign, such as to maintain his court, to receive ambassadors, to have separate postal and telegraph service, to keep the Vatican and Lateran palaces, etc. Pius IX refused to accept the subsidy.

Another difficulty, which has confronted the government since the union, has been the discord between the North and South. The northern provinces, especially Lombardy and Piedmont, have been making progress in manufactures and in commerce; whereas, on the contrary, the South, very ignorant and very poor, and devoted to agriculture, wine, grain, lemons, oranges, etc., without facilities for manufacture and without capacity for commerce, has made doubtful advance. Special causes have hindered it. In Sicily, in consequence of long-continued poverty, ignorance, and misgovernment, the secret societies, known as the Mafia, have overrun great parts of the island. The original cause of the Mafia was probably self-protection, the lower classes banding together to save themselves from the oppressions of the upper classes who clung to the remains of the feudal system. The landowners, for example, had used their control of the courts to maintain privileges and injustice. As a natural consequence, members of the Mafia deemed it ignoble to revenge wrongs by judicial process, and still more ignoble to give any information to any officers of the government. They settled their own disputes and righted their own wrongs. With the grant of suffrage the Mafia became a political power, and only permitted the election of such candidates as it approved.

In Naples there was also a power behind the scenes which resembled the Mafia, but in reality was totally distinct and individual. This Neapolitan power, a legacy from Bourbon times, was the Camorra, a society of criminals or ruffians on the edge of crime, organized for the purpose of levying tribute by blackmail; it was not unlike the worst municipal rings in this country, and gained its livelihood from the vicious, and from politicians who benefited by its support. Both Camorra and Mafia have been very great obstacles to social progress, and still exist.

The North, conscious of a higher standard of civilization, has wished to educate and reform the South, and also, perhaps, has not been unwilling to let taxation fall more heavily in proportion upon the agricultural produce of the South than on the manufactured products of the North. Resenting this assumption of superiority, and suspicious of unfair treatment, especially with regard to indirect taxation, the South has felt itself aggrieved; and so there have been continual misunderstanding and friction between it and the North.

In its foreign relations the country has also had hard problems. France and Italy ceased to be friends. Italy could not forget that the French had upheld the papal power in Rome, and had defeated Garibaldi at Mentana; and France was indignant that Italy had not come to her rescue in 1870. France also was jealous of a rival in the Mediterranean; while the Italians believed that France favoured a revival of the Temporal Power. This unfriendliness, fostered by the Italian clericals, constituted a most disturbing factor in Italy's foreign relations. The breach was increased by other causes, and Italy in alarm turned to find friends elsewhere. Austria and Germany, who had already made an alliance, were glad to have Italy join, as further security for the peace of Europe against any action by France or Russia. So the three joined and made the Triple Alliance (1882), which was renewed from time to time and still exists. This alliance has given Italy ample security against any attack by France, but has imposed upon her very heavy military burdens in order to keep her army at a certain standard of efficiency.

As time went on the actors of the great age dropped off one by one; Mazzini in 1872, Victor Emmanuel in 1878, Garibaldi in 1882. It is after their departure, their noble desires fulfilled, their noble tasks accomplished, that Italy looks little and inadequate. The parliamentary struggles have certainly been neither noble nor romantic. After the occupation of Rome, the Right, the conservative party, under Marco Minghetti, Quintino Sella, and others, was in power for half a dozen years, and by means of a burdensome taxation succeeded in making receipts equal expenses. But taxes and refusal to extend the suffrage led to its fall from power, and the Left, the progressive party, under Agostino Depretis, assumed the government. Depretis abolished an unpopular tax on grinding corn, made primary education compulsory, and extended the suffrage from 600,000 voters to 2,000,000. After these reforms the dominant party ceased to have a definite programme. There was general confusion, known as Transformism. The deputies split up into little groups under petty leaders and fell to log-rolling. The story is dreary and unimportant.

Depretis, who died in 1887, was succeeded by Francesco Crispi, the most striking political figure since Cavour. Crispi began life as an advocate at Palermo, and took part as a very young man in the early agitations for constitutional reforms. He was successful at the bar, and had moved to Naples to practise before the appellate tribunals there, when the events that led to the uprisings of '48 began to effervesce. Crispi took a leading part. After the uprisings had been suppressed, he lived in exile till the time was ripe to begin again. Then he returned to Sicily and plotted for the revolution which terminated in Garibaldi's expedition. He acquired great influence, took his seat in the Italian parliament, and soon became leader of the radical Left. In spite of vicissitudes and a not unattacked reputation, he was the chief parliamentary figure on the death of Depretis, and dominated Italian politics till 1896. In his youth Crispi had been a follower of Mazzini's republican theories; later, though still a republican in sympathy, he announced the opinion that "the Republic would divide us, the Monarchy unites us," and abandoned his old republican associates. For this reason among others he incurred the animosity of old friends and allies.

During the period of his ascendency the subdivision of the deputies into little groups made government difficult, and for a couple of years he was out of office. In that interval hard times, adding weight to republican and socialist propaganda, caused strikes, riots, and insurrections; and accompanying these disturbances came the "Bank Scandals." Sundry banks, conspicuously the important Banca Romana, had been violating the laws which regulated the government of banks, and had been engaged in most improper dealings with politicians, as, for instance, lending money to deputies on little or no security. These scandals, together with the strikes, wrecked the ministry, and the country called on Crispi, as the one strong man able to take control. He assumed office in December, 1893, and remained till 1896, when he fell with equal suddenness. The cause of his fall requires a separate paragraph.

About 1870 an Italian steamship company established a coaling station on the west coast of the Red Sea, and acquired a certain strip of land which it afterwards ceded to the government (1882). From this beginning the Italian government advanced, upon one pretext or another, to the establishment of a colonial dependency. It occupied Massawa, established the "Colonia Erithrea," and proclaimed a zone of influence along the east coast of Africa. Various battles were fought with the natives; and at last the government sent fifteen thousand men to perform some brilliant exploit for its own political benefit. The Italian troops were badly handled; they walked into a trap set by the Abyssinians, and suffered a terrible rout, losing half their numbers (1896). Crispi fell at once, and the new ministry under Di Rudinì, in spite of cries for revenge, prudently abandoned the colonial policy, and made peace as best it could. Italy renounced her protectorate, and contented herself with a strip of coast by Massawa. Thus ended the scheme of colonial aggrandizement begun in ignorance and folly.

The fall of Crispi removed the last interesting figure of the Risorgimento, and left Italian politics in a confused medley. Since then, various leaders of no marked ability or individuality have struggled with the permanent difficulties of Church and State, North and South, capitalism and socialism, and the shifting difficulties of foreign relations. All this time is too near to present any definite pattern to the casual eye. The century closed sadly with the assassination of King Humbert (1878-1900) by an ignorant workman who called himself a nihilist. Humbert was not a good ruler, but he had a kind heart and many pleasant qualities, which endeared him to the Italian people. He was succeeded by his son Victor Emmanuel III, the present king.

The greatest Italian figure of the last decades of the nineteenth century was not to be found in the service of the State, but of the Church. In 1810 Gioacchino Pecci was born in Carpineto, a dead little village perched on a hillside near Anagni, the town where Boniface VIII was nearly murdered by Sciarra Colonna five hundred years before. His father, Count Lodovico Pecci, had served in Napoleon's army; his mother was said to be descended from Cola di Rienzo. The count was the seigneur of the place, and lived in a somewhat shabby palace which had seen better days. Gioacchino was educated at a Jesuit school in Rome. He soon gave evidence of marked ability, and was taken into the papal service and sent as apostolic delegate to Benevento. Banditti infested the neighbourhood, and the nobility of the town were little better than the banditti. Pecci displayed character. He was promoted, and at the age of thirty-three was sent as papal nuncio to Belgium, with the title of Archbishop of Damietta, an archbishopric that had been in partibus infidelium since the days of St. Louis. In Belgium, where liberal ideas were jostling the old ecclesiastical system, Pecci distinguished himself for tact and address. From Belgium he went to Perugia as bishop, and governed the city for thirty-two years, during the trying time in which (largely at the expense of the Church) Italy was forcing her way to freedom. In 1860 his authority was overthrown by the Piedmontese soldiers, and many tales of brutality and wantonness charged upon the nationalists were brought to his troubled ears, and he unfortunately received a most unfavourable impression of liberals and liberalism. His reputation for ability, character, and diplomacy became so well established, that in the conclave on the death of Pius IX he had no serious competitor. Leo XIII (1878-1903) was already an old man when he was elected Pope, and had had the misfortune to receive his education and training in the narrow school of the old papal régime. Preceded by an incompetent Pope, he found himself confronted by the wreck of the Temporal Power, and by a liberalism which was not only triumphant in Italy, but in nearly all western Europe. He had not far to go to find thoughtful men who expected to see the Papacy collapse and die. Most difficult matters in Germany, in Ireland, in France, in the United States, required delicate and skilful management. It is not too much to say that Leo raised the Papacy higher in the world's regard than it had stood for two hundred years. Had he been a younger man, and trained in a more liberal school, he might, perhaps, have attempted the task of adjusting ecclesiastical conservatism and tradition to the needs of a fast changing world. But he was too old. With a few brilliant exceptions he accepted the conservative policy. He affected to deem himself a prisoner in the Vatican, and claimed the restoration of the Temporal Power; he declared Thomas Aquinas the best teacher for the priesthood, and stood firm on the dogmas of the Council of Trent. Nevertheless, his was a most impressive personality, and he stands in the long list of Popes in a rank inferior only to the highest.

In his old age, as he strolled in the Vatican gardens, meditating Latin verses, or thinking over his encyclical letters, "On the Condition of the Working Classes," "On Christian Democracy," "On the Holy Eucharist," or turning his emaciated, sweet, Voltairean face to the great dome of St. Peter's, he may well have let his mind wander in peace over the outside world, for never since Luther cast off his papal allegiance had the whole Christian world been so united in admiration for a Pope of Rome. All Christians could say amen to the prayer in his last poem, "Suprema Leonis Vota:"—

Expleat o clemens anxia vota Deus,
Scilicet ut tandem superis de civibus unus Divino aeternum lumine et ore fruar.

We have now reached our goal, the end of the nineteenth century, and if we look back and contemplate the vicissitudes of Italy, such as no other nation ever experienced, twice on the throne of Europe, three times crowned with its crown,—Imperial, Ecclesiastical, Intellectual,—and resurvey the three centuries during which foreign tyrant and native priest joined hands to smother and quench the Italian fire, and then read in detail the heroic acts of the men who sacrificed themselves for Italian freedom, we shall feel sure that the dull colours of the present generation are but signs of a time of rest, and that the genius of Italy lives within and will again enrich the world with deeds of men sprung from the "gentle Latin blood."

Made in the USA
Charleston, SC
02 December 2016